A HISTORY

OF

MODERN EUROPE

T0382376

A HISTORY

OF

MODERN EUROPE

FROM THE MIDDLE OF THE
SIXTEENTH CENTURY

by

JOHN E. MORRIS

D.Litt. (Oxford), Litt.D. (Manchester), formerly Assistant Master in
Bedford School

Cambridge:
at the University Press
1925

CAMBRIDGE UNIVERSITY PRESS
Cambridge, New York, Melbourne, Madrid, Cape Town,
Singapore, São Paulo, Delhi, Mexico City

Cambridge University Press
The Edinburgh Building, Cambridge CB2 8RU, UK

Published in the United States of America by Cambridge University Press, New York

www.cambridge.org
Information on this title: www.cambridge.org/9781107620773

First published 1914
First edition 1914
Second edition 1915
Reprinted 1916
First paperback edition 2013

A catalogue record for this publication is available from the British Library

ISBN 978-1-107-62077-3 Paperback

PREFACE

"A potentate who keeps a very small army and don't mean any harm." HENRY KINGSLEY.

THE said potentate's own statement was "L'Empire, c'est la Paix." But, whether he spoke sincerely or not, he was forced into war to justify his seizure of power and to show himself worthy of being a Napoleon. He found himself fighting, just because he had, or thought he had, the means. On the other hand, the grandson of his great and successful rival has also a small army, and has not yet used it.

It may seem queer for an author to preface a new book with an apology. But I must say that to present to young students the story of Philip II and Henry of Navarre, of Gustavus and Louis XIV and Frederick, of the Republic and the Empire, of United Germany and United Italy, and yet to abstain from giving details of wars, has seemed to me impossible. At least they can learn the need of readiness in face of possible dangers, the evils of disunion, and the influence of war as bringing out the best or the worst instincts, devotion or greed, according as a nation's cause is just or unjust. The part played by England, or by Great Britain, in several great wars is worthy of their study. Yet they will have but a distorted view of history if they read only of their own country. The best way for them to understand the aspirations of neighbouring nations is to look into the causes of the struggles, the means whereby the Dutch shook themselves free from Spain and the Houses of Hohenzollern and Savoy won their way to lead Germany and Italy, and the consequences of successful efforts, while our country was, as it were, on the fringe of European complications. So, after all, I do not apologise for putting war in the front place. A despot to satisfy personal ambition overawes his neighbours, or a nation in arms professes to spread to others the benefits of its superior "ideas," and at once resistance is laudable. Only the fighting machine may be made too strong, and then the instrument of honourable defence may become the instrument of wanton aggression, for the simple reason that the sovereign or nation possessing it wishes to use it.

BEDFORD,
  May, 1914.

PREFACE TO THIRD EDITION.

The text remains substantially as it was written in 1913, but references to the Great War made for the Second Edition have been changed from the present to the past tense.

Having read a good many of the recent books on the Great War I have come to the conclusion that it is better not to add anything after 1914. We have hardly yet got our focus right. The comments of some writers on both statesmen and generals are so naïve as to be almost ludicrous. Other writers seem to think that to denounce patriotism and national aspirations is the one duty of the super-intellectual man. The future of India and Egypt and Turkey is beyond our ken. So I prefer to leave untouched what is here written about the "ideas" which have influenced Europe up to 1914. The question of how to use a very small army in the future and yet not to mean any harm cannot be solved off-hand.

J. E. M.

January, 1925

CONTENTS

MAPS

PEDIGREES

CHAPTER I

EUROPE IN THE SIXTEENTH CENTURY

To say that the national fortunes of England and the very existence and growth of our Empire depended entirely upon the outcome of the national struggle against three great men in turn is a commonplace. But it is extremely important to understand what were the resources of these powers against which we fought, and it is not every Englishman who is willing to acknowledge that Spain and France had many other enemies than ourselves. In fact, it would not be too much to say that Philip II, Louis XIV, and Napoleon, failed in turn because each had too many irons in the fire and that, though England played an extremely important part in their overthrow, yet it was the number of enemies that each created against himself that ultimately decided each of the great struggles.

If we wish to take a distinct date from which to mark the development of England, we shall find that the ten years, 1550—60, are of great importance in the history of Europe as well as in our own. As far as we are concerned, the loss of Calais and the accession of Queen Elizabeth usher in a new era. At the same time Charles V —the fifth Emperor of the name, but King Charles I of Spain—abdicated and left Austria under his brother Ferdinand, Spain and the Spanish dominions and the Netherlands under his son Philip II. A long series of wars between Spain and the Empire on the one side and

France on the other, wars mostly fought out in Italy, came to an end by the *Treaty of Cateau Cambrésis* in 1559. The *Treaty of Augsburg* in 1555 gave to Germany a religious settlement which lasted into the next century.

The concentration of power in the Hapsburg family is well known. Maximilian of Austria married Mary of Burgundy, sole heiress of Charles the Bold; their son, Philip, married Joan of Spain, daughter of Ferdinand and Isabella; their son was Charles V. Therefore this prince was Archduke of Austria by paternal right, King of Spain by maternal, master of the Burgundian Netherlands and the County of Burgundy through his grandmother, and also Emperor by election. His strength was more apparent than real, for he could not secure the implicit obedience of all his subjects. He was most fond of the Netherlands, and in the eyes of the Spaniards was a foreigner and a Fleming. But Philip II, his son, lived in Spain, and was a foreigner and tyrant to the Netherlanders. In Italy both father and son were foreigners, holding Lombardy and Naples, Sardinia and Sicily, as conquerors in the struggle against France for the mastery in that fair land. In Germany the conflicting interests of many rulers were so individual that Charles could never be an autocrat there.

Taking Germany first, we find a host of church and lay potentates, archbishops, bishops, abbots, dukes, counts, princes, strong or weak, ruling over lands wide or small, Catholic or Lutheran or Calvinistic, and in their midst many great free cities. These formed the Empire, nominally the *Holy Roman Empire*. As the outcome of many struggles in the early Middle Ages a system of election had become crystallised, and on the death of an emperor, or it may be by anticipation before his death, seven great lords met together to choose his successor. The seven *Electors* were the three Archbishops of Köln (Cologne), Trier (Trèves), and Mainz (Mayence), the

Margraf (Marquis, count of the mark or borderland) of Brandenburg, the Duke of Saxony, the Count Palatine, and the King of Bohemia; the last named ruled over a non-German people. For a long period they elected an Austrian Archduke of the Hapsburg dynasty. While Charles V was yet alive they had already chosen his brother Ferdinand to be King of the Romans, a title preparatory to that of Emperor, and Charles had handed over to Ferdinand the government of Austria. The one thing that Germany needed was unity. The hundreds of great and small rulers could not combine when each was seeking his own good, and, although the Empire was divided into *Circles* for administration and for the raising of imperial armies, there was no possibility of any willing cohesion. There was a central governing body, the *Diet*, to which came the feudal tenants-in-chief and the representatives of the free cities, but rival interests prevented anything being done for the common good.

HOUSE OF HAPSBURG.

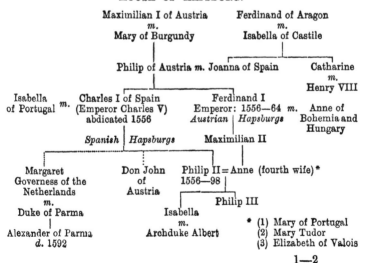

1—2

German unity might have been secured in the sixteenth century. Trade does a great deal to combine peoples together, and the free cities were great centres of trade. The root of a great commercial tree was Venice, and the trunk along which the sap flowed was the old Roman road which ascended the valley of the Adige from Italy into the Austrian Tyrol, crossed the Alps by the Brenner Pass, descended to the river Inn, and so reached the Danube. Many branches diverged, eastwards to Vienna, westwards from Ratisbon to Augsburg and Ulm, Basle and Strasburg, northwards over the gap through the mountains of North Bavaria to Nuremburg and down the Main to the Rhine. In central Germany the line of commerce stretched out to Magdeburg and Halberstadt, and thence to the cities of the coast. The cities were fortified and most of them were self-governed, and the feudal lords were too much indebted to them for the necessaries of peace and war to attempt to destroy them. There was a second possible factor of German unity besides trade, namely German learning; and the outbreak of the Lutheran movement was due to the German learned mind, which rejected the religious domination of an Italian Pope and examined points of doctrine for itself. Now Napoleon said that Charles V ought to have been a Protestant and put himself at the head of a national German movement to secure both religious and political unity; many historians have adopted this view. But Charles held the medieval theory of Church and State, Emperor and Pope each supreme in his own place. The consequence was that the Lutheran movement, deprived of the Emperor's support, was to a very large extent destructive only. The German conscience approved of Luther's defiance of the authority of Rome, but clung to the right of private judgement, which he invoked against Rome; if Luther challenged the right of the Pope on questions of doctrine, other Germans challenged the authority of Luther himself

The consequence was that the Reformation intensified the spirit of disunion. The constructive reformer was John Calvin, and his form of Church government as founded in Geneva was a model copied by the reformers of Scotland, of France, of Holland, when the great revolt broke out against Philip, and of some German states. The Calvinistic doctrines were hard and fast, and had to be accepted by all those who were subject to a national Calvinistic Church. On the other hand the Church of Rome, getting rid of its worst abuses and purifying itself, initiated the counter-Reformation, in which the chief agent was the newly instituted Order of Jesus. Thus a large part of Germany was lost to Protestantism.

In 1555 the religious *Peace of Augsburg* was made, being the work of Ferdinand, not of Charles. Ferdinand was not a bad Catholic, but he was an opportunist, that is to say ready to give up something for the sake of a greater advantage, and his object was to stop the dismemberment of Germany so as to be able to make head against the Turks. The principle of this peace was *Cujus Regio ejus Religio*; whoever was the lord of a region should decide what its religion should be. Therefore the rights of German peoples were disregarded, and individual princes settled the form of Church government for their own lands, whilst pledging themselves not to interfere with each other. Germany now remained comparatively quiet until the horrible Thirty Years' War of the next century. Church lands in countries already Protestant were secularised, that is to say administered for the benefit of their lay rulers. Thus in the next century there were possibilities of confusion and war whenever the Church of Rome should try to regain these secularised lands. In the meanwhile a *Council* was sitting at Trent on the Adige, and therefore on the high road between Italy and Germany, to discuss the policy of the Church. It held its last sitting in 1563; it left several points unsettled, but did much to revive the spiritual life of Roman Catholics.

The main object in life of Ferdinand, and of Maximilian who succeeded him, was to beat back the Turks, and therefore their eyes were always turned eastwards so that they had very little influence over the questions which agitated Spain and France. Ferdinand, marrying the heiress of the last king of Hungary and Bohemia[1], added those non-German lands to the Hapsburg dominions, and thus brought about the "Dual Monarchy" which existed to 1918. But then two-thirds of the Hungary that we know was in the power of the Turks, Buda included. Wars between Christian states always gave to the Turks their opportunity, even as the Crusaders had failed to effect a permanent lodgement in Palestine because of the rivalries and jealousies between them. But while the Emperors were devoted to the defence of Europe by land against the Turks, the commotions which had occurred in Germany in connection with the Reformation had so upset the country that the great promise of German unity, which seemed possible about the year 1500, had by 1550 disappeared. Most of the minor princelings devoted themselves to supplying German mercenaries to England or to France or even to Spain,—in fact to whoever could pay them. The great bulk of almost any 16th century army was composed of German Landsknechts, chiefly masses of foot pikemen, or of mounted Schwarzreiters, and both had an evil reputation as being neither loyal to their employers nor competent in their own profession, let alone the fact that they murdered and plundered pitilessly. But whatever the defects of these mercenaries, they were too useful to the King of France or to the

---

[1] The Bohemians belong to the great Slavonic group of nations, such as the Prussians, Poles, Russians, Croats, Serbians and others. The Hungarians or Magyars are a race apart; but only a proportion of the population of Hungary is Magyar, and the rest is Slavonic or Rumanian.

Netherlanders to be disregarded, and even the King of Spain would often enlist thousands of them, though so vastly inferior to his own trained Spaniards, simply to prevent his enemies from enlisting them. Another theory of German failure is connected with trade. When Venice began to decline in consequence of the discovery of the Cape route to India by the Portuguese and the divergence of Asiatic trade from the Levant to Lisbon, the loss of the trade from the overland Brenner Pass route might be compared to the drying up of the sap of the trunk of the tree. Germany now looked for her commerce to the Netherlands and the northern ports, not to Venice.

As the Emperor was the bulwark of Christianity by land against the Turks, so was the aristocratic Republic of Venice by sea. By the middle of the 16th century, not only was Venice feeling this decline of her eastern trade owing to the rise of Portugal, but she had to put forth efforts beyond her power to check the spread of the Ottoman dominion over Greece and the islands off the coast of the Adriatic. It was not only Turkish conquest that was against her. Wealth always causes jealousy; and the various Powers, though themselves benefiting by the trade which Venice gave to them, resented very much the conquest of the hinterland which we know as Venetia. As long as the city of the lagoons was merely a trading city, she stirred no kings against herself. When she gradually conquered Padua and Verona and the whole of the lower Adige, and even as far as the eastern borders of Lombardy, it was thought that she was going beyond her province, for she thus dominated the lands by which Germany was connected with Italy, namely the outlet of the Brenner route; and so the League of Cambrai was formed against her in 1508. Yet, on the conclusion of the war of the League of Cambrai, she regained all her mainland empire, for she was ever a clever and a lenient mistress. Now the problem for the Venetian Senate in face of the Turkish advance was a very difficult one. If she opposed the Turks with all her might, the Sultan had only to refuse leave for Venetian traders to come to his dominions. Thus we find, alternately, a compromise made with the Turkish government to leave to Venice such trade in the Levant as still remained, and an open state of war. And it was not only the government of the Sultan that had to be considered. The advance guard of the Mohammedans were the pirates who infested all the shores of North Africa. On one occasion Charles V stirred himself to make a mighty effort, and captured Tunis in 1535 from the great corsair Kheyr-ed-din, usually known as Barbarossa[1]; but in 1541 another great expedition against Algiers failed completely. The Spaniards continued to garrison Goletta, the port of Tunis, up to 1574, when it was finally lost for ever; and from this date right down to the 19th century no really serious attempt was made by any European Power to put down Mediterranean piracy. Christians during all this period were frequently made galley slaves. The greatest Christian Powers sent their consular agents to Algiers or Tunis and made agreements with the Sultan at Constantinople, but otherwise the traders had to look after themselves and to sail in company under arms. The one great effort that was made in 1571 resulted in the victory of Lepanto, when the Venetian fleet, under the command of Philip's half brother, Don John of Austria, reinforced by a comparatively small number of ships from Genoa and the Pope and Spain, broke the power of the Sultan for a time, but did not clear the Mediterranean of Mohammedans.

[1] The corsairs of N. Africa made war on the Christians and raided their coasts, sometimes independently of the Sultan to whom they owed nominal allegiance, sometimes as his allies. Burke says "The Turk cannot govern Egypt and Arabia and Curdistan as he governs Thrace; nor has he the same dominion in Crimea and Algiers, which he has at Bruse and Smyrna. The Sultan gets such obedience as he can. He governs with a loose rein that he may govern at all."

The long wars between France and Spain before and during the reign of Charles V had largely been fought for the possession of Lombardy and Naples, and Spain had finally triumphed. In 1559, at Cateau Cambrésis, it was finally acknowledged that France had no status beyond the Alps. Lombardy was now a Spanish province. Here was trained the best of the Spanish legions, the *tercio* of Lombardy. There was a certain amount of local freedom in Milan, and also in the smaller towns. Charles V actually supported the Senate of Milan against his own Governor. Philip indeed supported his Governor against the Senate, but not so far as to create a despotism. The Milanese continued quietly to enjoy the protection of their laws and of their Senate. It was in the next century that the Lombards suffered and wished Philip II alive again, for under him, in spite of heavy taxes which barely covered the cost of government and from which he drew no profit, and in spite of a certain amount of military duty in the cavalry, the Milanese preserved their rights. The Hapsburgs were greatly concerned by the question how they could communicate between Lombardy and Austria. Venice controlling the Adige route up to the Brenner Pass, it resulted that a Spanish army, except by the courtesy of the Venetian Senate which was neutral and disliked any violation of its territory, had to use the Valtellina leading up from Lake Como to the very steep and lofty Stelvio Pass, by which they reached the Upper Adige and the Brenner. It was an inferior and difficult route, but often it was a cause of war between the Hapsburgs and their enemies, and in later days France paralysed the Spanish arms by securing for herself the alliance of the Rhaetian Swiss who controlled the north of the Stelvio.

To the north-west of Lombardy the valley of the Ticino leads from the north shore of Lake Maggiore to the St Gotthard Pass, and this route was held by the Swiss.

They had conquered the present Canton of Ticino, and had planted three castles at Bellinzona, a few miles north of the lake, so as to control the district of Italy where the great highway debouched; to-day the Ticinesi being Italians do the rough work while high positions in their Canton are held by up-country Swiss, but they are personally free, whereas in the 16th century they were practically slaves. Thus the Swiss confederacy had their means of access to Italy. But the ascendancy of the Spaniards in Lombardy, and in particular the victory of the Spanish arms at Pavia in 1525, checked the further expansion of their power. In the days of Philip II the Swiss fought as mercenaries only, and were unable to extend their sway further into Italy.

Next to the west, the Duchy of Savoy spread from the Lake of Geneva across the main Alps between France and Italy into Piedmont. Gradually the Dukes lost the north side of the Lake where the Swiss created the Canton of Vaud, but they gained more than they lost, for by their occupation of Piedmont they controlled the West Alpine routes. Here again French and Spaniards were both anxious to secure influence; in the days of Philip II Savoy was almost a province of Spain, and under Louis XIV of France. Often we find the siege of some little fort taking a place in history which strikes us as being much too important for its size, until we see from the map that it was a military post controlling some mountain pass. Between France and Spain the Duchy of Savoy thrived because of its geographical position.

The Republic of Genoa had always been the rival of Venice. In the 16th century it was allied to Spain, and the great families of the Dorias and Spinolas supplied admirals and generals to Spain. It secured a large share of such Mediterranean trade as would otherwise have gone to Spain. It held most of the Riviera and ruled it despotically; many a little Riviera town still has its fort by which Genoa in those days held it in subjection. It also held the island of Corsica. Commerce in this part of Italy came along the coast by water. In many places the spurs of the Apennines come down precipitous to the sea, and only in the 19th century has the great coast road, the Cornice, been successfully engineered. Indeed so difficult has it been to lay down a track along the coast that the modern railway has only a single line of rails. Inland from Genoa passes over the Apennines led to Lombardy, and thus by the friendship of Genoa Spain secured her line of communication with Milan, just as by the Valtellina she had her line up to the Brenner and Austria.

Several of the small duchies, which had in the Middle Ages taken the place of the Republics, were still in existence, such as Parma and Modena. The dukes were usually the faithful henchmen of Spain, and Philip's half-sister Margaret married the Duke of Parma. The great city of Florence had lost her republic; the family of Medici, having overthrown liberty by their enormous wealth, now governed as Grand Dukes of Tuscany. In central Italy the Popes had extended their power beyond the Patrimony of St Peter, that is to say beyond the ring of territory near Rome, which more or less corresponds to ancient Latium. They held the district of the Marches across the Apennines, and the Legations of Bologna and Ferrara up to the right bank of the lower Po.

In the South, the King of Spain held Sicily by virtue of an old claim of the House of Aragon that goes back some centuries, though the Sicilians protested that they accepted the dominion of Spain of their own free will. There was ever strife between the royal power and the native Sicilians, and it was a land of feuds rather than of law. In the Island of Sardinia and in the Kingdom of Naples, which were now likewise Spanish, Philip's viceroy was far more powerful and more despotic. These three countries were occupied by permanent Spanish garrisons, the *tercios* of Sardinia and Sicily and Naples.

Spain herself, one would have thought, would have benefited by the accession of Philip in place of Charles, for Spain was his home. But he meant to be the master of his home. The Castilian nobles had already under Charles V become mere passive subjects, cut off from all participation in public life. They fell back upon the enjoyment of their wealth in their country seats; they enjoyed great incomes and had many families dependent on them; they passed their time in pomp and luxury, which indeed were foreign to the Castilian character and had been imported by Charles V into his court. Naturally the result of pomp and luxury was debt. Of course there were a few energetic Castilian nobles who served the King, such as the Duke of Alva, and the lesser nobles and hidalgos having lost their feudal rights and privileges looked for a livelihood to the King's service or to places of trust in the Indies. But the general result of the policy of both Charles and Philip was to destroy the natural adventuresomeness of the Castilian character, for Charles hardly ever kept his court in Castile, and Philip lived indeed in Castile, but lived apart and kept his nobles aloof from him. It has also to be considered that in Castile there were vast numbers of ecclesiastics. When a country has such an aristocracy and too many non-productive monks and nuns and friars, national life is stagnant. There was in Castile a representative assembly, the Cortes, but representing only the towns, and under Charles and Philip it became a body obedient to the royal power, meekly voted subsidies every three years, and was in no degree a basis of popular resistance against a despotic monarchy.

Aragon, including Catalonia, had been brought into partnership with Castile by the marriage of Ferdinand and Isabella, the grandparents of Charles V, but Aragon always had its own privileges. Under Charles V these privileges were more or less successfully maintained. Philip, quite at the end of his reign in 1592, seized his opportunity when Aragon rose to protect a certain Perez who stood upon his rights as an Aragonese. Chiefly by means of bringing the Inquisition over to his side, Philip gained his point and broke the spirit of the province. In Catalonia, the port of Barcelona had had a glorious past as both a naval and a commercial city. It began to decline under Charles; it sank into ruin under Philip, partly owing to the rivalry of the city of Genoa, a republic which was always favoured by the Spanish monarchs, and partly owing to the Turkish ascendancy in the Mediterranean. Venice on the one side and Genoa on the other defended their trade as best they could, making a compromise with the Sultan, even though such a course might seem to be undignified. But Spain never properly undertook as a Great Power the duty of protecting the Mediterranean.

The aristocracy of Spain under the gloomy rule of Philip being deprived of its position and no longer leading the nation, and the townsfolk having no vigorous municipal life, the nation became more and more stagnant. Gold and silver might come from across the Atlantic, but if the Spaniards had lost their power to use money profitably and to put it to use in the way of trade, it was only natural that the wealth which should have been theirs should pass to those who had the trading instinct. The Netherlanders were born tradesmen, and the wealth from America went to them. This cannot have been due only to the pride and slackness of the Spaniards themselves. It was part of Philip's policy of despotism to keep the Spaniards down by granting trade privileges to the Netherlanders, and in a general way it may be said that goods came to Spain only to be reshipped to Flanders. Moreover he laid a crushing tax of ten per cent. upon all sales. Therefore under this dead weight Spain went from bad to worse. When we add that the revolt of the Netherlands was the most important fact of Philip's reign, that the war continuing long after his death down to 1648 exhausted Spain as regards both men and money, it is clear that the connection with the Netherlands was deadly to Spanish life, and that the King only did hurt to his own nation.

In various ways, by marriage, by conquest, even by direct purchase, the counties and duchies of the Netherlands in the 15th century had been grouped together under the House of Burgundy[1], and from his grandmother, Mary of Burgundy, the sole heiress of Charles the Bold, Charles V held all the low countries as his inheritance. There he was popular and was at home as a Fleming, whereas Philip, having his home in Spain, was the foreign master. Of all the cities of the Netherlands, Antwerp most attracts our attention. Situated some miles inland up the deep and tidal Scheldt, Antwerp was an ideal centre for the redistribution of commerce into the heart of Germany and France. The discovery of a new world beyond the Atlantic and of a new route by the Cape to India brought commerce to Cadiz and Lisbon. The Flemings sailed to Cadiz and Lisbon, reshipped the goods and brought them to Antwerp. In the Middle Ages the chief port of Flanders was Bruges, an inland town, and sufficiently served by a canal by which she had access to the North Sea. But vessels large enough to weather the Bay of Biscay could not enter the canal and had to go up the Scheldt. Therefore Bruges is even to-day a mere medieval survival, and Antwerp, though she has had an intermediate period of ruin and decay, has in the last quarter of the 19th century become again one of the richest ports of all Europe. Thus Philip took over from Charles a

[1] The Duchy of Burgundy reverted on Charles the Bold's death to France, but the County of Burgundy came to Spain.

great city, in which was concentrated the main trade of Europe. There great commercial houses, not only Flemish but also German, had their headquarters, for instance the Fuggers of Augsburg, and they chiefly financed the Kings of Spain and France and England. Whoever could borrow from the Fuggers and kindred families could carry on a war; whoever could not repay the loans, or at any rate pay the interest on the loans, was nationally bankrupt and could not make war. To Antwerp came from Lisbon bullion and jewels, spices and sugar[1]; from Italy came silks and brocades; from the Baltic, corn and flax and wood; from England, not only wool but also cloth, for the Flemings had taught the English not to confine themselves to breeding sheep but also to manufacture. We are told that the trade with England rose in the first ten years of Elizabeth's reign from a quarter of a million to five million ducats, a very wonderful development, which at least marks the cleverness of the Flemish traders in London; it also goes very far to explain why Queen Elizabeth was slow to oppose Philip openly and strongly in the Netherlands, and why she, a poor sovereign unable to raise a great revenue from taxation in England, was able to borrow money from the merchants of Antwerp in return for trade privileges.

Now when we throw our eyes over all Philip's dominions, Lombardy, Naples and Sicily, Castile and Aragon, the Netherlands, and also the remnant of

[1] The spice trade was of vast importance, encouraged adventure, and led to war and rivalry. It is a little difficult to understand why pepper, cloves, nutmeg, &c., entered so much into the life of our ancestors, until we realise first that they had no roots as winter feed for cattle and therefore killed and salted the carcasses, and secondly that they could not freeze meat in hot weather. The spices enabled them to make palatable both salted and high meat. At first Portugal, later on Holland and England, grew wealthy on the spice trade. The importance of sugar in domestic life is obvious and explains the keenness of the rivalry of many nations in both East and West Indies.

Burgundy which we know by the name of Franche Comté, and when also we know that the Spanish Empire of the Indies had been founded, it is almost with a shock that we read that Philip was always hard pressed for money. Every one of his great undertakings failed. It was partly no doubt due to his slowness and continual procrastination. He would not let his nobles or his statesmen or his generals do anything. Every single detail must be sanctioned from his room where he dictated to his secretaries in solitary splendour in his new Palace of the Escurial. But it may be that his slowness in planning a war was due to his consciousness that he could not afford a war. We shall find that all his efforts in the Netherlands lacked stamina. The Armada that he sent against England was not nearly so strong as the Armada that he had originally designed. We are thus driven back from our first ideas about the riches of the Indies, and we simply ask ourselves, Did Philip really draw a tremendous revenue from the Indian trade? This brings us to another consideration. Did Drake and other English buccaneers really bring home from their raids such vast amounts of silver and gold and jewels as fancy has always depicted? The Indian trade in the days of Charles V was certainly not very wealthy. The silver mines of Potosi in Peru were only discovered in 1545, and were not in working order for some time afterwards. And next, even if the Indian trade was as rich as fancy paints it, it was very largely unprofitable. The precious metals arrived, and the King's "fifth," or 20 per cent. share of the total, was immediately required for repayment of loans. The merchants of the Netherlands or Germany had got as security certain places in Spain itself, and they profited, while the nation of Spain did not. They "cornered" the trade in various articles; for instance they trebled the price of quicksilver. They got control of the re-export from Spain, also of the export of native

Spanish produce, having licences from the Crown which the native Spaniards had not got. When a nation, partly by its own pride and sloth, partly by its subjection to the dead weight of tyranny, does not manage its own trade and manufactures and is also pressed by a rigid taxation, its apparent wealth goes to foreigners. Thus perhaps we can understand the state of affairs when we are told that in 1595 the Indian fleet brought to Spain 35 millions of ducats, the collective produce of three years, but within a single year not a coin of all that treasure remained in Spain. And so we are brought to the conclusion that Philip's great enterprises failed because he had too many plans against the Netherlands, against France, against England, while he had not got the money to defray the cost[1].

We have left the question of military strength. All contemporary authorities, Spaniards themselves such as Bernardino de Mendoza, Frenchmen such as the Seigneur de Brantôme, and the Welsh adventurer Roger Williams, are at one in praising the superb Spanish infantry—" La fleur de toutes les autres nations." The Emperor Charles, says Brantôme, knew that the issue of his wars depended on the lighted matches of his Spanish harquebuses. The Spanish veteran troops, the soldados viejos, were real regular troops. They date from the days of Ferdinand and Isabella, when under such captains as Gonsalvo of Cordova they won victories by their discipline although they had not got up-to-date weapons, when in fact they simply fought with sword and buckler; but very soon in the Italian wars against France the harquebus was introduced, and by the time that the Duke of Alva conducted the Spanish regiments into the Netherlands the musket had been invented, a gun with a longer barrel than the harquebus, heavy and having to be supported upon a fork or crutch, slow to load and awkward to carry, but in the hands of trained soldiers

---

[1] See Von Ranke, Lectures on Modern Europe.

very effective. Henceforward the ideal of a Spanish general was to have half his foot musketeers, and the other half pikemen as a solid mass for defence, and other nations copied Spanish methods. They were trained and constantly recruited from Spain so that a Spanish force was always up to strength, and they were divided into *tercios*, regiments of infantry, which took their name from the districts where they were trained and were kept in garrison. Philip inherited the *tercios* of Lombardy, Naples, Sardinia, Sicily, and Goletta. When Tunis was lost the *tercio* of Goletta was broken up. The remaining four, when combined for active service, were between 8000 and 9000 strong, but if weak in numbers they were intensely proud, conscious of their strength, and animated by an overpowering spirit of camaraderie. The Spanish cavalry was very good, but had not got the reputation of the infantry, and indeed young Spanish nobles eager for military fame preferred to join the infantry. The speciality of the Spanish horse was the use of the carbine or pistol fired from the saddle. Their method was to trot towards the enemy, fire, swing aside to right or left, and retire to reload whilst giving room to the second line to do the same. In an army of any considerable strength perhaps one-third, but more usually one-fifth, of the soldiers were native Spaniards. The rest would be Italians, Walloons[1], Burgundians, trained more or less in Spanish style, and perhaps Germans who adhered to their own national methods. For instance in 1586 Alexander, Prince of Parma, proposed for the invasion of England an army of 30,000 infantry, including only 6000 Spaniards; and in 1578 Don Juan had in his army 4000 Spaniards out of a total of 20,000. But small as were their numbers they acted as leaven to an army and made a victory sure; in fact they would put the finishing touch to a battle just

[1] Inhabitants of the French-speaking provinces of the S.E. Netherlands.

in the same way as did Napoleon's Old Guard. A King of France at this period had a small number of very gallant but entirely untrustworthy cavalry supplied by the nobility of France, and was forced to enlist thousands of Swiss foot who were certainly good and trustworthy, and it may be other thousands of Germans who were untrustworthy. Queen Elizabeth could only raise a militia from the counties of England, untrained and unorganised, liable to die off through the horrible ignorance of the period on matters of sanitary science. Thus we can understand that, had Philip's hands been free, and had he been able to pay and use this small number of choice Spanish old soldiers, he might have subjected Europe to his will, even as Napoleon did. But even Spaniards who were not paid would not fight. Proud as they were of their discipline in face of the enemy, they were ready to mutiny, and on one celebrated occasion they had the rich city of Antwerp absolutely at their mercy[1].

[1] See Colonel E. M. Lloyd, *History of Infantry.*

CHAPTER II

BEFORE we enter into the details of Philip's reign it will be profitable to consider the last war between Charles V and the French, which is typical of many wars between Germany and France, and only affected Spain indirectly. King Henry II took advantage of the pressure of the Turks upon Austria, and of the disunion in Germany which the Reformation had caused, to make alliance with Maurice, Elector of Saxony. Henry II himself was a persecutor of Protestants in France, and Maurice was a Lutheran, but we shall find this inconsistency always present; Cardinal Richelieu and Louis XIV did the same thing. Charles barely saved himself by flight from Innsbruck when Maurice tried to capture him by a sudden assault. The French occupied the three bishoprics of Lorraine, Metz, Verdun, and Toul. Somewhat later Philip married Mary Tudor and so brought England into the contest, with a disastrous result—or rather it was thought to be disastrous at the time—viz. the loss of Calais. Charles V shortly recovered from his troubles and laid siege, though uselessly, to Metz. After his abdication Philip's troops won two victories on the Flemish frontier at St Quentin and Gravelines, and thus a way was made for a treaty, the *Peace of Cateau Cambrésis*, which seemed likely to terminate the struggle for the time being. By it France withdrew altogether from Italy and Savoy, and on his side Philip allowed the three bishoprics of Lorraine to remain in French hands. Elizabeth was now on our throne and made an effort through her envoys to regain

Calais, but unsuccessfully, and indeed Cecil appears to have considered that the possession of a French port would really be a source of weakness to England.

Philip is now definitely the centre of the picture, and this means that the fortunes of Spain rather than of Germany are our chief consideration. Curiously enough he began his reign with a quarrel with Pope Paul IV. It is not at all unusual to find a despot, who is likewise a persecutor of Protestants, having such an enmity against some Pope; Louis XIV is another instance in point. Philip's sole idea was to be an autocrat, to crush out heresy in Spain, to support the Inquisition at all costs, and therefore if the Pope should resent the power of the Inquisition, then the Most Catholic King and the Head of the Catholic Faith would be at variance.

Henry II of France died at the end of 1559. His son Francis II, the husband of Mary Stuart, succeeded, and, under the influence of his wife's relations, the Guises, it seemed that religious questions would alone occupy his attention, *i.e.* suppression of heresy both in France and in Scotland. But here we meet with a problem that has always to be remembered: the Guises were Lorrainers and therefore foreigners. However, Francis II reigned only for one year and was succeeded by the feeble-minded Charles IX, his next brother; and the Italian Queen-Mother, Catharine of Medici, had great influence over Charles IX. There appeared three parties in France: the out-and-out Catholics, headed by the Guises; the independent Catholic faction of Montmorency, the Constable; and the Huguenots led by Admiral Coligny, and the two brothers, Antony of Bourbon and Louis of Conde, who belonged to the junior branch of the royal family and were "princes of the blood." If the Catholics had a measure of unpopularity because their leaders were from Lorraine, the Huguenots suffered from their relations with Elizabeth, who took the opportunity to throw an English

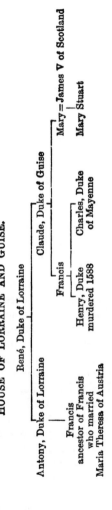

HOUSE OF BOURBON.

Charles, Duke of Bourbon and
Vendôme descended from
Louis IX

Antony = Jeanne d'Albret
Queen of Navarre

Margaret = Henry IV
murdered 1610
2nd wife was
Mary of Medici

Louis, Prince
of Condé
great-grandfather
of Le Grand
Condé

HOUSE OF VALOIS.

Henry II married Catharine of Medici

Francis II
m.
Mary Stuart
d. 1559

Charles IX
d. 1574

Henry III
d. 1589

Francis
of
Anjou

Elizabeth
m.
Philip II
of
Spain, 3rd wife

HOUSE OF LORRAINE AND GUISE.

René, Duke of Lorraine

Antony, Duke of Lorraine

Claude, Duke of Guise

Francis
ancestor of Francis
who married
Maria Theresa of Austria

Francis

Henry, Duke
murdered 1588

Charles, Duke
of Mayenne

Mary = James V of Scotland

Mary Stuart

garrison into Le Havre. This turned Montmorency to
the side of the Guises. Now Philip by the Treaty of
Cateau Cambrésis had married the youthful Elizabeth,
sister of Charles IX and daughter of Catharine. In 1565
it was given out that the young Queen of Spain would
visit her mother at Bayonne, and she was accompanied to
the interview by the Duke of Alva. There is no doubt
that Alva, as Philip's trusted representative, meant to
persuade the French Queen to renounce political jealousies
and to devote all her attention to the suppression of
heresy. That Catharine answered Alva with fair words
seems quite possible, but that she meant to pledge herself
to the cause of the Roman Church is hardly likely,
though Alva seemed to think that she had bound herself
to do so.

It is just now that Philip did one of the worst acts
of his whole reign. In the South of Spain there lived not
only Moors of pure blood, but likewise thousands of mixed
blood, generally known as Moriscos. A certain amount of
common sense, a compromise with his Catholic conscience,
would have enabled him to secure the loyalty of these
people for ever. But he began to persecute them, first in
little matters, interfering for instance with their dress and
prohibiting the use of any language but their own; then
came brutal penalties and, naturally enough, a revolt.
There were slaughter and atrocities upon both sides.
Philip finally called upon his half-brother, Don John of
Austria, to undertake the pacification of Granada. Don
John advocated clemency, but the forces of bigotry were
too strong, and before 1570 practically the whole of the
Morisco population of Andalusia had either been enslaved
or massacred or exiled.

But before the Moriscos had been finally crushed, the
troubles began in the Netherlands. Philip's first Regent
was his half-sister, Margaret, Duchess of Parma, and she,
like almost every other agent who was used for a time

and afterwards thrown aside by Philip, was in favour of a policy of compromise and leniency. But Philip had supplied her with a Spanish army and had established the Inquisition, though by a trick of language it was not actually called the Spanish Inquisition. William the Silent, Prince of Orange, now comes upon the stage; he was a German from Nassau, and was only titular Prince of Orange. He had been a favourite of Charles V, but he had taken hitherto no determined stand upon religious questions. Like Catharine of France, Elizabeth of England, and many others, he was an opportunist. He may have fashioned his policy according to the needs of the moment, and Catholic historians are never tired of pointing out that his public language at this date was entirely in favour of Catholicism. But the whole life of the man leads us to conclude that, though he began as an Imperialist and Roman Catholic, his love of political liberty brought him to consider more closely the question of religious freedom, and that in genuine earnest he became more and more Protestant until finally he was a decided Calvinist. But when the troubles first began in Antwerp and elsewhere in 1566, when excited crowds of extreme Calvinists indulged in anarchy and image-breaking, Orange was certainly not an instigator. At the same time he saw that, though vehement excess might give Philip a handle for fierce persecution, there was the national question behind. Also he had nothing to do with the boasting and drinking, in which men like Count Brederode, the buffoon of the Netherlands, indulged. A large number of the national party met at Brussels and went in procession to the palace of the Regent, Margaret, to put forward their claim to be free from the Spanish army and the Spanish Inquisition. It is said that a courtier whispered in her ear, "Madame, they are only a heap of beggars." Anyhow the name caught on, and that night at a banquet which degenerated into an orgy of intoxication Brederode

and his friends donned the bowl and wallet of the professional beggars, and adopted the nickname which always
stuck to the Netherlander rebels.

But it was one thing to protest and to drink. It was
a different thing to resist Philip in earnest. In 1567
appeared the Duke of Alva with his four Spanish *tercios,*
ready with them to crush any military movement that
might be made by Orange and his party, who were unable
to oppose to him any force except German mercenaries.
Margaret retired from the Netherlands, and Alva ruled
and initiated the reign of blood. For the time the Netherlanders were powerless, but then began Alva's insane
policy of taxation. From Spain he imported the ten per
cent. tax upon all commercial transactions. This struck
a blow at the merchants at Antwerp and the great cities,
which goaded them into rebellion when neither politics
nor religion would have moved them. And it was a policy
most fatal to Philip himself, for the very bankers of the
Flemish cities who declared themselves ruined by the
imposition of "the tenth penny" were the very men upon
whom he depended for his loans. For the time being,
however, there was but talk and excitement, while the
scaffold was kept busy. Loyal Flemish nobles, in particular the Counts of Egmont and Horn, whose sole crime
was protest, were beheaded. The Netherlands seemed far
from being likely to obtain freedom. It is true that
on one occasion Louis of Nassau, the younger brother
of William of Orange, lured one of Alva's veteran
Spanish regiments into ambush, but the success was but
momentary.

Our attention is suddenly called off to the Mediterranean. The Turks made another great move forward
by an attack upon the Venetian island of Cyprus in 1570.
A federation was formed against them. Neither Philip
nor the Pope, much less the Republic of Genoa, had any
fellow feeling for Venice; but it was clear that Venice

could not alone bear the brunt of a new Turkish war.
Like every confederacy, this one took a long time to form
and, when formed, was too late to save the Venetian
garrisons in Cyprus. But formed at last it was, and in
1571 a mighty fleet of galleys was put to sea and won
a decisive victory off Lepanto, in the mouth of the gulf of
Corinth. It is worth while to consider this battle, for it
was the last sea-fight of its kind. From time immemorial
the warship of the Mediterranean had been the rowed
galley, and sailing ships were for commerce or at most
mere auxiliaries in battle. 160 feet long, 25 oars to the
side, three or four or five slaves chained to each oar,
a crew of some 20 free but non-effective hands, some
60 officers and soldiers, two or three auxiliary masts with
lateen sails,—such is the picture of a typical galley.
Though galleys were not powerful according to more
modern ideas, on the comparatively still waters of the
Mediterranean they made up by mobility for what they
lacked in power, for they could be manœuvred as easily
as a regiment of cavalry. But the introduction of gunpowder had far more importance at sea than on land. It
was clear that when the gun became the deciding factor
in war, it could not be properly carried by a vessel of
which the broadside was needed for the oars; at most
three guns could be carried in the bows. A new ship had
indeed been invented, the *galeazza*, which, as in all periods
of transition in warfare, was a compromise. It was larger
than a galley and its whole crew, freemen and slaves
combined, amounted to 1000 men. There were 30 oars
to a side; the oarsmen were covered in by a deck on
which was a tier of guns; but the main strength was
in two lofty castles in the bows and stern, built to hold
several tiers of guns. At Lepanto the main fleets on each
side were of galleys, and on the Christian side there was
a centre of 62, two wings of 54 each, and a reserve of 30;
and half a dozen *galeazzas* were thrown forward in pairs

to distract and worry the Turks so as to allow the galleys
to charge with success. Most of the ships were Venetian,
and the commander-in-chief was Don John of Austria.
One point in the battle is noticeable. One of the Christian
wings swerved aside because the Turks threatened to outflank it, and another division of Turks immediately tried
to strike into the gap thus formed between the wing and
the centre. Immediately the reserve of 30 galleys, commanded by a celebrated and capable sailor, the Duke of
Santa Cruz, rowed with mathematical accuracy into the
threatened gap and restored the line[1].

From a political point of view the battle of Lepanto
only checked the Turks for the time being. Philip was
much too slow and too hard pressed for money to consent
to a vigorous offensive next year. The Venetians on their
side felt that they had to maintain their trade at all costs;
so they gave up all idea of reconquering Cyprus, made
peace with the Sultan, and continued to carry on such
trade as yet remained to them under the goodwill of the
Mohammedan Powers. If we look at the naval result of
Lepanto, we find that a new ship was invented which
should take the place of the *galeazza*, and this was the
genuine *galleon*, afterwards so conspicuous in the great
Armada. It was shaped like the *galeazza*, low in the
waist and with two towering castles, but it was not
intended to be rowed. It had the misfortune that it was
extremely unweatherly, and in an unfavourable wind
simply drifted.

We return to the Netherlands. Very many of the
Flemings fled to England, taking their knowledge of
handicraft to benefit the foreigner who received them,
and thus giving to England a definite step forward as
a manufacturing country. On the other hand the Hol-
landers and Zealanders from the west side of the Zuider
Zee and the islands at the estuary of the Rhine and

[1] See Julian Corbett, *Drake and the Tudor Navy*.

Meuse were not merchants and manufacturers, but chiefly poor fishermen and farmers. Also they were fiercer Protestants than the Flemings. Love for their religious doctrines, and doubtless in the case of many of them a mere love of adventure, induced them to put to sea. They are always known as the Water Beggars. One of their chief leaders was William de la Marck, "a wild sanguinary licentious noble, wearing his hair and beard unshorn, until the death of his relative Egmont should have been expiated, a worthy descendant of the Wild Boar of Ardennes." It is difficult to draw the line between patriotic adventure and piracy, and these men, whose wild spirit ultimately was the source of the success of the Dutch Republic, must have seemed to contemporaries to have been utterly lawless. They put to sea under letters of marque either from the Prince of Orange or from Admiral Coligny, for there was an understanding between the Protestants of France and those of Holland. The Spanish trade between Cadiz and Antwerp gave plenty of opportunity for privateering, but privateering is poor work when there is no place at which the plunder can be sold, and where the ships can fill up with food and water. Queen Elizabeth at first allowed the water-beggars to use the port of Dover. In 1572 she suddenly ordered them to quit Dover and, pressed by downright starvation, they attacked Brill upon their own coast, overawed the Spanish garrison, and then proceeded to seize Flushing and other places. The policy of Elizabeth has been criticised. Did she do this simply to please Philip at a time when Philip seemed to be dangerous to her, so that he might not be ready to support Mary Stuart? or had the descent upon Brill been devised months previously, and did she merely make a pretence of ordering them away from Dover so that she might not be suspected of conniving at their attack? "The accidental nature of the capture of Brill by the sea rover de la Marck on

April 1, 1572, which begot the Dutch Republic, has probably been exaggerated. Elizabeth had allowed Dutch freebooters the shelter of her ports, and la Marck used Dover as a regular basis of operations; and, while she issued public proclamations against him and all other pirates, she privately granted him safe-conducts. In November 1571 he was being greatly caressed by the English who, wrote Guerau, the Spanish Ambassador, at one blow with their practices in France will plunge that country into dreadful war. Subsequently Guerau stated that he had information of the design on Brill six months before it was effected; that he had duly advised the Duke of Alva at the time; and that the place had been reconnoitred before he left England in January 1572. In June Montmorency told Elizabeth to her face that la Marck had left Dover to seize Brill with her consent and aid, and she admitted the charge. Finally, William of Orange thanked her warmly for her efficient aid to la Marck in taking and holding Brill, and a Spaniard averred that la Marck's expulsion from Dover was all a deceitful trick to cover the taking of Brill. It was no sooner occupied than Elizabeth prepared to profit by the occasion, and Sir Humphrey Gilbert was allowed to take 1200 English across the sea[1]."

This was the beginning of English interference in the Netherlands. Elizabeth did not openly send royal troops, and made pretence to Philip that she was still his friend. Motley, the whole way through his celebrated history, continually sneers at Elizabeth and accuses her of double dealing and slowness in helping her fellow Protestants. But she knew what she was doing. She was not ready to defy Spain openly. She meant by every trick at her disposal to pose as the friend of Spain, and she disliked all rebels, even Protestant rebels. At the same time she

[1] Pollard, *The Political History of England* (Longmans), Vol. VI, pp. 331, 332.

pretended that she could not control her subjects, and
that both the sea adventurers like Drake and Hawkins,
and the land adventurers such as Roger Williams and
John Norris, were beyond her control.   What Motley
could never understand was that England was not at that
time ready for open war.   The county militias were mere
gatherings of untrained men, and the royal navy was
inadequate in numbers, so that the longer Elizabeth postponed her defiance of Spain the stronger she was likely
to be when the inevitable struggle came.   The ships had
not been built in 1572 which bore the brunt of the fight
against the Armada in 1588[1], for the Royal Commission on
the Navy, which discussed the defence of England and
produced the means whereby England was adequately
defended when the great Armada came, did not sit till
1583.   Moreover Elizabeth was desperately poor.   For
the sake of her popularity she dared not levy heavy taxes
or demand forced loans, however much she might domineer
and dictate to her parliaments.   She maintained her court
and state chiefly by paying long visits of several weeks
at a time to one nobleman or another; she had a private
understanding with Drake and Hawkins, and secretly
invested money in their buccaneering ventures, so as to
add an honest penny to the royal income.   Therefore for
her to have recklessly defied Spain at the wrong time
would have been fatal.   But in the meanwhile the sailors
were gaining experience of the Atlantic, even if Drake
himself did not bring home such vast piles of booty as
the popular imagination loves to think that he did, and
adventurous soldiers of the type of Roger Williams were
learning the art of war under the leadership of Orange
and his officers.   We are so accustomed to think of the
England of the 18th century continually maintaining
thousands of mercenaries with which to fight France or

[1] Accurately, ten ships of over 200 tons built between 1570 and 1587,
and eight ships rebuilt.

the rebel Americans, that it is with an effort that we acknowledge that in the days of Elizabeth, and also of James I and Charles I, it was the Englishman who was the most valuable mercenary, and the States General of the Netherlands paid him. From 1572 onwards there were always English volunteers or mercenaries in the Netherlands.

Meanwhile in France, in spite of their losses in the earlier civil wars between 1560 and 1566, the Huguenots had been gaining ground. The policy of Catharine was not to persecute the Huguenots as Alva thought that she had promised, but to play them off against the Guises. There were two main divisions of Huguenots: the nobles who often changed sides as did Antony and his more celebrated son, Henry of Navarre, nobles who probably saw in religious controversy an opportunity of regaining their feudal power which the Crown had been steadily weakening for the past century; and, secondly, the burghers of certain towns, not only La Rochelle and Toulouse, though the west and the south of France were the two great Huguenot strongholds, but also Rouen and Orleans. The Calvinistic creed was not acceptable to the majority of the light-hearted French; it was altogether too stern; but the burgher class had leanings towards Calvinism in what we might almost call a non-national mood. In the course of the civil wars Rouen and Orleans fell into Catholic hands, and Huguenotism was there stamped out, while La Rochelle was always the citadel of the Reformed Faith. The result of Catharine's opportunism was to create a party of *politiques*, and in alliance with this party Coligny got such ascendancy over the half-witted Charles IX that he seemed virtually to govern France. Then Catharine took fright after the seizure of Brill, regained her influence over her son, and suddenly persuaded him that Coligny was at the head of a vast conspiracy. She stirred up in him a savage feeling, and soon steps were taken and the result was the celebrated Massacre of St Bartholomew.

The country affected by the massacre was the Netherlands rather than France. The seizure of Brill and of Flushing had been followed by an outbreak throughout the whole land, and in particular the border town of Mons in Hainault had been seized by young Louis of Nassau with Huguenot help, and he was expecting Huguenot reinforcements. The massacre deprived him of the expected aid, and he had to capitulate to Alva upon honourable terms, just at the moment when it seemed as if he would be successful in spreading the revolt in the southern Netherlands.

Yet though deprived of Huguenot aid for the time being, the Netherlands of the north never lost ground. Alva might capture Haarlem and the Spanish soldiers might there vent their fury, but Leyden defied his successor though reduced to the last gasp. What with the defiant Hollander and Zealander water-beggars destroying the Spanish commerce, Elizabeth sending volunteers, and Huguenots threatening the border, Alva felt the task too strong for him and demanded his recall. The successor, Requesens, was unable to do much more, and in 1576 Philip had to send up his brother Don John, the pacifier of the Moors and the victor of Lepanto.

When Requesens was governor of the Netherlands the grievances of the Spanish soldiers came to a head. For a long time past Philip had not paid them, and yet his hold over the Netherlanders depended entirely upon them. Coolly and under good discipline they first seized upon Mechlin, and afterwards upon Antwerp itself. They systematically looted and massacred, and Motley must be quite right in saying this was the first of the various causes that ruined the greatest commercial city of Europe of the day. "It was called the Spanish Fury, by which dread name it has been known for ages. The city which had been a world of wealth and splendour was changed to a charnel-house, and from that hour its commercial prosperity was blasted. Other causes had silently girdled the yet green and flourishing tree, but the Spanish Fury was the fire which consumed it to ashes[1]."

The result of the sack of Antwerp was that the Roman Catholics of the South Netherlands were thrown into the arms of the Prince of Orange. They did not indeed wish to break away from Philip, for the source of their wealth was mostly the carrying trade from Spain, but they were determined to insist upon the departure of the Spanish soldiers. On the 8th of November, 1576, the States General, the Assembly of the United Netherlanders, drew up a document known as the *Pacification of Ghent*; it was a real edict of unity, and recognised the Reformed Faith in Holland and Zealand, yet acknowledged Philip as king. Such was the state of affairs when Don John arrived. For the time being he was quite powerless and had to accept the Pacification. Borrowing large sums of money at reckless rates of interest, and thus satisfying the Spanish soldiers, he withdrew them for a time. But the Union lasted for only a short time. Back came the Spaniards and other troops under the command of Alexander of Parma, son of Margaret and therefore nephew of Philip, a hero already distinguished at Lepanto as much almost as Don John. A motley army got together by the States General was scattered without much trouble at Gemblours in 1578.

The great difficulty in the way of Orange was that the original rebels of Holland and Zealand were utterly different in character from the Flemings and the Walloons. Not only Holland and Zealand, but five other provinces of the north, Utrecht, Guelderland, Overyssel, Friesland, and Groningen, formed in 1579 a confederacy known as the *Union of Utrecht*. They were the Seven United Provinces,

[1] Motley, *Rise of the Dutch Republic*, Part iv. chap. 5.

or United States, but by a natural mistake we call the
whole country Holland from the biggest and strongest
member; by a further mistake we call the inhabitants
Dutch. Their power was always based on the sea, and,
as the years of successful rebellion passed by, from being
poor refugee fishermen the Dutch, after the seizure of
Brill, grew to be the richest ocean-traders of Europe.
Inland dwelt industrious farmers or boers. They were
almost all ardent Protestants, mostly Calvinists. They
could defend their walled towns stubbornly, and by
cutting their dykes could bring the sea to assist them,
whether now against the Spaniards, or a century later
against Louis XIV. But they had no taste for land-
fighting, and for troops to face the Spaniards they
depended on foreign mercenaries and volunteer adventurers. William of Orange was the Stadtholder, let
us say the chief administrator and leader, of Holland
itself and Zealand, but not of all the seven, and originally
he held the office for Philip; in 1581 he formally disowned
Philip's sovereignty.

But, on the other hand, the Netherlanders of the south,
Flemings, Brabanters, Hainaulters, French-speaking Walloons of the south-east, were manufacturers and bankers
as well as merchants. They did not really wish to break
with Spain, for they valued the trade. They were mostly
Catholics; though it has to be remembered that some of
the fiercest image-breaking Calvinists were to be found at
one time or another at Antwerp and Ghent, these men
were not the solid burghers whose wealth made them
important. The leaders were Catholics and had no wish
to see Orange too powerful. Consequently the unity
brought about for a time by the atrocities of the Spaniards,
and expressed by the Pacification of Ghent, could not
last. Orange did his best to find some prince who would
be acceptable to both north and south. More than one
German was proposed, but the choice of a Frenchman

seemed to be more promising. Vile as was Francis of
Anjou and Alençon, the youngest son of Catharine of
Medici, the help of France at such a crisis was too
valuable to be missed, and Orange persuaded the States
General to accept him. Moreover Elizabeth,—who as far
back as 1559 saw her chief danger in the alliance of
France with Scotland in support of Mary Stuart,—was
now drawing near to France, and seemed even likely to
risk losing her popularity in England by marrying him.
Anjou reached Antwerp in 1582. But he had no con-
ception of the duties of the high station offered to him
and of the greatness of his chances as sovereign of the
Netherlands. He tried to loot on the Spanish model.
The Antwerpers were not yet so far sunk as to submit to
Anjou, who had not the military capacity of the Spanish
mutineers of 1576; they promptly barricaded their streets,
and forced him to surrender. He returned in disgrace to
France, and of course Elizabeth at once repudiated him;
soon he died.

Before Anjou's escapade Don John had retired, to die
unhappily after a life of early promise. Alexander of
Parma was now governor, and proved to be the ablest of
all Philip's generals. He played upon the feeling of the
southern Netherlanders against Orange, and easily occupied the Walloon provinces. Gradually he was winning
his way towards Antwerp and Brussels. The Seven United
Provinces, in their inability to combine with the others,
would have made Orange their sovereign, but suddenly
he was assassinated in 1584. The situation was at once
changed. There was no one capable of filling the place
of Orange, and his son was young. Would Alexander be
able to occupy the cities and provinces one by one, profit-
ing by their disunion and lack of a leader? Elizabeth
was now moved to take up a decided policy. Ever since
1572 there had been a steady stream of English volunteers
ready to fight for the Netherlanders, but now she thought

it necessary to do something more openly. Her sea-rovers
had shown her the way to defy Spain, and already she
was strong enough to refuse to give Philip satisfaction for
Drake's raid in the Pacific. Thus she felt herself ready
to oppose him openly, and her new fleet was also ready.
While Orange lived she could not take decided steps;
this may seem mean, but there is no such thing as gratitude in politics, and had Elizabeth helped Orange at an
earlier date and enabled the Netherlanders to win complete independence from Spanish rule, there would surely
have been a conflict between defenders and defended. It
was best for her to keep aloof until her aid was urgently
required. So in 1585 she made a regular treaty with the
States. She would provide royal troops on condition that
certain towns were yielded up to her, and these are known
as the "cautionary" towns, Brill, Flushing, and Ramekins.
Philip Sidney was put in command of the garrisons, and
Robert Dudley, Earl of Leicester, was the Queen's Commander-in-Chief.

The negotiations took time, and before the effect of
English help could be felt, and whilst the Netherlanders
had no leader to succeed William of Orange, Alexander
besieged and finally captured Antwerp. He had not a
force large enough to blockade the city on all sides, but
the country was flooded and he held central positions on
the dykes amidst the submerged fields, and a short way
down stream from Antwerp he built a great bridge of
boats over the Scheldt to bar the approach of the Dutch
water-beggars. The Antwerpers made a desperate attempt
to break down Alexander's bridge. A vessel was filled
up with bags of gunpowder and paving stones, and a
mechanical genius of the city inserted a clock, and, when
the vessel fell down with the ebbing tide towards the
bridge, the clockwork went off accurately, the gunpowder
was exploded, and Parma's bridge with some hundreds of
his best Spanish soldiers was hurled into the air. But the

water-beggars had already appeared and had failed to capture the bridge and had retreated beyond recall, so that there were no ships to take advantage and sail up to the besieged city. In a wonderful way Alexander repaired the moral of his army, rebuilt his bridge, and ultimately forced Antwerp to surrender. From this time onwards her destiny was fixed. The Dutch always held the mouth of the river, and built there several strong forts as well as Flushing. No commercial or fighting ship could pass up or down stream, and the result was that the city, which of all cities was in the finest position for European trade, languished and starved under Spanish rule. Louis XIV and Napoleon in turn coveted Flanders for France, and would have made Antwerp a great centre in case of success, but it was a cardinal point in the policy of both England and Holland from 1585 onwards that Antwerp should be in a perpetual state of blockade; overseas trade, whether from the East through Lisbon, or from America, was diverted to Amsterdam or London as the redistributing port. It was only in the last part of the nineteenth century that all restrictions were withdrawn, and modern Antwerp dates from 1863.

Elizabeth must have been quite aware of what would happen from her policy when, in defiance of Philip, she knighted Drake and when she sent her troops to Holland. But the culminating point was reached when she was persuaded into signing the death warrant of Mary Stuart. This is not the place to enter into the controversy as to whether Elizabeth played the hypocrite when, after Mary's execution, she vented her wrath upon her secretaries, Walsingham and Davison, who persuaded her to give her signature. But one cannot help feeling that she had given it only under pressure, that she meant to revoke it, and that the death warrant was hurried off to Fotheringhay and Mary was executed before Elizabeth had an opportunity at the last moment to change her mind. She saw,

what apparently Cecil did not see, that the presence of
Mary in England was indeed a danger to her because
she was the centre of assassination plots, and assassination was in the air, but that on the other hand Mary
was a hostage, and that Philip could not fight England
in the cause of Mary and of the Roman Church whilst
Mary herself was closely confined. Whatever the ex-
planation of Elizabeth's conduct, it was now too late
to hesitate. She had the ships which had been newly
built under the eye of John Hawkins, who had entered
her service as her chief naval architect, and it only
remained to decide whether the policy of Drake or
the policy of Elizabeth herself should be followed when
the Armada, which Philip had planned to send to sea
and which the Duke of Santa Cruz was organising,
should be ready to sail. In 1587 Drake gave the first
practical proof that the theory of seeking the enemy upon
the enemy's side of the sea was the right one. It was
not only that he sailed into Cadiz harbour and inflicted
tremendous damage upon the portion of the Armada
collected there, but also, by hovering off Cape St Vincent,
he completely prevented the various units of the Armada
from collecting together. He had no naval base where to
fill up his ships with water and provisions; he had no
ally; but he did exactly what the great admirals of two
centuries later were able to do under more favourable
circumstances, that is, he made the enemy's coast England's frontier. In this connection one of the most
important points to be considered is that the crown of
Portugal suddenly became vacant and was claimed by
Philip, and Alva was sent with a Spanish army to overrun
the country and secure Lisbon. It was promised that
Portugal and the Portuguese Indies should be ruled by
Portuguese in Philip's name and not by Spaniards, but
everyone could see that Philip would in time treat Portugal
as a conquered province, even as he treated Aragon or

Naples. In the war the result was that, instead of the
English finding in Lisbon a neutral or a friendly port
which would be the basis of a naval attack upon Spain,
the harbour and the ships and seamen of the Portuguese
navy were now on the side of Spain. Therefore Drake's
ability to keep the sea and to paralyse the Armada in
1587 was a great feat. It is well known that next year
he wished to repeat his experiment and catch the Armada
before it crossed the Bay of Biscay, and it was Elizabeth
who compelled our fleet to wait off Plymouth.

The story of the Armada has been retold for us by
modern historians. The old-fashioned idea that Englishmen rose in all their might to defend their faith and
country, and poured out in their little ships from every
port to harass and vex the great Spanish hulks, that the
fire-ships of Calais were the invention of the Queen herself, and that finally came a lucky wind which blew the
Armada into the North Sea and round the shores of Scotland, has now to be given up. The best ships, upon which
fell the brunt of the fighting, were Queen's ships. A few
vessels of tolerable size were provided by Drake himself
and his adventurous friends and by the city of London,
but the multitude of small vessels, even a tyro can understand, could not carry heavy guns sufficient to batter the
Armada. They may have contributed to make a display
in the eyes of the Spaniards, but the work was done by
the couple of dozen Queen's ships. And moreover they
were not very small. The "little Revenge" was Drake's
flagship, though most people only know of her as the hero
of the fight against the fifty-three, and she carried a crew
of 250 and some twenty heavy guns. The best of the
Spanish ships were really Portuguese, genuine ships of war
and manned by trained crews. There were likewise some
good Italian ships, but the Spaniards indeed themselves
had never been a naval race, and the so-called squadrons
of Andalusia and Valentia were merely composed of

traders in Philip's service and their crews were certainly
not experienced. The galleon could not tack against the
wind. On our side fore-and-aft rigging had been invented
by Fletcher of Rye in the reign of Henry VIII. Various
other inventions had been worked out by Drake and
Hawkins, and the result was that the Queen's ships could
tack against the wind. A writer at the end of the reign
says: "There are two manner of built ships, the one with
a flush deck fore and aft, sunk and low in the water; the
other lofty and high, charged with a half-deck, forecastle,
and copper-ridge heads[1]." Various seamen of the time
preferred one or other of these classes. Walter Raleigh
wrote that he preferred the flush-decked class; the ships
were more nimble and would carry guns as great as the
other class did, and, though such guns were fewer, the
ships could turn and fire more often and more steadily.
Lastly one must mention that Hawkins covered the keels
of his ships with boards of elm closely nailed over with
layers of felt, his own device against barnacles and other
things that would make the timbers rot, a device which
was not beaten until the invention of copper-sheathing
was made at the end of the 18th century.

When the Armada, having drifted up to Calais, was
scared out of the roadstead by the fire-ships and drifted
aimlessly into the North Sea, then took place the pitched
battle off the coast of Gravelines which decided the campaign. It would seem that the English captains, who
were divided into four squadrons, got their ships into line
as best they could, and having the wind sailed in under
the Spanish galleons, delivered their broadsides as quickly
as possible, then hauled out and tacked so as to repeat with
the other broadside. Admiral Winter wrote the following

[1] A copper-ridge head we should call a bulkhead, and the advantage
of a forecastle is that if the enemy were to board in the waist of the ship
then from the bulkheads a deadly volley could be fired upon them. See
Corbett, *Drake and the Tudor Navy*, passim.

to Walsingham: "I deliver it unto your honour upon the credit of a poor gentleman that out of my ship there were shot 500 shot of demi-cannon, culverin and demi-culverin, and when I was furthest off in discharging any of the pieces I was not out of shot of their harquebus, and most times within speech one of another." This would mean that on an average each of his 20 guns was let off twenty-five times in the day. On all our ships the gunners were trained men and the science of gunnery had been worked out elaborately. Of course at this date in a land battle the solid shot of the typical cannon of the day did very little harm indeed. But at sea, when there was a large mark to aim at and the guns were fired at harquebus range, they must have done very considerable damage. But we can hardly compare them to the guns of Nelson's day, though the statement has been made that Nelson's guns were only 25 per cent. better than Drake's. A broadside from the "Victory" at Trafalgar had a smashing effect, for almost all the guns were doubly loaded and some trebly, and they had been most carefully made and tested. The demi-cannon mentioned by Winter was a 30-pounder with a 6½-inch or 7-inch bore, the culverin a 17-pounder with a 5-inch or 5½-inch bore, and the demi-culverin a 9-pounder with a 4½-inch bore.

Next year was made a serious attempt to retaliate upon Philip. The campaign was well planned. Drake's fleet was to escort the army of Sir John Norris, a veteran of the Netherlander wars, who was to land near Lisbon, summon the Portuguese to arms, and advance on that city. But Drake was ever a difficult man to work with. The army was landed too far from Lisbon, the fleet did not co-operate further, hardly any Portuguese rose, the Englishmen were untrained and ill-disciplined, and the expedition resulted in abject failure. Drake lost much of his reputation. Later when he and Hawkins fitted out their last retaliatory expedition against the West Indies, they both died out there, and yellow fever made the expedition quite profitless. It is another of the superstitions of Elizabeth's reign that Drake and his compeers year after year crossed the Atlantic and came home with their ships deeply sunk in the water with a vast weight of Spanish gold and silver, and that Philip's Atlantic trade was absolutely ruined by them. It would seem that in truth the only voyage which was really profitable to Drake was the cruise around the world, 1577—80; on his return the recorded value of his spoil was £55,000, and it is thought that perhaps £120,000 more had been secretly got rid of by him before he rendered his account to the Queen. Perhaps his plunder on that occasion would represent one million of money of our day, though it is true that Philip claimed that the damage done was nine times as much. On the other hand it has been mentioned already that in 1595 Philip's fleet brought from the West Indies to Cadiz 35 millions of ducats, the produce of some three years. Taking the ducat at about 2s. 6d. and multiplying by six to give the value of the present day, we can calculate how much was Philip's income from America; and the fact that this 35 millions reached Spain safely shows that the English buccaneers had not destroyed his Indian revenue.

The last attack made upon Cadiz by Howard and Essex gave the finishing touch to Philip's hopes of equipping a second Armada.

Alexander of Parma had not approved of the invasion of England at all. He had his definite work to subdue the Netherlands, and, had he been able in 1588 to carry over his entire army from Flanders to England, what he had already done in the Netherlands would probably have been undone; even the fact of having to wait for the Armada made him lose the whole of the year 1588. Philip was trying to do too much with the scanty means at his disposal, but he was always doing that, and now we find him acting in just the same way towards France. The French Civil Wars had come to such a pass that it appeared that Spanish interference was absolutely required. There was nobody but Alexander to give the aid of Spain, and so the third task was put upon him of fighting Henry of Navarre. In France towards the end of the eighties we come to the two last stages of the long-drawn agony of her religious feuds. It is called the War of the Three Henries. There was Henry III the King, a mere puppet with neither intellect nor morals; there was Henry of Guise, the Catholic champion, who meant to put forward his own claim for the throne of France in case of the death of King Henry; there was Henry of Navarre, who had already once recanted and turned Catholic at the time of the Bartholomew, but had come back to the Huguenot camp, and who was the son of Antony of Bourbon and Jeanne d'Albret, Queen of Navarre[1]. He is known in French history as *le grand Béarnais*, Béarn being the portion of the Kingdom of Navarre north of the Pyrenees, and he had been born at Pau, its capital. He was of course an opportunist; he trimmed his sails to the wind of the moment. He was a born fighter, blunt and genial, and able to put up with the blows of fate. His intimates adored him, and he just suited the French character.

In January 1585 had been formed the League of French Catholics in definite alliance with Spain. Henry of Guise was supported at the head of the League by his brothers, the Cardinal of Guise and the Duke of Mayenne, and the Pope issued a bull in their favour. Their avowed object was to secure the crown for a Catholic on the death of King Henry III. The King was shifty, and inclined in turn to the League, which acted as if it had sovereign rights, and to Henry of Navarre. At one time the two Henries, France and Navarre, advanced on Paris.

[1] See pedigree, p. 22.

But treachery and assassination were favourite weapons
of low minds, in this as in other ages. Henry of Guise was
lured to a conference at Blois in 1588 and was murdered;
then Henry of France was murdered in 1589 in revenge,
and at last the male line of Catharine was extinct. The
way was now clear for the third Henry, both of France
by descent from the main line of French kings, and of
Navarre. There was no one else of blood royal. A certain
Cardinal of Bourbon was thought of, but died; besides
him there were only Philip of Spain by right of his wife
Elizabeth in violation of the much cherished Salic Law,
or the young Duke of Guise, son of the murdered Henry,
or Mayenne, in defiance of any right at all.

There were jealousies amongst the Catholic leaders
themselves, and their cause was damaged by their reliance
on foreigners, Spaniard and Lorrainer. Many Catholic
nobles followed Henry of Navarre. But even the famous
victory at Ivry in 1590 over Mayenne did not secure for
him the crown. Paris and Rouen and other towns were
staunchly Catholic, and would not have even a patriot to
be King to save them from the foreigner at the price of
accepting a Huguenot. Philip now ordered Alexander of
Parma to turn his back on the Netherlands, and to take
his Spanish army to the relief of Paris in 1590 and of
Rouen in 1592. The two great captains never fought a
pitched battle. The impetuous Béarnais would have liked
to come to blows, but Alexander was cautious and dared
not risk the lives of his valuable Spaniards who could not
be replaced. Alexander triumphed so far that the crown
of France seemed quite out of Henry's grasp. Then Henry
made his great coup, recanted for the second time, became
Catholic, and said that Paris was worth a mass; the
city opened its gates and Alexander's work was undone.
Alexander died at the end of 1592.

And so we have come to the end of a critical chapter
in the history of France and Europe. After the brood of

Catharine of Medici at last a real man was on the throne
of France, a man who was no bigot but a true Frenchman,
who, by the *Edict of Nantes*, gave complete toleration to
the Huguenot lords and Huguenot cities, who was himself
a Catholic and at the same time the ally of the Protestant
Queen of England and the Protestant Netherlanders.
With the advent of Henry of Navarre to the throne of
France begins the period of the decisive interference of
France in affairs outside her borders. There was a
momentary pause when he was assassinated in 1610, but
finally Richelieu took up the work. On the death of
Richelieu and during the minority of Louis XIV there
was another pause, and then Louis XIV in his manhood
assured the ascendancy of France, though he completely
spoilt it by revoking his grandfather's Edict of Nantes.

Therefore the triumph of Henry IV was just the final
touch which ensured the failure of Philip. For indeed
Philip had failed, however strong Spain might still appear
to be to contemporaries. Of course the steady opposition
of the Dutch, based on their sea power, was the greatest
cause of the ultimate exhaustion of Spain. The English contributed their share, especially by defeating the
Armada, for by so doing they drew Alexander off from
his proper task; the men and the money wasted in vain
against us would have been invaluable to him against the
Dutch. But neither the continuous draining of Spanish
resources in the Netherlands, nor the shrewd blows struck
by English sailors, should allow us to slight the work of
Henry IV. He, too, in 1590 and 1592, spoilt Alexander's
prospects by bringing him from the Netherlands into
France; he was the open enemy of Spain and ally of the
Dutch down to the *Treaty of Vervins* in 1598, and even
then helped them by money and sympathy; he foiled
Spain by getting the better of the League and Mayenne
its chief. As we look back to Philip's and Alva's attempt
at Bayonne in 1565 to secure the co-operation of Catharine

in putting down heresy in both countries, to the Huguenot support of the Dutch in spite of the terrible set-back caused by the Bartholomew, and to the episode of Anjou's attempt to take the sovereignty of the Netherlands, we have to acknowledge that French affairs deeply influenced all Philip's plans. A French crown devoted to Catholicism would have caused civil wars in France worse than those which actually took place, and then Philip would have been less distracted from the Netherlands. Henry's final triumph made the ultimate success of the Dutch quite safe. The critical years were those from 1584 to 1592 when Alexander seemed to be on the point of victory, William of Orange dead and Maurice too young, and the Dutch for the time leaderless, and include the years of the Armada and of Ivry. Henry safe on the throne of France and Alexander dead, the cause of the Dutch was won.

CHAPTER III

THE GROWTH OF FRANCE. THE THIRTY
YEARS' WAR

WITH the death of Philip in 1598, and of Elizabeth in
1603, the stage is filled with new characters. In the same
year 1598, Henry IV made peace with Spain at Vervins.
Very soon after his accession James I made peace with
Spain, and we cannot call him either short-sighted or
unpatriotic in doing so. Naval power is an excellent
defence to a country, but only a direct offensive on the
enemy's soil can bring a war of such magnitude to a
decisive conclusion. As long as England had no standing
army, as long as untrained men were swept into the
militia, put into uniforms and sent abroad untrained; in
fact as long as the military state of England was as
depicted by Shakespeare in the plays of *Henry IV* and
Henry V, with fraudulent musters, bribes accepted from
the strong men who did not want to serve, mere gaol
sweepings and weaklings swept into the ranks, braggarts
of the Bardolph type abounding,—and there can be no
doubt that in those plays Shakespeare was describing
what he actually saw,—serious war was impossible, and
neither Elizabeth nor James I dared to make the smallest
attempt to tax the nation for a standing national army.
Not only did James make peace with Spain and even go
so far as to wish to marry each of his sons in turn to
a Spanish Infanta, but also he came to terms with the

Dutch. For a sum of money down he sold the three cautionary towns, and henceforward there was no disguise; the Englishmen who still served in thousands in the armies of the States were no longer royal troops but downright mercenaries. They were organised and trained scientifically, and at this time the Dutch army rather than the Spanish was the model for Europe.

The Stadtholder was Maurice of Orange and Nassau, the second son of the murdered William the Silent, now grown to manhood. He was fighting a war which still was severe and exhausting even for the conquerors. On the death of Alexander of Parma, the Netherlands were formed into a separate Government for Philip's daughter Isabella and her husband Albert, an Austrian Archduke. They conciliated the Walloon and Flemish Provinces, granted freedom of worship, and a certain measure of municipal freedom in the towns. Under them neither Walloons nor Flemings wished to pass under the rule of the House of Orange, and so the present line between Holland and Belgium was fixed. The great military undertaking of the early years of the 17th century was the siege of Ostend. Albert Spinola, a Genoese noble and soldier of fortune, was the able commander of the Spaniards and Catholic Netherlanders, and he set himself down to capture Ostend, for it was of vital importance to the Netherlands to have a port, as Antwerp was blockaded and useless. After three years' siege Ostend fell, but in those three years Spinola had lost so many men that it was almost a disastrous conquest in the long run. The rest of the war down to the truce of 1609, and then again from 1619 onwards, became an affair of sieges along the border and was chiefly concentrated round Bergen-op-Zoom, Breda, Bois-le-duc (Hertogenbosch), Maestricht. Well disciplined and well led, the Dutch and their mercenaries, Englishmen, Scots, Frenchmen, and Germans, devoted themselves to the science of sieges and the

defence of a limited frontier. By sea their trade grew
at the expense of both Spain and Portugal, and indeed
the curious thing is that Portugal suffered most, yet the
original enemy was Spain only, and Portugal was dragged
into the war simply because Philip II annexed it. When
Dutch ships were unable to go to Lisbon for the spices
that found so ready a market in every land, the natural
result was that they went direct to the Spice Islands of
the East Indies, and there they ruined the trade not of
Spain but of Portugal. The English followed, and the
two nations then became rivals for what in the 16th century
had been a Portuguese monopoly.

For the last sixty years the history of Germany has
lacked interest. The Treaty of Augsburg of 1555 was
a compromise, and every compromise lasts for just as long
a period as the contracting parties choose to keep it. In
the early 17th century the Jesuits gained new influence
in Austria, and the Roman Catholic sovereigns thought
themselves strong enough to break the treaty. The
question was whether the States where Church lands
had been secularised could be compelled to restore them.
In fact the Counter-Reformation, in Austria and Bavaria
in particular, was ready to attack the Reformation. In
1610 a general conflagration nearly burst out. Two
German duchies adjoining the Netherlands, Cleves and
Jülich, fell vacant. The claimants were Protestant, the
inhabitants Catholic. Neither the Emperor nor the
Church would willingly let the duchies pass to heretics
and the lands be secularised, and the Emperor claimed
the right to administer them while vacant. To check
the imperial pretension Henry IV made alliance with
Maurice of Orange, and only his murder prevented a
great and general war; and when the Thirty Years' War
did begin France took no part at first, as Louis XIII was
young and Richelieu not yet established in power.

The actual occasion was the election of Frederick,

Elector Palatine[1] and a Calvinist, to the throne of Bohemia in 1619. The Catholics had already nominated Ferdinand of Styria, cousin and heir of the Emperor, and himself shortly afterwards elected to be Emperor[2]. Thus the struggle was precipitated, but would have occurred sooner or later. The point of interest for us is that Frederick was married to Elizabeth, the beautiful daughter of James I, the object of the adoring allegiance of so many of the poets and statesmen of the time. But James could do nothing to help the new King and Queen of Bohemia. He had no force that he could send inland, and, clever talker as he was, he could not by mere words prevent Spain from taking the Catholic side. The first part of the Thirty Years' War is the Bohemian period. Frederick was in 1620 crushed at the battle of the White Mountain and beaten out of Bohemia, and then out of his own Palatinate. The Emperor Ferdinand declared that the electoral vote was to be transferred from the Palatinate

---

[1] Frederick ruled the Lower Palatinate on the middle Rhine with Heidelberg as his capital. The Upper Palatinate was on the upper Main.

[2]

HOUSE OF HAPSBURG.

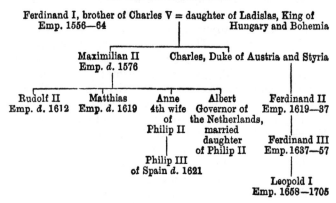

Ferdinand I, brother of Charles V = daughter of Ladislas, King of
   Emp. 1556—64   Hungary and Bohemia

Maximilian II   Charles, Duke of Austria and Styria
Emp. d. 1576

Rudolf II   Matthias   Anne   Albert   Ferdinand II
Emp. d. 1612   Emp. d. 1619   4th wife   Governor of   Emp. 1619—37
                             of   the Netherlands,
                             Philip II   married
                                         daughter   Ferdinand III
                                         of Philip II   Emp. 1637—57
                             Philip III
                             of Spain d. 1621
                                                          Leopold I
                                                          Emp. 1658—1705

to Bavaria, whose Duke belonged to a younger branch of the same family.

But the religious passions spread far beyond Bohemia. There were two main Catholic parties in Germany with divergent interests. There was the party of the Emperor who looked to the interests of Austria and the House of Hapsburg; and there was the league of minor Catholic States, the Duke of Bavaria at their head, Count Tilly their General, and Spain their ally, whose chief idea was to win back to the Church the secularised Church lands which had been covered by the Treaty of Augsburg. Tilly's army was strong, and advancing through central and towards northern Germany he seemed likely to crush all the petty Protestant princes. The Spaniards occupied the Lower Palatinate. In the meanwhile the two great Lutheran Electors, George William of Brandenburg and John George of Saxony, held aloof. They were pronounced Protestants, but Frederick was a Calvinist; also they did not want to disunite the Empire by a great civil religious war on a large scale. As they would do nothing, it rested with Christian of Denmark to become the champion of the Protestant cause, for he held the secularised archbishoprics of Bremen, Verden, and Lubeck.

The fortunes of the second period of the Thirty Years' War depended therefore entirely upon the position of the Baltic powers. The King of Denmark commanded the passage of the Sound, and held Norway in subjection, thus controlling all the commerce between the Swedish, North German, and Russian ports on the one side, and Holland and England on the other. The *raison d'être*, so to speak, of Denmark was the guardianship of the Sound. The cautious Dutch were willing enough to pay tolls to the Danish Government for their ships, which went in search of the corn and timber, hemp and skins, which have ever been the main articles of commerce in the Baltic. But there was another power to be considered. Sweden always felt aggrieved at being cut off from the North Sea by the Danish power. The question therefore was: would the three Protestant countries, Sweden, Denmark, and Holland, make a confederation to help the German Protestants, and would England join? Or would Christian of Denmark have to fight entirely upon his own responsibility?

Now in the first place Holland could do very little to help. The truce of 1609 was broken and a new war broke out between Holland and Spain, a war marked by exactly the same features that we have noticed before,—the defence of a land frontier, and the sieges of cities on the one side or on the other. Frederick Henry of Orange continued year after year to fight Spinola, even as his brother Maurice had done, with an admirably trained and scientific army of mercenaries, Englishmen and Scots, Frenchmen and Germans.

Gustavus Adolphus of Sweden would have joined in the struggle if he had been allowed to. He was at war against Poland, for the King of Poland was his kinsman and the Roman Catholic claimant to the Kingdom of Sweden. Therefore if he were to take part in a German war he required some sort of security against Poland. He likewise required some remission of Danish tolls upon Swedish ships, and he claimed the right to be commander-in-chief of the Confederacy if it was formed. Christian of Denmark could not grant his terms, and so he fell out.

Before James I of England died he had been so greatly offended by the refusal of the King of Spain to marry the Infanta to Charles that he was willing for war against Spain. The Duke of Buckingham had come home from Madrid with Charles bent upon vengeance against Spain, because this refusal appeared to him in the light of a personal insult. So Charles I came to our throne with a distinct policy of taking a part in the Thirty Years'

War as the ally of Christian[1]. He married Henrietta Maria, the sister of Louis XIII, and certainly hoped to draw France into the alliance. Now it is so much the custom to sneer at our earlier Stuarts and to consider them mere men of straw in comparison with Elizabeth who came before them, or with Cromwell who came after them, that one has to make somewhat of an effort to view the state of affairs from Charles' own point of view. Firstly he seriously wished to help the Protestant cause and his uncle Christian. Next he made a real effort, according to his powers, to induce the Lord-Lieutenants of the counties to raise useful soldiers in the militia, compel them to have up-to-date arms and train them, instead of holding a farcical inspection once a year. It is impossible to read the orders which he sent without seeing that his wishes were neither tyrannical nor impracticable. At the same time he wished the cavalry of various counties to be collected in some central place for joint training. But he was met with a quiet and stubborn refusal to carry out his orders. If he had been the typical despot of tradition he might have set the Star Chamber in motion against the offenders, but he was unable as a constitutional sovereign to do more than he did. Then as regards money, the very party who had always cried out against the wicked Catholics of Spain, that is the Puritans, had control of the House of Commons and refused to grant Charles supplies, and all that he could do for the help of Christian was to sell a few jewels. The picture of Puritan England refusing to let their King help brother Protestants in Germany, while they haggled over a vote of a few thousands in the House of Commons, is not one which Macaulay presents to us, but it is a true picture all the same. The justification of these men would be that Charles had married a Roman Catholic wife, though they

[1] Christian IV was brother of Anne of Denmark, and therefore Charles I's uncle.

forgot that she was the daughter of Henry of Navarre, that the Edict of Nantes was in force in France, and that Richelieu was quite ready to join the Confederacy on Christian's side. Another justification was that Buckingham was high in favour, and one must confess that here we see how it was that Charles failed, for Buckingham no historian has ever presented otherwise than as an incompetent and gaudy trifler.

The next point is that, just as Richelieu was on the point of committing France to the war, the Huguenots of La Rochelle were mad enough to revolt against the Crown of France. Of course Richelieu could do nothing to help the German Protestants whilst the French Protestants were in open rebellion, and therefore it is remarkable to see how the Protestants of both France and England damaged the cause of the Protestants of Germany.

Therefore the second period of the war, which begins just about the time when Charles I succeeded to our throne, has as its chief figure Christian of Denmark. He was supported by the lower Saxon States, and Ernest Mansfield, a soldier of fortune, had collected a scratch army of volunteers and mercenaries. Besides this, in the far east of Hungary Bethlen Gabor, Prince of Transylvania, won some successes and was distracting the Emperor's attention. On the other side was the army of the Catholic League headed by Tilly. We now find the Emperor giving a special commission to that wonderful and mysterious character Wallenstein, a nobleman descended from a German family settled in Bohemia, whose real name was Albert von Waldstein. He had already shown distinction as a leader of mercenaries, and the Emperor made a bargain with him to raise 50,000 men as the Imperial General with the rank of Duke of Friedland. In the war Tilly completely broke up the power of Christian at the battle of Lutter in 1626, and overran all lower Saxony. Wallenstein scattered the

army of Mansfield and overran Silesia. For the next
three years the state of the conquered country was very
bad indeed, and the Emperor felt himself strong enough
to issue an *Edict of Restitution*, by which he seized for
the Church all bishoprics and lands which had become
Protestant before the Treaty of Augsburg. Christian was
in abject terror and made a humiliating peace.

In the midst of military triumphs the Catholic party
now definitely split into two. The German princes of the
Catholic League, especially the Duke of Bavaria, who had
the support of Spain, had no other view than the restoration of the Roman Church; but on the other hand the
Emperor was aiming at the expansion of the power of the
House of Hapsburg, and one cannot but acknowledge that
he was in the right, for if ever the much distracted Germany
was to be united it must be under the strongest German
power, that is to say under the Hapsburgs alone. But
then, by identifying himself so strongly with the Counter-
Reformation, and being so largely under the control of the
Jesuits, Ferdinand completely failed to carry through his
policy, and to other Germans it seemed that he was merely
trying to advance the interests of Austria in particular
and not Germany as a whole. In these years of triumph
he had the great design of pushing his power to the
shores of the Baltic. He made Wallenstein Admiral of
the Empire, and it would seem that on the collapse of the
power of Denmark he aimed at controlling the trade of
the Baltic. This frightened the German Cities of the
Hanseatic League; more than that, it frightened Gustavus
of Sweden. Therefore when Wallenstein laid siege in 1628
to Stralsund, which was the key to the possession of the
Baltic coast, not only the dejected Christian of Denmark
plucked up courage to throw in supplies and troops, but
also Gustavus was called upon the scene. Wallenstein
swore that he would have Stralsund and assaulted it with
fierce keenness, but a corps of Swedes and of Scots in the

Swedish service was thrown into the place and made it safe. This was the turning point of the war.

Indirectly Richelieu, looking carefully after the interests of France, helped the Protestant cause to some extent by interfering in Italy. He wished to prevent Savoy from being the mere vassal of Spain; he supported as heir to the Duchy of Mantua a claimant who had a French mother and French sympathies; he tried to bar access to the Valtellina to the Spaniards in Lombardy. He was, in fact, causing the French once more to assert themselves on an old battle-ground. In doing this he had an eye to geographical position, Savoy commanding the western Alps, Mantua the neck between Lake Garda and the Po, and the Valtellina the line of communication from Lombardy to the Brenner and therefore to Germany. French success in the Valtellina crippled the Spaniards of Lombardy, and both a Spanish army under the able Spinola and an Imperial army under one of Wallenstein's officers had to be called away from Germany; consequently the first efforts of Gustavus in the Thirty Years' War were much influenced. Moreover Richelieu was instrumental in bringing about a truce between Gustavus and Poland.

Gustavus, during the last few years carrying on his war against the King of Poland, his own cousin, had been training his native Swedish troops. His army was exceedingly well disciplined and trained, and his two years of triumphant marching and fighting in Germany mark the next epoch in military history. Gustavus discarded the old method of fighting in great masses, and therein he differed from both the Spanish and the German commanders. He was in favour of rapid marches which disconcerted his enemies, and was entirely opposed to the Dutch method of reducing war to a series of sieges, a method useful enough on the limited frontier between the Independent and the Spanish Netherlands, but out of place in this war which spread over the wide area of well-nigh the whole of Germany. He was the first of the modern commanders who trusted to a direct charge of horse in place of skirmishing methods. His ideal was for his cavalry to be interlaced with musketeers, so as to shake the enemy with their shot, and then he would order the charge at a trot with the naked sword. He altogether revolutionised the method of handling artillery, and introduced light field-guns in place of the great fixed batteries of heavy guns then so dear to the German mind. His infantry he arrayed in longer and thinner lines and in smaller units than the Germans; he made the musket lighter and more efficient, and got rid of the crutch on which it was fired; but he still kept the proportion of half musketeers and half pikemen. The bulk of his troops were native Swedes, but it can hardly be imagined that his own small and poor kingdom could supply sufficient men for war on a large scale, and he had numbers of Scots in his service and Germans also, but he trained them on the Swedish method. The Scots were particularly attracted towards his service, whereas such Englishmen as wished to fight, whether for the sake of adventure or of religion, still preferred to serve the Stadtholder of Holland.

Gustavus began his career quietly in 1630 with the invasion of various places upon the coast of Pomerania and West Prussia that he might obtain, to use his own language, a bastion, that is to say, a basis on the coast from which he could strike securely inland. When he wished to push forward from his bastion inland in 1631,— we note by way of parenthesis that he was the first to adopt the method of fighting right through the winter instead of going into winter quarters, for the hardy Swedes made light of the cold of a German winter,—he was foiled for the time being by the extreme obstinacy of George William, Elector of Brandenburg, who, though a Lutheran Protestant, refused to let him march through Brandenburg territory. John George, Elector of Saxony, was equally obstinate. These two powerful Electors, in spite of their religious feelings, did not like to see a foreigner on German soil. Matters were critical when the great city of Magdeburg declared in favour of Gustavus. Either the King of Sweden would violate the rights of neutrality in Brandenburg so as to save Magdeburg, and would thereby offend other Lutheran Powers, or he would have to submit to the mortification of seeing Magdeburg conquered when his presence in Germany was the sole reason for Magdeburg's revolt. Unluckily, while the negotiations with George William were going on, Tilly stormed the town and the usual massacre took place[1]. One German city had declared itself on Gustavus's side, and that one city had been destroyed. So far therefore the King of Sweden seemed to have failed, but he was now put upon his mettle, and he threatened George William with his direct enmity if he persisted in remaining neutral, and then, but too late, Brandenburg joined the Protestant side. Next John George of Saxony, frightened by the fate of Magdeburg, was drawn out of his state of neutrality, and Gustavus had therefore an excuse for pushing southwards. After a good deal of manœuvring and counter-manœuvring, he and Tilly met face to face at Breitenfeld, a short distance north of Leipzig, where the new Swedish formation triumphed completely. Tilly's army was not merely beaten; it was annihilated.

The rest of the year saw Gustavus pushing westwards through central Germany and down the line of the Main to the Rhine. In or near the valley of the Main were several great ecclesiastical estates, the bishopric of Bamberg, the bishopric of Wurzburg, the archbishopric of Mainz, and

[1] A massacre when the blood of the assailants is hot is common in history; Alexander at Maestricht and Tilly at Magdeburg have their Protestant parallel in Cromwell at Basing House and Drogheda. Wellington was unable to control his men at Badajoz. In fact military rather than religious madness causes such scenes.

so on, so that the country was known as the "Priests' Alley." Here then Gustavus brought the horrors of war upon the Catholics, and so relieved the distressed Protestants of Lower Saxony upon whom had fallen the brunt of misfortune previously. Not that Gustavus deliberately plundered and massacred as Tilly had done, but he demanded subsidies and fines and brought home the reality of war to the Catholics, surely though not cruelly. The winter of 1631—32 saw him with his court at Mainz or Frankfort alternately. He partly relieved the Palatinate from its Spanish garrisons, and for the time being the Catholic League was prostrate.

During 1631, while Gustavus was moving against Tilly and the Catholic League, the Emperor and Wallenstein had been comparatively quiet. Now that Gustavus was at the height of his triumph a new commission had to be given to Wallenstein. He was to make war entirely upon his own responsibility, and have absolute power of nominating officers and disposing of lands confiscated from enemies and rebels. Such was Ferdinand's distress that, to stem the tide of Swedish victories, he was forced to make this incredible bargain. In 1632 Gustavus invaded Bavaria, assured Nuremberg of his protection and alliance,—for a great independent city of that type required assurance that it would not be left in the lurch as Magdeburg had been the previous year,—and finally he penetrated to Augsburg, the very home of Lutheranism, where he was enthusiastically received. Tilly was once more beaten and died of his wounds. But then Wallenstein came upon the scene with his new army and enjoying his new powers. Wallenstein threatened Nuremberg, and Gustavus hastened back to defend it. Wallenstein occupied a position upon high ground and refused to be drawn into a battle. Gustavus occupied Nuremberg and tried to lure Wallenstein out on to the open. The army on each side was at about its greatest as regards numbers, some 60,000 to 70,000 strong, and therefore the policy of waiting resolved itself into the question as to which could feed itself longest. The light cavalry of Wallenstein, the Croats and Hussars from the Slavonic part of the Austrian dominions, were born plunderers and utterly pitiless in their methods. They managed to sweep in more victuals than Gustavus's scouts, and in consequence starvation seemed to threaten the Swedish army first, let alone that there was a plague in the city of Nuremberg. Therefore it was Gustavus who had to move first, and he assaulted Wallenstein's entrenched lines with his entire force and, amid scenes of terrible carnage, he was beaten back. Consequently he had to abandon Nuremberg and retreat towards the north. Wallenstein was very nearly as hard pressed for victuals as Gustavus and, having suffered almost as much in the assault on his lines, he likewise drew off from Nuremberg; but the honours of war were with him, for Gustavus had moved away first, and the triumphant Swedes were checked.

Later in the same year the rivals met for the last time in Saxony. John George resorted to his old game of neutrality, and the Saxon commander-in-chief, Count Arnheim, was very much under Wallenstein's influence; thus it seemed as if Saxony would change sides. Therefore Gustavus hastened towards Saxony, and there he met Wallenstein at Lützen, half a dozen miles to the south of Leipzig. On November 6th, in the midst of most desperate fighting during a foggy day, Gustavus, separated from his cavalry, was recognised and killed. But his army, led by Bernard of Weimar, was roused to such a pitch of fury that it drove in Wallenstein's very much superior numbers, and so the year 1632 ended with the death of the great Protestant champion and the annihilation of Wallenstein's unique army. Fifteen months later, in February 1634, the Emperor found that a general of such overpowering importance was no longer useful to him, and by a miserable conspiracy he procured the assassination of Wallenstein.

The last sixteen years of the war, 1633—48, entirely lack interest. The native Swedish veterans of Gustavus died off, and their places could not be filled. The so-called Swedish armies were now largely composed of mercenaries of all types trained on the Swedish method. The discipline was relaxed, and horrible tales of cruelty were told of the Swedes just as of the Spaniards or the Germans of Tilly's old army. If any name can be applied to the last stage of the war, one would feel inclined to call it the French period. In fact, it was Richelieu who kept the war alive where otherwise sheer exhaustion would have produced peace, and French armies appeared in Germany. And Germany suffered horribly, Catholics and Protestants alike, at the hands of both friends and foes. The war even dragged on for a few years after the death of both Louis XIII and Richelieu. It was ended in 1648 by treaties drawn up at Osnabruck and Munster, but we usually talk about the *Treaty of Westphalia.* Religious toleration was secured and the old doctrine was established —*Cujus regio ejus religio*—owing to the exhaustion upon both sides. Austria's gain was the control of Bohemia, where the war had begun, now purged of Protestantism. France gained Alsace and absolute right to Metz, Verdun and Toul, the three bishoprics of Lorraine; but the main triumph of France was that she had interfered so skilfully in German matters as to make disunited Germany even more disunited. Sweden gained her bastion, viz. parts of Pomerania and Mecklenburg, Bremen and Verden. The Elector of Brandenburg secured the rest of Pomerania and the mid-German bishoprics of Magdeburg and Halberstadt. The Duke of Bavaria, in whose interests, one might almost say, the war had been waged, gained definitely the Upper Palatinate and recognition as an Elector. The son of Frederick, the former Elector Palatine, regained the Lower

The Peace of Westphalia

THE DUTCH AT SEA 63

Palatinate; and thus there were now eight Electors. The
sacred number of seven no longer existing a ninth was
later created, and the Duke of Brunswick became Elector
of Hanover in 1692.

Meanwhile the dreary war between the Dutch and the
Spaniards had been fought to a finish, and in 1648 Spain
formally recognised the United Provinces as a Sovereign
state. It was a war, as noticed previously, of sieges of
fortresses along the border. The Dutch never allowed
themselves to look away from home, and Frederick Henry
of Orange with his foreign brigades made siege-craft a
fine art. But the Spaniards had interests elsewhere, and
helped the Catholic League in Germany. Spinola, the
clever Genoese general, was called away to the Palatinate,
thence to Italy to combat Richelieu's war policy[1], and in
Italy he died. By sea the native Dutch navy reduced
the Spanish naval and commercial power to a shadow.
A crushing victory in 1635, when Spain made a great
effort, can be compared to our victory over the Armada.
Indeed so formidable were the Dutch by sea that Charles I
was seriously anxious lest they should control the straits
and channel. Out in the East Indies they had turned the
English settlers away from the Spice Islands, and no
satisfaction was forthcoming for a massacre of English
traders and their servants at Amboyna, the island where
cloves were grown, in 1623. Here we see one of the
reasons why ship-money was so important a question:
the men who thought only of their position in England
and Parliament's control of taxation were, from one point
of view, as short-sighted as those who prevented Charles
from assisting Christian of Denmark in 1625; Charles I
was the patriot in that he aimed at recreating England's
navy to protect her trade[2]. Sooner or later the English

[1] See page 56.
[2] The ship-money fleet fought the Mohammedans of the Mediterranean, and captured Salee near the Straits of Gibraltar, thereby freeing

and Dutch would fight at sea for profit and commerce, though old allies and brother Protestants. As traders the Dutch got a name for being grasping, and they reduced the quantity of the spices that they brought from the Indies in order to raise prices. This is a well-known commercial heresy, and few would now deny that it is better to sell a greater quantity at a lower price so as to make a larger total profit. Also the Dutch were great merchants, bankers, and carriers of the world's trade, but not manufacturers; here was a weak point in their armour, for if they lost the carrying trade between foreigners they would have no other source of wealth. But every nation has had commercial blindness in some form. Spain had tried to keep Drake and Hawkins, and the generations that followed them, from trading with Spanish America, so that raids of retaliation and smuggling and piracy were normal in the West Indies. England in the day of her power made laws to keep her colonial trade in her own hands. Wealth and monopoly stir up hatred against the strongest commercial power of any period, and in the 17th century the strongest were the Dutch and therefore the jealousy was against them.

France and Spain fought each other in the last years of the Thirty Years' War, and still after 1648 they were fighting. Richelieu and Louis XIII died, and Anne of Austria was regent for the boy Louis XIV in 1643. She was really Anne of Spain, being sister of Philip III, and lived down the unpopularity that naturally arose against her as a partisan of her native land. The young Duke of Enghien, who later became Prince of Condé, descended from the uncle of Henry IV and therefore of the blood royal, won near the Netherlands a crushing victory at Rocroi, and another at Lens, blows fatal to the fame of

many Christian galley-slaves ; but trade rivalry and fear of Holland were the chief reasons of the renewal of the navy by Charles I, and therefore of ship-money.

the Spanish infantry. But a minority usually brings trouble, and the reign of Anne and of her Italian adviser, Cardinal Mazarin, was not an exception to the rule. Here was an opportunity for the feudal nobility of France to raise its head again after Richelieu's heavy hand was withdrawn by death. Even Condé opposed the crown. Of course aid came to the rebels from across the border, Condé fought as the ally of the Spaniards whom he had recently beaten, and the Spanish Queen-mother with an Italian cardinal was the patriot and champion of the grandson of Henry IV. This is known as the war of the Fronde. The rebels were the *frondeurs*, *i.e.* slingers, a term of contempt applied from the gutter-snipes of Paris; they were suppressed in 1652.

In 1640 Portugal became once more free from Spain, and the House of Braganza secured the throne. She had to fight for independence, but Spain was fast weakening, and both France and England helped in turn. Though now independent the Portuguese had lost their old power. They seemed to be exhausted, as if the strain of maintaining a great empire had been too much for so small a nation. Their fatal readiness to marry native women had weakened the race. The Dutch, who really were the enemies of Spain, and only accidentally of Portugal because annexed to Spain, had ruined their eastern trade and empire. Therefore restored Portugal had no weight in Europe.

We were having our own civil war, and brought it to a conclusion just about the period of the Treaty of Westphalia and of the Fronde. The result was that the Rump Parliament after the battle of Worcester possessed a magnificent army, the first real, trained, standing army that England ever possessed, thanks entirely to one man, Oliver Cromwell[1]. And when a nation possesses such an

[1] Cromwell consciously imitated Swedish methods. He trained his cavalry to attack or retreat by alternate bodies, while Rupert broke his

instrument of power, it is not long before it makes its
power felt. But the first enemy of the Roundheads, when
there were no more Cavaliers or Scots or Irish to fight,
was Holland, the great sea power. The jealousy, which
began in the Spice Islands, came to a head and broke out
into open war when the Rump introduced its new financial
scheme by the Navigation Act. A definite national income was wanted, for Cromwell's army had to be paid,
and the best and most steady income is that which comes
from trade; so, by the Navigation Act, trade was to be
forced into English ports, so that customs duties could be
collected and the profits of England's trade should be for
England herself alone. Hitherto the Dutch had been
accustomed to ship colonial products, Virginian tobacco
let us take for example. Now by the Navigation Act all
England's colonial trade was to be in English ships and
brought to English ports, and such Virginian tobacco as
was required by foreign countries would have to be reshipped in English ships for those countries; that is to
say it shattered the carrying trade of the Dutch. As
a matter of fact the war which resulted was not directly
caused by the Navigation Act, but the bitterness between
the two countries was brought by it to a culminating point
at the end of fifty years of commercial rivalry, and the
question of the English right to demand salutes from
Dutchmen to our flag on the narrow seas was the occasion
rather than the cause. The two Protestant powers fought
each other in 1652 and 1653 very fiercely by sea. The
Dutch had the larger and the more experienced fleet, but
had begun to economise since peace had been made with
Spain in 1648. England, thanks firstly to Charles I and

enemy by one dashing charge ; the men were to fire from the saddle and
then fall on at a good round trot, weight and steadiness taking the place
of impetus. The foot were still half pikemen and half musketeers, and
he taught them to be effective in a charge, not only solid on the defence.
He lightened the musket, and did away with the crutch.

the iniquitous tax of ship-money, and secondly to the Rump Parliament which built very quickly a fleet to put down those Cavaliers like Prince Rupert who had taken to the sea and to privateering after the battle of Naseby, was not so very far behind. The generals converted by the needs of the war into admirals, Blake and Monk in particular, fought several fierce actions against van Tromp and de Ruyter, fierce, hard-hitting fights without much science. There was no Trafalgar when two such nations as England and Holland met at sea. But the geography of the naval war was in favour of England. All Dutch commerce from the ocean had to come up-channel to reach Holland, and the battles were fought by the Dutch fleet to cover and protect their commerce, so that they fought at a disadvantage. Cromwell hated such a war between two Protestant powers and, whatever we may think of him, at least it has to be acknowledged that his piety as a Puritan was absolutely genuine. As soon as ever he had ejected the Rump Parliament, he made it his first aim to make peace with Holland. The profit of this naval war certainly rested with England. The Navigation Act was not repealed, and the Dutch, having been forced to fight us immediately after their long eighty years' war against Spain, suffered considerably. Holland, we have to remember, was not a manufacturing but only a trading country, and the result was that the payment of interest upon war loans became ever more and more difficult for the Dutch Government.

It was after the conclusion of the Dutch war that Cromwell, now Lord Protector, with full control over the foreign policy of the country, had to decide whether he should take part with France or with Spain. Certainly at first he inclined to alliance with Spain. It seemed that France during the minority of Louis XIV, while the Frondeurs were in arms and helped by Spain, was a country on the decline. Cromwell deliberately offered

5—2

terms to Spain. Would the King of Spain allow to the English Free Trade with the Spanish colonies, and would he exempt Protestant Englishmen living and trading in Spain from the control of the Spanish Inquisition? The King refused to grant either request, so Cromwell entered into negotiations with Mazarin, and made a treaty by which he provided a contingent of soldiers to the French army on the borders of the Spanish Netherlands. The result was that a joint force of English and French under the command of Marshal Turenne laid siege to Dunkirk, beat the Spaniards who came to save the place, and captured it[1]. And so Dunkirk was handed over to Cromwell as the price of England's help in 1658.

Cromwell's alliance with Mazarin has been much criticised. It is always said that he helped to depress the power of Spain and to raise the power of France at the critical moment. The fact of course is true; but the real question at issue is whether Cromwell, or any man then living, could have foreseen that the power of France would rise so rapidly in the next twenty years as to become a direct danger to the whole of Europe. We, knowing all the future history, know of course that Cromwell did contribute to make Louis XIV the most powerful and the most dangerous king at the close of the century. But hitherto France, under Henry IV, under Richelieu, and under Mazarin, had been tolerant to the Huguenots unless, indeed, they were in open rebellion, had maintained the Edict of Nantes, and was in alliance with Protestant powers. Cromwell could not possibly have foreseen that the youthful Louis XIV would later on revoke the Edict of Nantes, persecute the Huguenots, and use his military power in a wanton and aggressive manner so as to become the tyrant of Europe.

[1] The English veterans after the battle said that the discipline in Turenne's army was "not bad for Frenchmen," an amusing proof of what Cromwell had done for the military pride of England.

Lastly, before closing this chapter we must look to the East. Terrible as was the harm done to Germany by the Thirty Years, the horrors would have been intensified to a degree beyond the power of calculation if the Turks had taken advantage. But for nearly a century they were inactive, and the deterioration of the worst foes of Christendom was marked, the discipline of their armies relaxed, and intrigue rampant at Constantinople. Thus for a time Austria was not distracted. Most of Hungary, however, was still held by the Turks, and a Pasha ruled at Buda. There was a strong anti-Austrian feeling, which claimed that the reigning Hapsburg had no hereditary right to be King of Hungary unless chosen by the Hungarian Diet; moreover this feeling was largely Protestant. The Transylvanians had no tie of allegiance to either the Germans of Austria or the Magyars of Hungary, but were aiming at independence; their champion, Bethlen Gabor, did something to help the Protestant cause in the Thirty Years, though he influenced the war but little. In another direction Poland was strongly Roman Catholic and the natural ally of Austria, and had elected a Swedish king of the House of Vasa, the Romanist rival to the Protestant branch of Gustavus Adolphus; thus Poland's share in the war, as we saw before, was to prevent Gustavus from coming earlier on the scene. But, though once the greatest of the Slav countries, she had lost her energy, for where a monarchy is elective[1], and the nobles are bent upon proving themselves superior to the king, a strong policy beyond the frontier is impossible. Poland's help to Austria, therefore, was at best but spasmodic and indirect.

[1] The hereditary Polish dynasty of the line of Jagellon came to an end in 1572, and the monarchy then became elective.

CHAPTER IV

FRANCE AT HER ZENITH

As France dominates Europe ever more and more during the 17th century, it is well to throw our eyes back, and see the steps by which that country reached her pinnacle of power under Louis XIV. The foundations of the strength of France were undoubtedly laid by Henry IV. He had distracted Alexander of Parma from completing the conquest of the Netherlands during the minority of Maurice of Orange. For a time, indeed, he had been foiled by Alexander, but by the very fact of his distracting the Spanish power he had saved the Dutch during their most critical period. Alexander died in 1592, and the Treaty of Vervins in 1598, the same year in which Philip II died, marks the comparative impotence of Spain. It is not to be supposed that Henry no longer tried to thwart the Hapsburg ambitions. He considered himself the permanent enemy of both the Spanish and the Austrian branches of that family, and with France thoroughly united for the time being, the Huguenots pacified by the Edict of Nantes, the great nobles thwarted and crushed, Henry was, for the time being, the arbiter of Europe. As regards territorial expansion, we can only point to the addition of the Kingdom of Navarre to France, and the annexation of a portion of Savoy, which gave to France the last link in securing the whole of the

Rhone Valley from the Lake of Geneva to the sea. In his government of France at home he was helped by the first of an able line of ministers who saw that France was a self-sufficient country, and that, if the natural resources could be thoroughly developed, not only would she suffice for herself, but would also gain by an external trade. This minister was the Duke of Sully, the predecessor in every sense of the word of the great Colbert of the reign of Louis XIV. The silk industry and the porcelain industry received their start. It is said that France, at the end of the 16th century, imported silk to the amount of 2½ millions of our money; but by 1620 she not only supplied her own consumption, but exported to Germany and to England as much as 5 millions. Internal trade was promoted by the cutting of the first canal between great rivers, namely that between the Seine and the Saone, and France has had the reputation of being the most skilful country in connection with water-engineering from those days down to the period of the Suez Canal.

The policy bequeathed by Henry was, of course, the policy of strengthening the Crown and thereby unifying France. Previous kings such as Louis XI had worked much in this direction, but it was Henry IV who really gave to France her great impetus, for, by terminating the wars of religion and weakening both the great Catholic nobility and the Huguenot nobility alike, he left a Crown which, in spite of two periods of relapse, never lost its domination. As a counterbalance to the power of the nobles, he partly created, partly strengthened, the *Noblesse de la Robe*, those families of professional lawyers who, claiming to hold their office from father to son, at first made the King independent of the old nobility, and later on put a stumbling-block in the way of reform. The *Parlement* of Paris began now to get new powers; it was a law-court which gradually secured the right to register the King's edicts, and from this it was but a short step towards claiming the right to invalidate a royal edict by refusing to register it. This evil was not conspicuous under Henry IV himself, but was glaring under Louis XVI, nearly two centuries later. Lastly we must notice his employment of professional armies, so that he might not be dependent upon the retinues of the great nobles in war. Efforts had been made before him to create a national French force of infantry, but with no great success. France under him was still dependent upon Swiss and German mercenaries, but at least he showed the way to his successors who in course of time evolved a national and professional army. In the Jülich-Cleves affair Henry formed a confederation in alliance with Maurice of Orange to check the Emperor. Perhaps the Thirty Years' War might have begun, with France taking a leading part, some nine years earlier than it actually did, had not he been assassinated at the critical moment in 1610.

Under the Queen-mother, Mary of Medici[1], the expansion of France was for a time checked. The old personal ambitions once more came to the front, and court intrigue was ever in the air. But, when at last Louis XIII saw that it was to his profit to utilise the services of Cardinal Richelieu, order was once more restored and the second chapter in the history of the growth of France was opened. Richelieu secured the peace of France at large by crushing the political powers of the Huguenots. He had no choice in the matter; he simply had to stamp out what has been described as an "imperium in imperio." We are told that by the Edict of Nantes public worship, according to the Reformed Faith, was legalised in 3500 castles as well as in specified towns, and this simply means that feudal rights and Huguenotism were bound up together. In the great

[1] Henry's second wife.

towns of the west and south of France the right of
assembly was so strong that one might say that each
Huguenot town was an organised republic. Moreover
the Huguenot ministers were certainly very intolerant
towards their Catholic neighbours. On the other hand,
after the capture of La Rochelle toleration was still
granted, but all political power was swept away. Of
course it was not only the Huguenot castle, but the
castle of any feudal lord who was too strong for the
Crown, that Richelieu set himself to destroy. Like our
own Henry II he saw that the possession of private
fortresses was incompatible with the unity of the country,
and henceforward fortified places are to be found only
on the borders of France, garrisoned by royal troops, a
defence to France herself and no longer a menace. Outside France we saw in the last chapter that Richelieu
because of this same Huguenot problem at home was
unable to interfere openly in the earlier stages of the
Thirty Years' War. It was only after the fall of
La Rochelle and after the death of Gustavus Adolphus,
when the Protestant cause in Germany was leaderless,
that the power of France was thrown definitely into the
Protestant scale. Richelieu's ambition was not in any
degree religious; he simply wished to weaken the House
of Hapsburg, to keep Germany disunited, and to secure
the balance of power in the direction which suited France.
His campaign in 1630 to secure Savoy, the Valtellina, and
Mantua, was planned to cut the Spaniards of Lombardy
apart from the Austrian armies of central Germany by
barring to them the use of the Valtellina[1]. His object
was attained in course of time, and the control of this
route ultimately passed to the League of the Rhaetian
Swiss[2].

[1] See p. 56.
[2] They formed a confederacy in alliance with the genuine Swiss, but
were not incorporated in Switzerland until the days of the French
Republic, and now they form the Canton of the Grisons.

That Richelieu suppressed the French aristocracy is a mere commonplace of history, and it is unnecessary here to give details. The aristocrats, who resented his influence and frequently conspired against him, were time after time encouraged by Gaston, Duke of Orleans, Louis XIII's very unworthy brother, and then betrayed by him. Montmorency, and many other great nobles who openly revolted, were executed on the scaffold. The last effort, which was made the very year of Richelieu's death, by Henry d'Effiat, known as Cinq Mars, has been celebrated in literature, and has therefore attracted perhaps more attention than it deserves, for apparently it never had much chance of success.

Richelieu, able and ruthless, did much to destroy, but nothing to create. He removed no social evils, he left to the aristocracy their privileges, and indeed may be said to have spoilt France, though not so much as he benefited France, by removing such feudal powers as could counterbalance the Crown, and at the same time leaving the social privileges which finally led to the great Revolution. Against this we must put his patronage of literature, and by his support of Conrart, a man fond of letters who collected at his house a private assembly of literary men, he became the founder of the French Academy.

France had her second relapse when Anne, the Queen-mother, was opposed by the Frondeurs, and the strange thing was that a Spanish woman upheld the Crown against Condé, a royal prince yet a rebel in alliance with Spain. Louis XIII had decided that a Council of Regency, not Anne, should govern France; Anne appealed to the *Parlement* of Paris to set aside the dead king's wish, and thus gave to the lawyers too prominent a position. The Frondeurs were a miscellaneous crowd. Condé and the feudal nobility, their Spanish allies, the *Parlement*, and the Parisian mob, had no common interests. For a moment there was danger when Turenne, the great marshal and Condé's rival, wavered. Then Mazarin temporarily gave way on minor points, and went into exile voluntarily till disunion spoilt the chances of the rebels. Finally the leadership of Turenne, powerfully helped at Dunkirk by the Cromwellian contingent in 1658, made the Crown to triumph.

The critical date in the history of Louis XIV is 1660, when he married Maria Theresa of Spain after signing the *Treaty of the Pyrenees*. From this time onwards it was clearly seen that Spain was a thoroughly baffled power, and would not count for much in any European alliance. Maria, on marrying him, renounced all claim to the throne of Spain. Yet such a renunciation might in the future be repudiated, and indeed forty years later actually was repudiated. This same year Charles II was restored to the throne of England, and both by his own leanings and by the influence of his mother, Henrietta Maria, sister to Louis XIII, he was inclined to look to alliance with France, even though France had but recently been the ally of Cromwell. We are therefore on the eve of a new development, and with Louis XIV reigning alone in his own right, Mazarin dead, Spain humbled, and England ready to be the ally of France, we have now to see how the internal resources of France were fostered till she became *the* dominating, and no longer merely *a* dominating, factor in European combinations. Two names stand out prominently, Colbert and Louvois, and it is mainly through these two men that Louis XIV became so strong.

The evils which the Duke of Sully had combated in the reign of Henry IV had all reappeared. Without going into detail, we may say that the greatest evil was that the people were heavily taxed and yet very little money came into the royal exchequer. Colbert continued and perfected the work of Sully, seeing clearly that, the more prosperous a country becomes, the more easily it can pay taxes, and that the weight of taxation is less evil when the taxpayer has direct relations with the king's ministers and is not fleeced by middlemen. Now, Mazarin had done a great deal of good to France by crushing the Frondeurs, yet he not only had done nothing to help the taxpayer, but on his death left behind him an ill-gotten fortune equivalent to two millions of English money. After his death the chief minister was Fouquet, who behaved himself almost as though he were the king's rival, or even superior, and who also, holding the office of Superintendent of the Finances, amassed an enormous fortune. The young king, helped by Colbert, laid a plot against the all-powerful minister and he was condemned after a long trial to banishment, but then Louis substituted a sentence of perpetual imprisonment. Fouquet once out of the way and his vast private fortune confiscated, Colbert had a free hand. He re-assessed the chief tax, the *taille*, which was partly a tax on property and partly a tax on land, and from which the nobles were exempt; he forced the tax-gatherers to show their accounts; and so quickly did his measures have effect that in his first year of office he was able to show a surplus, and in a short time amassed a reserve of money such as no previous King of France had ever had at his disposal. Like Sully, he wisely protected the silk industry and the porcelain industry. Unlike Sully, he forbade the export of corn which France produced so abundantly that an export trade would have added materially to the resources of the country. Again, like Sully, he turned his attention to engineering, and under him was constructed the great canal by which the Garonne is joined to the Mediterranean Sea through the gap between the Pyrenees and the Cevennes. As the distance from the Mediterranean coast to Bordeaux is about 250 miles as the crow flies and about 1600 miles by sea, the importance of such a triumph of engineering is self-evident. In the same way the engineering of roads was encouraged, yet in this policy there were the seeds of a future grievance, for the King claimed the *corvée*, the right to call for compulsory service upon the roads, which fills so large a place in history at the time of the Revolution.

The betterment of the various harbours of France, the promotion of the interests of Canada and of the French East India Company, were also part of Colbert's task. But the culminating point of his scheme was the creation of a French navy. Richelieu had done a little, but it must be confessed very little, towards the foundation of a navy, and usually he had to borrow ships from England or from Holland. Colbert set himself steadily to build ships and to train Frenchmen. He had ready to hand the smugglers and fishermen of a very long coast and the provincial nobility of Normandy and Brittany, Gascony and Provence, and when once their ambitions were turned to the Royal Naval service, French sailor and French noble officer alike were very capable. There were elements of weakness in the new French navy, for every young French noble, even if a mere under-lieutenant, thought himself the social equal of his captain, or even of his admiral. The service being promoted by the Crown and the Crown's ministers, and not being a natural service of a people turning willingly to the sea, like the English, it resulted that in the moment of adversity the French navy had no reserves of strength; in fact, we may say that it was nursed into excellence, and had no natural power to keep up this excellence, whereas the English navy during the same period, that is to say roughly from the date of Louis XIV down to the days of Napoleon, though frequently weakened during the days of peace by the politicians in power at the moment, had an inherent vitality and was ever able to grow stronger in the face of danger. And what is true of the navy is more or less true of most of Colbert's work for France. It was all done *for* the people and not *by* the people, and thus, though France is and always will be the most self-sufficing power in Europe, producing corn and grapes and mulberries, and dependent upon herself alone for her coal and her iron, she has, at two crises of her history, been unable to stand the strain. France, nursed by despots, has not been quite strong enough to contend against all the enemies that those despots have raised up against her, and in particular has been unable to maintain both a strong army and a strong navy. " What Louis XIV and Napoleon I failed to do, will modern Germany succeed in doing ? " was the question before us in 1914.

On the purely military side, the strength of France was the work of the war minister, Louvois. Whereas former kings of France found the native French foot worthless, Louvois set himself to train and give to Louis a good national infantry. It was based upon a territorial system, and each of the old provinces of France henceforward had its own regiment with its own depot and recruiting office. The officers were directly responsible to the Crown, and not to some noble who was titular colonel. With a system of camps and manœuvres and reviews upon a large scale, Louvois was able to work the material up in the early days of the reign, between 1660 and 1672, so that the new regiments should enter upon war thoroughly trained. He gave to France some 150,000 men on a peace footing. He did not entirely do away with the mercenary regiments, and there was always in the service of the French Crown a large number of Swiss and of Germans, but even here he made such changes as were necessary to secure proper discipline and obedience to the Crown rather than to the proprietor of the regiment. In the cavalry indeed the predominant element was German, and right down to the days of the French Revolution we find such names as " Royal Allemand " for mounted regiments. Not only

is this a period of change in the constitution of the French
army, it was also a period of military development in arms
and equipment. The old matchlock gradually disappears
during the reign of Louis XIV and its place is taken by
the fusil, which had a flint-lock, the gunpowder being
ignited by a spark struck by a trigger which brought
a flint on to the pan of the gun. Likewise the pike
gradually disappeared, and its place was taken by the
long knife of Bayonne which was fitted into the barrel
of the gun, and so is the ancestor of the present bayonet.
It was a long time before a satisfactory bayonet was
developed from this beginning, but at last Vauban invented and brought to Louvois' notice the socket bayonet,
which could be fitted by a ring to the outside of the barrel
so that the men could load while it was fixed. It is a fact,
however, that the use of flint-lock and bayonet was finally
brought to a greater state of perfection by the rivals of
France. Marlborough at the end of the reign trained
the English in the use of the fusil[1], which they fired better
and more rapidly, and which threw a heavier and therefore more effective bullet; and Leopold of Dessau invented
the iron ramrod which improved the loading. Louvois
also paid a very great deal of attention to the equipment
of an army; the military trains, the food and ammunition
wagons of a French army that took the field in any campaign of Louis XIV, were admirable.

The two greatest of the men who used the new army
provided by Louvois were Vauban and Turenne. Vauban
brought to perfection the study of fortification, and he
either constructed or improved the triple line of the French
fortresses from Dunkirk and Lille through Champagne
to Lorraine and Alsace, and finally down to the Alps. It
will be remembered that the Dutch and Spaniards during
their long war of eighty years up to 1648 had confined

[1] Curiously enough the English while using the *fusil* still called it a
musket, and the French to-day have no word for a *rifle* but still say *fusil*.

war to the attack or defence of fortresses along their common frontier. Now the new armies of France did not depend solely upon fortification and entrenchment, but in the line of Vauban's fortresses they had a base to which they could always fall back if they were temporarily checked. Marshal Turenne, the father of modern ideas of warfare as far as France is concerned, depended, as Gustavus Adolphus of Sweden had depended, upon marching rather than entrenchments as the chief element of victory, and he struck, so to speak, the right balance between defence and attack in his great campaigns.

It has been said that Louis XIV was not at all original in his ideas. The men who served him best were those who had already received their training under Mazarin, and this is certainly true of the four men whom we have already mentioned. Colbert had been one of Mazarin's chief officials, and Turenne had won some of his greatest victories before Mazarin died. The same statement could be made as regards Louis' position as a patron of learning and literature. Richelieu had been before him as the political founder of the Academy. Corneille and Racine had flourished already. Yet the Augustan Age of French literature is his reign. It is now that the French language began to dominate all European languages; it became the medium of diplomatists, and in fact it is only in our own day that it has ceased to be what one might call a universal language. The ascendancy of the French literature and language was not of course caused by, but undoubtedly it was promoted by, French military successes. We may very fairly point to what has happened since the last humbling of France. Up to 1870 German writers frequently used French phrases, and many words in the German language were French. Since 1870 the Germans have deliberately and carefully got rid of French idioms, and coined new German words to take the place of imported French words. Therefore it may be argued that success in war impresses the minds of contemporaries, and has an influence over language and literature.

Before dealing with the details of the age of Louis XIV, it would be as well to extend our retrospect to Holland. The House of Orange had certainly done most to win independence from Spain, and one can hardly think even of a Holland without the family of Orange. But there were signs that the Dutch did not always acknowledge the benefits they had received from their ruling family. During a ten years' truce with Spain, 1609—19, there was a violent quarrel between Prince Maurice and John Barneveldt, the chief Dutch statesman of the period. The quarrel was partly religious, partly political. Maurice represented the strict Calvinistic Church; Barneveldt was more tolerant and, according to Calvinistic ideas, unorthodox. The Reformed Church in Holland wished to regard the property of the old Catholic Church as its own peculiar property, whereas men of the Barneveldt type thought that ecclesiastical property should be controlled by the State. Of course Maurice likewise represented a military policy, and Barneveldt was the leader and spokesman of the great republican merchants who regarded militarism as injurious to the country. The trouble came to a head, and Barneveldt finally died on the scaffold. When the Spanish war came to an end in 1648, and the Dutch had time to breathe and enjoy their independence and the commerce that had come to them as the harvest of their independence, the family of Orange seemed to find its work gone. They had been military leaders pure and simple, and had no place in the days of peace. Prince William II, feeling this, tried to carry out a *coup d'état* and failed. He died in 1650, and the republican party headed by the brothers de Witt declared the Stadtholdership to be at an end. The child William III was brought up under the supervision of his political enemies, and for the time being the House of

Orange was almost extinct. This was just the period of
the Dutch wars of the Rump and Charles II, and also of
the interference of Louis XIV in the Netherlands. The
special grievance of the Dutch Republic was the Rump's
Navigation Act, which was accepted and made stronger
by the Parliament of Charles II. England and Holland
were certainly ready for another war, so great was the
rivalry between them in the East and in the West Indies,
and so great the bitterness that still remained from the
Rump's war of 1652.

War broke out in 1664 actually on the west coast of
Africa and was concerned with the question of the slave
trade. It extended to America, where New Amsterdam
was captured by the English and its name changed to
New York. Then followed a series of battles in the
Channel between the English and Dutch fleets, fierce
and hard battles between navies of nearly equal strength,
and, as in 1652, it was seen that the war would not be
terminated by one great victory of the Trafalgar type
but was a question of endurance and stamina. Now
these very years of fighting, 1665 and 1666, were the
years of the Plague and the Fire of London, and one
cannot help thinking that historians who blame Charles II
have forgotten this plain fact. In 1667 so great was the
scarcity of coin in England, due to Plague and Fire, that it
was simply impossible to keep the ships afloat. Sailors
even deserted to the Dutch and shouted out to their old
comrades, "We used to fight for tickets but now we fight
for dollars"; which means that Charles II's government
had tried to pay them their wages by tokens and not in
actual coin. Here we get the real reason of the national
disaster of 1667. The ships of our royal navy were laid
up in harbour; the Dutch sailed the high seas unopposed,
picked up many prizes, finally came up the Medway three
days running at high tide, and inflicted considerable loss
besides sending London into a panic. By a great effort

the veteran George Monk, now Duke of Albemarle, brought back sailors and workmen to their allegiance, repaired the batteries of Chatham, and showed so strong a front that the Dutch did not sail up again. Yet they held the mouth of the Thames for two months and the naval glory of England seemed to have vanished. At the peace then made at Breda, humbled though England appeared to be, she retained New York, and, says an American historian, "What was the loss of a few ships and a momentary panic in London in comparison with the permanent possession of practically the whole Dutch colony in North America?" The policy of John de Witt does not strike one as being very clever. Either he should not have sent de Ruyter to attack Chatham, in which case he could have more easily made friends with England, or, sending de Ruyter to attack, should have struck harder while he had the chance and not made the Treaty of Breda. For the fact is that the new power of France was now coming to be recognised. The problem that confronted European statesmen was, Should Louis XIV be resisted by a grand alliance? should England and Holland maintain their commercial and naval jealousies against each other, in which case France would get all the profit, or should they combine as friends against France, the creation of Colbert and Louvois, the new naval and commercial power?

The danger was not at all imaginary. In 1665, on the death of Philip IV of Spain, Louis XIV in the most bare-faced way put forward a claim on behalf of his wife to the Spanish Netherlands, as being daughter of the late King of Spain by his first wife; whereas Charles, who succeeded to Spain itself, was son by the second wife. The local custom in Brabant was that the daughter by a first wife should succeed to land over the head of her step-brother, but local land customs do not usually control succession to a crown, and Louis' claim on his wife's behalf was a

6—2

downright violation of the Treaty of the Pyrenees. Of course this attack upon the Spanish Netherlands entirely upset the traditional policy of the Dutch. Ever since their first outbreak against Spain they had looked to France for help, and France was at the moment actually their ally against England. De Witt and his government had therefore reached a crisis. Should they desert their traditional ally, France, and make terms with their commercial rival, England? It was a difficult point to decide. At this moment the English Ambassador at the Court of Brussels was Sir William Temple, who has been termed with great justice "an unusual man." He opened negotiations with de Witt, then went to England to interview Charles, and returned to Holland to negotiate in 1668 the *Triple Alliance,* Sweden being brought in to form the third Protestant power for the humbling of France. The Triple Alliance was so strong that Louis had no choice but to evacuate the Spanish Netherlands, but at the same time the Allies allowed him to retain the strip of borderland containing the great fortress of Lille; that is to say, the Allies did not object to a slight loss which fell upon Spain in order that they might secure the retirement of Louis from the bulk of the Netherlands.

Here, on the one hand, we see that "a French ascendancy stood revealed to the world, an ambitious purpose, avowed by Louis, of asserting his superiority among the European States, and sustained by an evident superiority in fact[1]." Temple spoke of Louis as "this great comet that has risen of late." On the other hand, Spain was distinctly the sick man of Europe, and the Spanish Netherlands, lying in the centre between England, Holland, the Empire, and France, was destined to be the battle-ground of conflicting powers. Not one of the four could allow any one of the others to seize the line of the river Scheldt and the great port of Antwerp, which, though

[1] Sir J. R. Seeley, *The Growth of British Policy,* vol. II. chap. 2.

always sacrificed to the commercial needs of London and Amsterdam and deprived of all the trade which its grand position would otherwise command, was too dangerous a prize to be allowed to fall into the hand of some predominant power.

Now Charles II, supported by the Earl of Arlington whose initial forms the second letter in the "Cabal" ministry, gave way to Temple's policy of alliance with Holland, but at the same time he was negotiating for an alliance with Spain on the old Cromwellian lines. Would Spain grant Free Trade to the English in the West Indies, and would Spain exempt English residents from the control of the Inquisition? Moreover, he was bargaining also with Louis. His adhesion to the Triple Alliance is therefore easily explained. He still looked upon Holland as England's chief enemy, and there can be no doubt that the great majority of Englishmen agreed with him. Holland was Carthage, our commercial rival; Carthage must be destroyed, and the Medway disaster of but one year back must be avenged. If France was not willing to make alliance with England on England's terms, France must be taught a lesson; and England would make alliance with Holland even though she was Carthage. Charles knew perfectly well that he could throw Holland over and join France at any moment, when Louis could be brought to see that it was to his advantage to secure terms with England. Very soon indeed Louis was brought to this point of view. Henriette, Charles' favourite sister and wife of the Duke of Orleans, Louis' younger brother, came over to Dover, ostensibly to visit her brother, in reality to bring the treaty between France and England, which was thereupon signed and is always known as the *Secret Treaty of Dover*, 1670. It is customary with most writers to blame Charles as a merely selfish king, who cared only for self-indulgence and pleasure and was willing to sacrifice the interests of

his country. Historians point at him playing and laughing
with his courtiers at the very time when the Dutch ships
were sailing up to Chatham. But second thoughts are more
fair. Charles was frequently pretending to play the fool
while he was really scheming for what, after all, was
England's political and commercial gain, however shabby
the intrigues which led to it may appear. It may seem
mean and sordid to trick the Dutch into an alliance in
1668 and to throw them over in 1670, but very few politicians have hesitated to lure their enemies on to destruction
in the same way. Had the Treaty of Dover been merely
a political affair it would not have attracted so much
abuse; but there were secret religious clauses attached
to it, and Charles and James were to declare themselves
Roman Catholics, and to rid themselves of the domination
of Parliament by means of French money and French
soldiers if need be. It was the coming to light of these
terms that caused the subsequent storm.

Having won over England to his side, or rather
having been tricked by Charles into acknowledging the
importance of having England as his ally, Louis turned
all his wrath against Holland in 1672. The war was
partly commercial, for Colbert's policy of building up a
tariff to protect the home industries of France was as
directly opposed to the wishes of the Dutch as was the
Navigation Act of England. But probably ambition far
more than a policy of tariffs led to the war. Louis had
the new army which Louvois had created; he had in
England a naval ally who would bear the brunt of the
war at sea, whilst the new French navy was still too
weak to face the Dutch openly; and he had a grudge
to work off against the Dutch because they had thwarted
him in his wish to secure the Spanish Netherlands in
1668. Led by Turenne and Condé, the French army
pressed into Holland from the south-east by way of
Maestricht and fought its way near to Amsterdam.

Then occurred the famous scene in the streets of the Hague. The brothers de Witt were made scapegoats when Holland was in danger, and the populace demanded the restoration of the House of Orange; they were murdered in the streets while the Calvinistic clergy urged the people on, and William III, the young Stadtholder, who had just been restored to the place of his ancestors, conveniently looked the other way. It is hard indeed to estimate the motives which controlled the actions of William. Being our own deliverer sixteen years later he has been put upon a pedestal in history, and is the idol of Lord Macaulay; but hostile writers are never slow to point out how he was accessory to the murder of the two de Witts, at least after if not before the fact, even as he was accessory after the fact to the massacre of Glencoe. Very young at this date, brought up in a miserable boyhood by the enemies of his house, naturally inclined to suspicion, yet at heart intensely patriotic and looking only to the good of Holland, he was tempted to appear to be ignorant of a frightful crime, which probably in his heart he justified to himself because of the danger to which his country was exposed. Under his orders the dykes were cut, and Amsterdam was saved.

In the meanwhile the English fleet under Prince Rupert had done its work in opposing de Ruyter, but had not met with conspicuous success. In all probability, had not de Ruyter held our fleet off, a small English army might have been landed on the coast of Holland just in time to prevent the cutting of the dykes. But at home feeling was already beginning to veer round. The spectacle of Holland deluging herself with water to save her capital, the heroic struggle of William against Turenne's overpowering army, and the thought that France had but as it were hired us to beat the Dutch at sea, where our own ships would inevitably receive much damage, so that the new French navy of Colbert

might look on and gain all the advantage, brought
Charles II's Cavalier Parliament into an anti-French
frame of mind. We should always remember that this
Parliament which so strongly opposed Charles, which
hated the Treaty of Dover, which passed the Test Act by
way of answer so as to secure all government offices and
commands by land and sea to orthodox Churchmen to
the exclusion of both Roman Catholics and Protestant
Dissenters, was the same long Cavalier Parliament which
had been elected after Charles' Restoration in all the
fervour of Cavalier joy at his return. The very men,
or at least the sons and nephews of the very men, who
had fought and bled for Charles I at Marston Moor or
Naseby, were wild at the idea of Charles II going over to
Rome to secure the alliance of Louis XIV. The result
was that in 1674 England made terms with Holland by
the *Treaty of Westminster*, and the French were left to
continue the war alone. It is well known that James
declared his conversion to Rome, and Charles, having
recognised that he had raised a storm of antagonism such
as it was not wise on his part to face, shrugged his
shoulders and did not publicly go over to Rome. Pepys,
the diarist, has an exact phrase which explains Charles:
"The king has a bewitching kind of pleasure called
sauntering"; that is to say, he meant to get the best out
of life, as much pleasure and power as possible, but he
did not mean to exert himself beyond the point where he
saw that the very Cavaliers would oppose him.

In 1673 many of the Powers of Europe, in particular
the Emperor Leopold and the "Great Elector" of
Brandenburg, frightened by French successes, made
alliance together to save Holland. Immediately Louis
saw that even the mighty army of Turenne could not
hold down Holland and at the same time make head
against the Germans, and the war was at once transferred to the middle Rhine. The Imperialists were not to

be despised and had a clever leader in Montecuculi, but Turenne was more than his match. His winter campaign of 1674—75 was a masterpiece of manœuvring and counter-marching, and he completely cleared the Imperialists out of Alsace and drove them over the Rhine. Following them up into the Black Forest, after a series of clever manœuvres he seemed to hold Montecuculi in the hollow of his hand, but just at that moment a chance cannon ball struck and killed him. With the death of Turenne the luck of Louis XIV seemed to desert him. Exhausted by his great efforts and aware that Colbert's financial reforms had been severely strained, Louis was forced three years later in 1678 to conclude the *Treaty of Nymegen.*

Europe had thus, for the time being, been freed from the domination of this forerunner of Napoleon, but probably nobody doubted that when he had got a new opportunity Louis, with his funds repaired, his treasury refilled, his army reorganised and brought up to strength again by Louvois, would plan some similar stroke. From 1678—88 there was indeed a period of peace for Europe at large, but it was a treacherous peace when the air was full of thunder and all men anticipated the thunderstorm. These ten years have very properly been called "the Ten Thunderous Years," and they are notorious for the three great crimes, as they may be fairly called rather than blunders, of Louis: the seizure of Strasburg, the Revocation of the Edict of Nantes, and the alliance with the Turks which led to their march upon Vienna. As regards ourselves in England, they were likewise years of thunder. They are the years of the Exclusion Bill and the Popish Plot, of the panic engineered by Shaftesbury's intrigues, of the Rye House Plot, of the accession of James II and the rebellion of Monmouth, of the expulsion of the President and Fellows of Magdalen College, and the Trial of the Seven Bishops, up to the culminating point when the letter was sent to William of Orange to summon him to England.

Firstly, Louis had by the Treaty of Westphalia in 1648 obtained most of Alsace subject to some conditions, and been confirmed in his possession of the three bishoprics of Lorraine. He had secured the strip of the Spanish Netherlands, which still belongs to France and is known as French Flanders, in 1668. By the Treaty of Nymegen he got Franche Comté, of which the capital is Besançon. He intrigued now to extend his borders, and created certain *Chambres des Réunions* from the Parlements of Metz and Besançon, who gave a verdict that the dependencies of Alsace and Franche Comté and the three bishoprics were really French territory, which meant that Louis was practically free to annex the whole of Alsace and Lorraine. The great free German city of Strasburg was included; he seized Strasburg in 1681, and immediately Vauban turned it into a fortress of the first class. Matthew Arnold always used to point to the French government of Strasburg and Alsace as a conspicuous example of the ability of France to win over those whom she conquered. The Alsatians have for two centuries boasted themselves to be French, and it would not be too much to say that the presence of flourishing colonies of Alsatians in distant Algeria, founded after 1870, are a justification of the policy of Louis XIV.

Secondly, Louis had a quarrel with the Pope. Even before the days of the Reformation many a King of France, though orthodox as regards doctrine and dogma, wished to be politically free from the power of Rome, to appoint his own bishops, and to hold as royal property whatever sees were momentarily vacant. Louis XIV followed this policy, and in 1682 an assembly of clergy under the presidency of Bossuet passed certain resolutions at Saint Germains which were simply defiant and anti-Roman. Thus in a sense Louis was anti-Papal at the

very time when to English eyes he was the persecuting
Catholic, and when we got rid of our own King because
he was a Roman Catholic and a possible persecutor in
England, the Pope himself was a member of the Grand
Alliance against Louis.   Thus it came to pass that a
French King who defied the Pope signalised his independence from Rome by persecuting the Huguenots and
revoking the Edict of Nantes.   One cannot avoid the
conclusion that a despot must be illogical simply because
he is a despot.   Louis, like our own Henry VIII,
persecuted those who agreed with Rome and those who
were the arch-heretics against Rome.   It is thought that
Madame de Maintenon, whom he married secretly a few
years after the death of Maria Theresa, pushed him on
into persecution, yet probably he would have done something similar had she never come across his path.
Persuasion turned many Huguenot nobles to Catholicism,
persecution destroyed thousands in the south who were
dragooned without mercy, and exile gave to England,
Holland, and Brandenburg, who were only too willing to
receive them, some of the very best artisans of that middle
class of which France was in sore need in the days of the
great Revolution.

Thirdly, there was new trouble on the side of Turkey.
We have to go back to the days of the 16th century when
the Turkish advance was for the time stopped by the
battle of Lepanto at sea and the resolute defence of the
Hapsburgs by land, so that during the Thirty Years' War
there was no Turkish peril in rear of Austria[1].   In 1645
the Sultan roused himself to attack the Venetians in
Crete, and the siege of Candia, "Troy's rival," lasted
from 1648 to 1669, when the Crescent finally prevailed
over the Lion of St Mark.   In 1663 began a new land

---

[1] "Fortunately for Europe, the unique opportunity offered by the
Thirty Years' War had been lost by the Turks." Professor Lodge in the
Cambridge Modern History, vol. v. p. 341.

war. In spite of intrigues in court and harem, of deterioration and growing slackness, the Turks were still formidable and held the major part of Hungary. The Emperor Leopold I appealed to the Diet of the Empire. Louis XIV played the part of champion of Christendom and sent troops. Thus an army of Austrians and Hungarians representing the Hapsburg dominions, of Germans of the Empire, and of French allied with them almost against precedent, fought and won an action near the convent of St Gothard on the river Raab. But then France and Austria fell apart once more, and in 1674 the Emperor engaged in war against France to help Holland. The Hungarians were never loyal if they thought that the Germans of Austria disregarded their nationality, and a serious conspiracy had to be suppressed in 1670; in a most ill-advised manner suppression was followed by persecution, as if the Hungarians could be dragooned to renounce Protestantism even as Bohemia had been crushed in the Thirty Years. Yet the Turks profited little by Austrian policy. A new war broke out between the Sultan and Poland, and a new champion appeared in the person of John Sobieski who won a great victory in 1673. His services were rewarded when he was elected next year to be King of Poland.

The efforts of the Turks were at this period serious indeed but spasmodic. Attacking Poland at the wrong time, in place of attacking Austria when weakened by Hungarian conspiracy and French war, they now advanced again on Austria when Hungary was crushed and the French nominally at peace. Louis XIV was credited with being the cause of this advance, but it appears that he hoped to profit by it rather than originated it. In 1683 an enormous army of Turks laid siege to Vienna. Its defences were weak, but the defenders fought desperately to almost the last gasp. The conscience of Germany was aroused. Lutheran Saxony and Catholic

Bavaria, the Diet of the Empire and the nobles of Poland,
sent aid. On September 12 under the supreme command
of John Sobieski the decisive action was fought, and
Vienna was saved after a siege of two months. Europe
put the blame of the danger on Louis, whose aggression
on the west flank of Germany had given to the Turks
their opportunity.

Leopold was now able to retaliate. In 1683—86 more
victories were won by Charles, Duke of Lorraine, who
had been the chief leader of the Germans in the defence
and relief of Vienna though he then gave up the command to Sobieski; after the relief Poland's help was
withdrawn. Buda at last fell and was restored to
Christian rule in 1686. Practically all of what we now
know as Hungary and Transylvania was effectually
occupied by the House of Hapsburg[1]. War continued
down to the *Peace of Carlowitz* in 1699; during these
"nineties" most of Europe was banded against Louis,
and thus a French war and a Turkish war went on
together and came to an end together. This explains
why, in spite of victories, more ground was not recovered
and Belgrade remained in Turkish hands. Meanwhile
Venice had roused herself to attack Greece, and occupied
the Morea and a good deal of the Dalmatian coast; the
most famous incident in this part of the war was the
bombardment of Athens in 1687, when the beautiful
buildings of the acropolis of the ancient city, especially
the Parthenon or temple of Pallas Athene, were wrecked
by Venetian guns.

Thus the story returns to Louis and France, though it
has to be remembered that in the years 1688—98 Austria
was distracted from giving the full weight of her assistance to the Allies. One has a feeling of sympathy with
Austria now as at other times of crisis, however greatly

---

[1] Peter the Great also was pushing the arms of Russia southwards
and in 1696 occupied Azov: he lost it in 1711.

one dislikes her persecution of Protestants. To be at
one and the same time the bulwark of Europe against the
Turk and of Germany against Louis was an exhausting
task. Other Powers benefited; England and Holland had
no share in the eastern war, and were content to protect
their Mediterranean trade by bargaining with the
Moslems; Prussia was fated to oust Austria from the
headship of Germany without ever having borne her
share of past burdens; Russia became the chief protector
of the Christians of Turkey.

The ten years of thunderous peace were dragging out.
In 1685 James II came to our throne, and the Sedgemoor
campaign was followed by his attack upon the Church of
England, the expulsion of the President and Fellows of
Magdalen College, the trial of the Seven Bishops, and the
birth of a son to his second wife Mary of Modena. In
1686 was founded the *League of Augsburg* to resist Louis.
Thus the readiness of England to drive out the Romanist
Stuart coincided with the readiness of the Allies for
war. William of Orange accepted the invitation to go
to England just when the Allies wanted England to join
them. James II refused the aid of Louis against William,
and wisely enough, because his best chance was to trust
to English national dislike of the Dutch without making
England the tool of France. Louis on his side made no
effort to invade Holland in William's absence, probably
arguing to himself that, if his bitterest enemy were locked
up in England and engaged in war owing to that anti-
Dutch spirit, he would be free for a campaign on the
Rhine. But the result was very different. James' army
and fleet went over to William, James ran away, and
so England came into the Grand Alliance, while Louis
gained nothing but detestation by his ruthless devastation of the Palatinate, which shocked an age accustomed
enough to pillage. He had let England slip away from
him, failed to do harm to Holland, yet had done himself

no good. The moral is that such a despot, eager to extend
his frontier in several directions and with too many irons
in the fire, is liable to give way to the wrong ambition at
the wrong moment.

The war of the League of Augsburg (1688—98) is
remarkable in that France was in arms against nearly
all Europe, and secondly in that France put to the test
the efficiency of her new navy which had been created
for her by Colbert, though Colbert himself was now
dead. At first it seemed as if the French would control
the Channel, for the English and Dutch admirals, misunderstanding each other, were beaten at the battle of
Beachy Head, 1690. But the critical year was 1692 when
Louis autocratically insisted that his ships should put out
to sea though the Mediterranean squadron had not yet
come round to reinforce the Brest squadron, and even an
autocrat cannot be sure that fleets will meet when they
are separated by 2000 miles of sea. The result was the
great victory of Cape La Hogue. Admiral Russell was
not a Nelson, and the battle of La Hogue was not in itself
a crushing victory to be compared to Trafalgar, but the
results of it were almost as great. Russell, following up
his success, burnt 15 ships upon the coast of Normandy
and thoroughly upheld England's naval superiority.
Louis came to the conclusion that, if after Colbert's
death Colbert's navy was so easily beaten, he had better
devote all his attention and all his spare funds to Louvois'
army. The failure of the French attempt to win Sea
Power under Louis XIV is, therefore, a strong argument
in favour of the theory that no nation yet has ever
been able to maintain both a great army and a great
navy for any length of time, a theory which may be
falsified in the future but which certainly is justified by
the experience of the past. It must not be supposed
that Louis never had ships at sea after 1692. He gained
a conspicuous success when a squadron destroyed our

fleet of merchantmen bound for the Mediterranean, which
was known as the Smyrna fleet. The skilful and energetic
sailors of Brittany and Normandy also turned their attention to privateering and inflicted many a loss upon the
English. But we can refer to the dictum of the famous
American naval writer, Admiral Mahan; a nation which
has secured the ocean as a highway of commerce by
right of victory and the superiority of her ships of war,
as trade follows the flag, can view with equanimity the
capture of a few stray merchantmen by privateers; and if
a victory such as that of La Hogue doubles England's
trade, the capture of five or even ten per cent. of our
trade by privateers is trifling.

By land the main fighting was once more in the
Spanish Netherlands. At first Louis easily secured
Mons, Charleroi, and Namur, the border fortresses on
the Spanish side of the frontier, whilst William's troops
were chiefly engaged in Ireland. But in 1690 and 1691
the Battle of the Boyne and the ultimate surrender of
Limerick freed William's hands, and he was able to
devote the whole of his force to the Netherlands. Though
twice beaten by the Duke of Luxemburg, Turenne's ablest
successor, William made such a stubborn resistance that
at last in 1695 he was able to lay siege to the citadel of
Namur. His chief characteristic was that he never knew
when he was defeated and could rally his forces so as
to lose all the disadvantages of defeat, and he kept together so successfully all his Allies, English, Dutch,
Austrians, Brandenburgers, Bavarians, and Spaniards,
that he brought the siege to a victorious conclusion. The
fall of Namur brought a shock of surprise to Europe.
Its first capture by the French had seemed to be a great
triumph. It had been strengthened by all the arts of
Vauban, yet it had fallen to the motley army of William,
and Boileau's poem of laudation at the capture of Namur
was caricatured by an English ode of greater triumph at

its recapture. Once more Louis felt that his means were being exhausted, and he said himself that the last piece of gold would win. Unluckily for himself, his instincts towards persecution and aggression had spoilt all that Colbert had done for France. England with some surprise discovered that she could carry on a war for nine years without finding herself plunged in a financial crisis. The beginnings of our National Debt and the foundation of the Bank of England during this war prove that England's trade was prosperous, and that our government could borrow in the country enough to carry us over years of danger. The Tory landowner growled that his land was severely taxed in order that the Whig merchants who had lent money to William at a high rate of interest might be recompensed, and probably many heads were shaken and people thought that England's credit could not stand the strain; but it did stand the strain, and the last piece of gold did win, in spite of an intrigue set on foot by the goldsmiths of London to ruin the new Bank of England. By the *Treaty of Ryswick* in 1697 between England and France, Louis acknowledged William as King of England and disowned the exiled James II. A year later the Allies likewise made peace with France on condition that Louis gave up all that he had won since the Treaty of Nymegen; yet he kept Strasburg. It was in 1699 also that Austria was freed from the incubus of the Turkish war by the Treaty of Carlowitz.

Thus a second time Louis had been foiled, and for a second time he rested to nurse his strength and watch for a new opportunity. It was not long in coming. Charles II of Spain was at death's door, and the Allies arranged two *Partition Treaties*; by the first the bulk of the Spanish dominions was to go to a Bavarian prince; by the second, after the Bavarian died, to the Archduke Charles of Austria, second son of the Emperor Leopold. But the pride of Spain had not been taken into consideration.

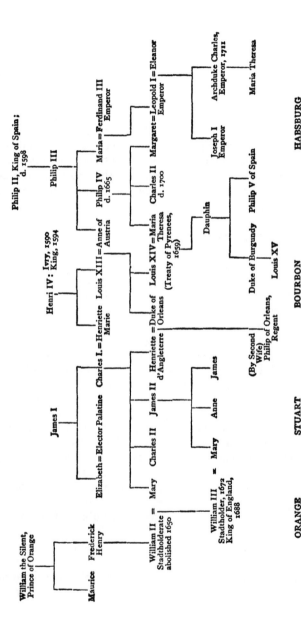

Philip II, King of Spain;
d. 1598

Philip III

Henri IV: Ivry, 1590
King, 1594

James I

William the Silent,
Prince of Orange

Maria = Ferdinand III
Emperor

Philip IV
d. 1665

Louis XIII = Anne of
Austria

Charles I = Henriette
Marie

Elizabeth = Elector Palatine

Maurice   Frederick
Henry

Margaret = Leopold I = Eleanor
Emperor

Charles II
d. 1700

Louis XIV = Maria
Theresa
(Treaty of Pyrenees,
1659)

Henriette = Duke of
Orleans

Charles II   James II

Mary

William II =
Stadtholderate
abolished 1650

Archduke Charles,
Emperor, 1711

Joseph I
Emperor

Maria Theresa

Dauphin

Duke of Burgundy   Philip V of Spain

Louis XV

(By Second
Wife)
Philip of Orleans,
Regent

Mary   Anne   James

William III
Stadtholder, 1672
King of England,
1688

ORANGE   STUART   BOURBON   HABSBURG

Spain might be the "sick man" of Europe, but had not sunk so low as to accept an Austrian Hapsburg as her King at the dictation of Europe. Charles bequeathed his crown to Philip of Anjou, second grandson of Louis XIV. Louis accepted the will of Charles, and Spain greeted the young man as the best answer to the insulting partition. Moreover Louis could argue that neither he, nor the dauphin, nor the dauphin's eldest son was now King of Spain, and that the Treaty of the Pyrenees did not stand in the way of the dauphin's second son. Philip's grandmother was the sister, the Archduke's grandmother was the aunt, of the late King. Therefore his was the better claim, and it was supported by the good will of the Spaniards.

In Philip's name French troops occupied the Spanish Netherlands and Spanish Lombardy. Therefore Louis had the opportunity for which he had been waiting. His troops were in possession, and the Allies had the difficult task of turning them out. He could pose as the champion of Spain, and the Allies openly were committed to dismember the empire of Spain. In spite of the Treaty of Ryswick and the recapture of Namur, France was yet the dominant military power. France, moreover, was in a fine central position, and the Allies were scattered and far apart. But Louis had an autocrat's weakness, excessive belief in himself, and in no way did he show this more clearly than in his choice of generals. He passed over his best men who would have represented the traditions of Turenne, such as Catinat and Villars, and pushed to the front Tallard and Villeroi. And such men, mere favourites of an autocrat, fate willed it should meet two great captains of war.

Handsome John Churchill had several years ago attracted the attention of Turenne; yet it was only known that he had been second in command to Feversham in a fight on a very small scale on the marshes of

7—2

Sedgemoor. Eugene of Savoy, a cousin of the Duke of Savoy, had been brought up at the court of Louis as a young French noble, had been ordered by Louis to enter the Church, had made up his mind that he would be a soldier and not a clergyman, had fled from France to throw himself upon the mercy of the Emperor, and had already served with distinction against the Turks. Louis lived to find out that the combination of these two men would destroy his apparently impregnable position as the ally and protector of Spain. Within a few years Eugene had driven the French out of Spanish Italy, and Churchill had conquered the whole of the Spanish Netherlands.

The people of England were not at all anxious to enter into war and cared little for the partition treaties, but they were moved by the seizure of the fortresses of the Spanish Netherlands by French troops. Then Louis committed a great blunder in acknowledging James III, son of the dying James II, as King of England. William III died just at this moment, bequeathing to Anne a war, the justice of which from our point of view was acknowledged by Tory and by Whig alike.

The Allies now were England, Holland, Austria, and a large number of the minor German States, such as Brandenburg whose Elector had just recently been raised to be King of Prussia, and Hanover whose Elector had been acknowledged as the heir to the throne of England; also after a short time Savoy and Portugal. Savoy was important as giving access by the Alpine passes from Italy to France, and Portugal as giving to the Allies the naval base of Lisbon. On the side of Louis were not only the whole of the Spanish dominions, but also Bavaria and Cologne. In days gone by Richelieu had always tried to conciliate Bavaria, and a century later Napoleon was to find in Bavaria, also in Saxony and Wurtemberg and Baden, his warmest allies against the larger Powers,

Austria and Prussia. Therefore, not only was Louis in a
strong position because he was actually in possession of
the Spanish forts of the Netherlands and of Lombardy,
but likewise he had through Bavaria a direct line of
attack upon Austria. He promised to the Bavarian
Elector such territories as would be conquered at the
expense of Austria, particularly the Tyrol, but the
Tyrolese were devoted to the family of Hapsburg and
rose against the Bavarians. This happened again in the
days of Napoleon, and is a proof that mountaineers may
sometimes be willing to be the subjects of a despotic
monarch, and are not always devoted to republicanism
and independence as in the case of the Swiss.

In the celebrated campaigns which follow we see
that the new ideas of warfare have now taken root.
Almost all the infantry were armed with the new flint-
lock guns and bayonets, but throughout the English
under Marlborough's careful training were the most
skilful in their use, and the fire, which is so marked a
century later under Wellington in the Peninsula, was
a feature also of Marlborough's army. Likewise he and
Eugene made the utmost use of their cavalry, neither like
Rupert sending their men in at a dashing gallop un-
supported, nor yet like Cromwell charging steadily at the
trot and firing from the saddle, but organising them in
several bodies, one to support the other, and charging
with the naked steel, wave upon wave, until the last
reserve broke the enemy's last reserve, and victory fell to
the general who had the last word. Field artillery was
becoming more important, and Marlborough himself
personally directed the fire of his batteries at Blenheim.
As regards fortifications and entrenchments, neither
Marlborough nor Eugene believed in them, and were
ready to out-manœuvre the enemy from his chosen
position or else to mask his fortresses. Except where
the French were stubbornly on the defensive, this is a

war rather of marches and manœuvres according to the
school of Gustavus and Turenne than of many sieges.
But while Marlborough and Eugene worked very well in
unison on these lines, they were much hampered by the
Dutch. They regarded the war as a whole, Spain and
Italy and Germany being so many squares upon the
chess-board, whereas the Dutch cared only for their one
square and wished to see Marlborough with their own
contingents confined to the Netherlands. Thus, if one
may pass a criticism on Marlborough that he did not
always show signs of the perfect strategist, it has to be
remembered that this stubbornness of the Dutch did
much to upset the grander plans which he had laid. As
regards personal qualities, he was the calm and cool
soldier who kept his head in the midst of the stress of
fighting, though he was quite capable of putting himself at the head of a victorious charge of horse, while
Eugene was the dashing soldier who seemed to go mad
with excitement in the heat of battle. But Marlborough
had the defects of his qualities, and the stern self-
repression which made him cool at a crisis had its
revenge in a period of break-down after he had won
a victory.

The war begins with minor actions upon the Rhine
and in Italy, while the Allies were preparing themselves
for greater efforts and creating their armies. This is true
of England in particular, for the jealousy against a
standing army, inherited from the days of Cromwell's
military despotism, was always so strong that on the
conclusion of each war the army was cut down to danger
point, so that when a new war begins the army has to
be recreated. It was in 1703, just as Marlborough was
beginning to feel his way, that Louis let slip his chance.
His ablest marshal, Villars, planned the direct attack
upon Austria by way of Bavaria of which we have already
spoken, but for various reasons it did not succeed. In

1704 Villars was recalled, and the work was put into the hands of the less competent Tallard and Marsin. Eugene came up from Italy; Marlborough made his celebrated cross-march from the borders of the Netherlands by the Rhine and the Neckar through the Black Forest to the upper Danube, stormed the heights of Donauwörth to secure a passage across the Danube, joined Eugene, and finally headed off the French and Bavarians at Blenheim. A series of powerful cavalry charges upon the French centre, which had been weakened whilst the infantry of the Allies were pounding at their flanks, gave to the pair their first great victory. The fall of Namur before William III had been the first sign that the soldiers of France were not invincible, but Blenheim was the first crushing blow which broke the prestige of Louis. Bavaria was devastated and henceforward useless to France. The French armies were put upon the defensive, and the initiative in the war passed to the Allies.

The year 1704 is celebrated also for our capture of Gibraltar, but, though the Rock still remains to us as a memorial of this great war, its seizure in that year was not really so important as the naval action which followed. The French Mediterranean squadron met the English and Dutch off the Spanish port of Malaga. The action seemed to be indecisive, but the French retired to Toulon and never again risked a pitched battle. Therefore the Allies won Sea Power quite easily and without any very great effort. In 1705 Barcelona fell to a mixed force, which came by sea; and in 1706 was defended against the French by land and sea, being relieved by the English fleet under Admiral Leake which the French dared not face. The fall of Barcelona to the Allies was followed by the up-rising of the whole province of Catalonia, always bitterly opposed to Castile and ready to welcome any enemy of Castile. Marlborough now planned a great attack upon the south of France and particularly upon Toulon. It is

clear that he realised to the full the value of Sea Power,
which gave to the land forces of the Allies the initiative
to attack France wheresoever they would. To carry out
this plan Eugene in 1706 marched westwards up the river
Po, delivered Turin which was being besieged by the
French, and drove them completely beyond the Alps into
their own country. But the opposition of the Dutch was
fatally felt. They insisted so strongly that Marlborough
should not leave their frontier, looking, as we suggested
before, merely at one square upon the chess-board and not
at the board as a whole, that his great plan broke down.
He found himself forced to fight in the Netherlands, and
compensated himself for his disappointment by the brilliant
campaign of Ramillies.

The French, put on the defensive, had a series of entrenchments in a long curve between Brussels and Namur
by which they hoped to cover Brabant. It was not
difficult for Marlborough by making a feint and breaking
through at the weak point to render these 70 miles of
entrenchments useless. Then he came upon Marshal
Villeroi who was posted upon some rising ground
behind the village of Ramillies, made a feint with his
English troops as though he would attack the French left
wing, threw the main force of his infantry upon the
village and, with a typical series of cavalry charges in
succession, carried the rising ground so as to completely
break the French right and centre; then, swinging round
his line and charging at a right angle to his previous
attack, he swept off the French left and Villeroi's army
was exterminated. Brussels and Antwerp fell to him at
once, and Ostend the next year after a siege. Therefore,
foiled in his designs upon South France, he was now in
full possession of all the Netherlands except the strip
covered by the border fortresses.

Affairs were not however going well in Spain. It is
clear that Marlborough's idea was to break the military

power of France, whereas to the Archduke Charles of
Austria it was the conquest of the Spanish throne for
himself that was the main purpose and excuse of the
war. Accordingly in 1706 and again in 1707 the Allies
marched upon Madrid. In 1706 they captured the capital
but had to evacuate it, so great was the hostility of the
Spaniards. In 1707 the army of the Allies, partly
English but mostly Portuguese, commanded by the
French refugee, the Earl of Galway, was beaten at
Almanza by a Franco-Spanish army commanded by the
Jacobite refugee, the Duke of Berwick. This battle
was decisive, and was a proof that Marlborough's plan
of leaving Madrid alone and attacking Toulon by sea was
superior. Eugene, fresh from his Italian victories of 1706,
attempted single-handed in 1707 to capture Toulon and
was beaten back. Clearly, isolated campaigns were not
likely to be successful when the Allies were fighting in
different directions, each for his own hand.

It has been suggested that the Allies ought to have
come to terms with Louis in 1706 after the triple successes
at Ramillies, Turin, and Barcelona. Yet it is doubtful if
so proud a King as Louis XIV could have accepted terms
such as would suit the Allies whilst he still had a chance
of rallying. To terminate a war before the enemy is
decisively beaten would merely have the effect of giving
him yet another breathing space and encouraging him to
make a greater effort later on. The Treaties of Nymegen
and Ryswick had given already to Louis such a chance,
and the Allies could not afford a treaty which would leave
him defeated but not exhausted. Some point to the wars
of 1813—15 and of 1870 as instances of the sound, though
it may seem to be inhuman, argument that an aggressive
enemy must be absolutely humbled to the dust, and
Europe required that Louis should be humbled. Others
who criticise the Allies for failing to make peace may
point to Almanza, and say that the allies never had a

chance of conquering Spain itself and therefore should
have been contented.

In 1708 it appeared as though the French would be
able to win back lost ground.   The districts of the
Netherlands occupied by Marlborough after Ramillies had
been handed over to the Dutch, and the bitter rivalry
between the Protestant Dutch on the one side and the
Catholic Flemings and Brabanters on the other was such
that the latter were ready to welcome the French back
again.   The Duke of Vendome in 1708 made a dash
across the French border, recaptured Ghent and Bruges
and, though failing to surprise Antwerp, held the line of
the river Scheldt.   Taken by surprise for the moment
Marlborough quickly recognised the position, and marched
to cut Vendome off from France.   The armies met at
Oudenarde on the middle Scheldt, and Marlborough's
van might have been isolated and destroyed by Vendome
had not Louis' grandson, the Duke of Burgundy, been
present and by his royal influence caused a retreat.
Later on in the afternoon of the same day the French
attacked when the whole of Marlborough's army was up,
and the third great defeat was inflicted upon them.
Then, joined by Eugene's army, Marlborough advanced
on Lille.   Eugene undertook the siege and Marlborough
covered him, and the great fortress fell.   In the winter of
1708—9 Louis again offered terms, and the Allies might
have found it to their advantage to have accepted them,
but a condition was made, contrary to Marlborough's
advice, that Louis should actually join the Allies to expel
Philip from the throne of Spain.   Of course it was impossible for him to submit, and he braced himself up and
appealed to the patriotism of France to renew the struggle.
In 1709 the border fortress of Tournai was captured by
Marlborough on the upper Scheldt.   Then followed the
siege of Mons, and Marshal Villars for the first time was
put into the command which he might have exercised

The Netherlands: to illustrate reigns of Elizabeth,
William III, and Anne

with much profit earlier. He advanced to save Mons, Marlborough and Eugene came out to meet him, and stormed with very great loss the entrenchments which he threw up at Malplaquet. Mons then fell.

The "fag-end" of the war is remarkable only for a new effort of the Allies to regain Madrid, which ended in disaster like the previous efforts, and for the advance of Marlborough and Eugene into the territory of France. Marlborough's plan was to leave alone Vauban's triple line of fortresses and advance on Paris; Eugene and the other Allies preferred to attack the fortresses one by one. Villars defended them sturdily, so that there is no great event to be chronicled in the years 1710—12. The interest of these years is entirely political. In England arose the usual cry that the war merely benefited the Whig merchants who lent money at a high rate of interest to the Government to carry it on, while the poor Tory landowners had to pay out of the land tax. There was no object gained by a continuance of the war except that my Lord of Marlborough would gain military glory for himself. We were simply fighting to help our Dutch and Austrian Allies. If the Dutch wanted a series of barrier fortresses against France, or if an Austrian Archduke wanted to become King of Spain, let them fight for their own hands without all this expenditure of English blood and money. Moreover by the deaths of his father and brother Charles was now Emperor, and to join Spain to Austria under the same Hapsburg would be fatal. These arguments had immense weight upon the English people, and Jonathan Swift drove the point home in one of the most powerful and most popular of political pamphlets, "The Conduct of the Allies." In 1710 Queen Anne dismissed her Whig ministers and dissolved Parliament. The Tories obtained a majority, thwarted Marlborough in every way, secured his dismissal, and finally brought about the *Treaty of Utrecht*.

There was one period in this long war when Louis might have obtained a very valuable ally. Ever since the days of Gustavus Adolphus the Swedish army had been a power in Europe, and Sweden held various positions on the south of the Baltic. The Swedish menace was not so dangerous to Europe as might have been thought, for Denmark and Brandenburg, Poland and Russia, were all offended by this supremacy and on various occasions banded together. However, if the enemies of Sweden were many, they were disunited. In 1700 the youthful Charles XII had recently come to the throne. He was a lover of adventure and a sort of knight errant, devoted to war as his only pleasure. In turn the Danes were beaten and Copenhagen captured; and the Russians, not led on that occasion by Peter the Great, were routed at Narva by a force one-fifth of their own strength. Then followed an invasion of Poland, the deposition of Augustus of Saxony who was King of Poland, and the invasion of Saxony itself in 1706. Had Charles XII now turned to France as the old ally of Sweden and taken the Allies in the rear, the combined plans of Marlborough and Eugene would have been seriously endangered. But it is well known from Voltaire's account that Marlborough himself interviewed the young King, played upon his ambition, and influenced him to turn his eyes once more towards Russia. He commenced a wild and blind march into the heart of Russia. Peter, anticipating the policy which foiled Napoleon the Great, retreated until the Swedish army, reduced in numbers and with a quarter of the men sick and unable to fight, was surrounded by a vastly superior force of Russians and beaten at Poltawa in July 1709; 11,000 are said to have been killed or taken prisoners in the battle, and 13,000 capitulated. Charles himself barely escaped and crossed the border into Turkish territory. After various adventures, at one time welcomed by the Turks and stirring them to attack

Russia—it was in 1711 that the hitherto victorious Peter
was forced to give up Azov—at another time treated as
an enemy and besieged in the house which had been
allotted to him at Bender, at last in 1714 he escaped and
reached Sweden. He found all his enemies arrayed
against him, including George I of England who wanted
Bremen and Verden for Hanover. In 1718 he was killed
in front of a fortress in Norway. Finally Bremen and
Verden were added to Hanover, Stettin and part of
Pomerania to Prussia, Livonia and a large part of Finland
to Russia. Sweden was no longer a power to be feared.

This story has introduced us to a new Great Power,
destined to shift the centre of historical interest from
western to middle Europe. Modern Russia is the creation
of Peter the Great. Before him several Tsars had extended their way towards Kiev. But he first laid down
the lines of a traditional national policy, that Russia
must expand to the sea. He founded Petrograd, and for
a short time held in the opposite direction the port of
Azov. He reorganised and settled the conditions of the
national Russian life, creating a class of officials devoted
to the Crown as a counterbalance to the hereditary
nobility, and so strong were his foundations that at the
present day officialdom or, as it is sometimes called,
bureaucracy is the dominant element in Russian life.
He organised a Russian army of which it has been said
that, though dirty and ignorant, it has always been able
to take more pounding that any army of its more civilised
neighbours. In those days the chief enemies of Russia
were Sweden and Poland and Turkey; in the days to come
they were Germany and Austria. The Western Powers
sometimes have found Russia a valuable ally, sometimes
have hurried into war against Russia so as to press her
back from the sea. But whoever have been the enemies
and whoever the friends of Russia, the great Empire has
always expanded.

EXPANSION OF RUSSIA AND PRUSSIA 111

There was yet another Power whose friendship each country found to be valuable, yet whose ultimate expansion could hardly have been anticipated, namely Brandenburg-Prussia. The story of the expansion of the power of the Hohenzollern dynasty is fascinating, as it tells of steady growth and readiness to seize opportunities. As far back as the 10th century there were Counts of Zollern in the far south-west of Germany. In 1417 Frederick of Hohenzollern, Burgraf of Nuremberg, was chosen to be Elector and Margraf of the Mark of Brandenburg, which was a German border district on the lower-middle Elbe over against the less civilised Slavonic races. There his neighbours eastwards were the Teutonic Order of Knights, who in the middle ages were an outpost of Christendom and crusaders against the heathen Prussians[1]; as they declined they sold the New Mark of Brandenburg on the Oder to a successor of Frederick. Then the Kings of Poland were lords of Prussia, divided into a West or Royal half, and an East or Ducal half. In 1525 Albert of Hohenzollern obtained East Prussia under the overlordship of Poland. Next were obtained the Duchy of Cleves near Holland, Magdeburg and Halberstadt on the Elbe, and part of Pomerania, after the Thirty Years; though a Lutheran, George William the Elector of that day had not welcomed the presence of Gustavus and the Swedes. Frederick William, the Great Elector 1640—88, thus succeeded to a number of states, held by various titles, and scattered over Germany from the Polish to the Dutch frontier. He was a great organiser of central government, which he could only bring about by a strong paternal despotism, himself appointing officials so as to limit the powers of the local

[1] Adventurers from any country were welcomed by the Order; in fiction the Knight of the *Canterbury Tales*, in history Sir John Chandos in the interval between Crécy and Poitiers, and Henry of Bolingbroke when exiled, crusaded in Prussia.

governments, and extending the authority of his Council of Brandenburg over the other states. He welcomed some 20,000 landless Huguenots, who were invaluable as teachers of agriculture and industry where the soil was poor and manufactures did not exist. He had canals cut, especially one between the Oder and the Spree. His son Frederick in 1701 took the title of King of Prussia by virtue of his non-German territories, and henceforward Brandenburg is, so to speak, lost in Prussia. In the wars of William III and of Marlborough the Prussian troops gave a foretaste of their quality at Namur, Blenheim, and Oudenarde. But he was yet a poor king and had to be subsidised. The time was to come when, as a principal rather than an ally, Prussia would dictate to Europe. Meanwhile Frederick I added Stettin and part of Swedish Pomerania to his dominions; his grandson, Frederick II or the Great, was to add Silesia at the expense of Austria, West Prussia at the expense of Poland.

From unfavourable beginnings a solid kingdom was formed out of disconnected parts. The non-German districts were more and more Germanised under the Hohenzollerns until Slavonic ideas and language disappeared. A national standing army was formed under the strictest discipline and centralised authority; a strong line divided the noble officer from the peasant in the ranks, another strong line the tax-paying non-military burgher from the less taxed soldier families. Foreigners were continually attracted, and even were kidnapped for the army, and soon these would be genuine Prussians. Royal patronage of industries and a measure of public education were not wanting. And if one looks forward to Frederick the Great as the King who did most as an "enlightened despot," at least his ancestors showed him the way, and throughout modern Prussia was the creation of the Hohenzollern dynasty.

CHAPTER V

THE PREDOMINANCE OF PRUSSIA

THE War of the Spanish Succession came to an end by a series of treaties, and the most important of these was the *Treaty of Utrecht,* finally signed in 1713, between Britain and Holland and France. The Emperor Charles VI continued the war alone for another year, but as Villars had the upper hand over Eugene he made peace by the *Treaty of Rastadt* in 1714. The map of Europe was altered and the results were of vast importance.

Firstly, the Frenchman Philip V was recognised as King of Spain, and the Catalans who had taken the side of the Allies were left to his tender mercies. Thus the Hapsburg-Bourbon rivalry across the Pyrenees came to an end after two centuries of almost continuous war, and a Bourbon held each throne. Yet the Allies had fought to prevent this very thing. It had been a successful war except in Spain itself, and now the original object of the war was lost. The crowns, however, of France and Spain were never to be united. When Louis XIV died in 1715 and was succeeded by his great-grandson Louis XV, it was clear that the French Bourbons and Spanish Bourbons were positively hostile. Louis XV was very young. The regent, Philip Duke of Orleans, son of Louis XIV's younger brother, was heir to the French throne; therefore he looked for the support of the late enemies of France,

Britain and Holland, in case Philip V should try to unite the crowns. The hostility of France and Spain was of but short duration. Louis XV married in 1725 Maria, daughter of Stanislas, ex-King of Poland, and in 1729 an heir was born to him. So then there was no reason why the two countries should not become friends. In 1733 they made an agreement which in later years blossomed into the *Family Compact*; henceforward the two Bourbon dynasties were to be found on the same side and were Great Britain's enemies. But it was a weakened and exhausted France that fought us in the Seven Years, and it is absolutely true that Marlborough's victories made possible the later victories of Clive and Wolfe. Not till the War of American Independence did the allied Bourbons obtain their revenge. The permanent gain of the British was Gibraltar; and a temporary gain was Minorca, which thrice taken and thrice lost remains to-day Spanish.

Secondly, Philip only obtained Spain and the Spanish Indies. Charles VI obtained, as compensation for losing Spain itself, nearly all the European dominions, viz. the Spanish Netherlands, Lombardy, Sardinia, and Naples. This satisfied the British and Dutch, for their main interest was to save the Netherlands from French control. But it did not satisfy Charles VI himself. He had to submit to two conditions; the Dutch were to garrison the fortresses of the "barrier," *i.e.* the Belgian border towards France; the Scheldt was to remain closed to trade, and therefore the possession of Antwerp was valueless. He felt that Britain and Holland had only made use of him for their own ends, deserting him when they made the treaty, crying out that their blood and gold ought not to be spent to make him King of Spain, giving the Netherlands to him simply to keep out the French, but taking good care that Antwerp should not have the chance of attracting the overseas trade from London and Amsterdam.

Thirdly, the Duke of Savoy obtained Sicily. This fact is important as the House of Savoy is to-day the reigning House of Italy. The geographical position of the duchy astride the Alps, one foot in Savoy, the other in Piedmont, led to some gain at every crisis, for in every European combination and war the duke's friendship was valuable out of proportion to the size of his dominions.

In making peace as in prosecuting war the Allies neglected an important factor, namely the pride of the Spaniards. They were offended and sore because no consideration had been shown for their feelings, an archduke whom they did not want had at first been forced upon them, and now had received their Italian and Netherland lands. No nation can be expected to submit tamely to contemptuous disregard, and Spain was not so abjectly low in fortune as to remain quiet as the "sick man." The Netherlands were too far away. But Gibraltar and Minorca and the lost parts of Italy might be recovered. Philip V was much under the influence of his second wife, Elizabeth of Parma, known as the "termagant of Spain," and her immediate wish was to secure Parma for her own young son, Don Carlos; the son of Philip's first wife was heir to Spain itself. Thus the troubles which arose between the Treaty of Utrecht and a final settlement twenty-five years later were primarily due to Spain's offended pride and Elizabeth's ambition.

The first move of Spain was due to Cardinal Alberoni, an Italian of humble birth, whose aim was to win back Naples and Sicily. He hoped that Britain, at any rate, might be unable to interfere because Charles XII of Sweden was threatening to support the Jacobites against George I; but this danger passed away when Charles died[1]. A Spanish force occupied Sardinia, but when the attempt was made to occupy Sicily Admiral Byng fell on the fleet off Cape Passaro and destroyed it in 1718; there

[1] See p. 110.

was no declaration of war by us as Spain was the aggressor. The British and Dutch and the Duke of Orleans, as the rival Bourbon to Philip V, formed a Triple Alliance, and Alberoni's scheme collapsed.

In 1725 Baron Ripperda, a Netherlander who had come to Spain, formed another combination. Philip and the Emperor Charles, the original rivals, were to come to terms; Elizabeth's two sons were to marry Charles' two daughters; the British were to be driven from Gibraltar, and an Austrian East India Company, with its base at Ostend as Antwerp was useless, was to have all their privileges of Spanish trade. It was an unnatural alliance and no success attended it, though there was a half-hearted effort to attack Gibraltar.

In 1733 died Augustus, Elector of Saxony and King of Poland. France supported the ex-King Stanislas, Austria and Russia supported Augustus' son for the vacant throne. At the same time, Orleans being dead and Louis XV having an heir, there was no reason why France and Spain should continue to be enemies; and by the Treaty of Turin the two reconciled Bourbons, together with the Duke of Savoy, agreed to drive the Austrians out of Italy and rearrange the map. Walpole was at that moment in power in England, and his aim was solely for peace; he is said to have gloated that much blood was shed and none of it British. There was in fact a great deal of fighting. A French force appeared as far off as Dantzig in the interests of Stanislas, but was unsuccessful. Russia alone was the ally of Austria, but Russia cared only for the throne of Poland and a Turkish war. Therefore the Austrians had to defend themselves both in Italy and on the Rhine, and were everywhere beaten; even Eugene, now an old man, could do nothing, for the Austrian military organisation had sunk very low. The Emperor Charles had to come to terms, and at last the "definitive" *Treaty of Vienna* gave a general peace in

1738.   He gave up a great deal in Italy.   But one thing was very near to his heart, and for it he was ready to give up a great deal.   The House of Hapsburg had no male heir.   Therefore he wished to secure for his daughter, Maria Theresa, his hereditary dominions, and for her husband, Francis of Lorraine, the title and dignity of Emperor.   If the Powers, and in particular France, would agree to the so-called *Pragmatic Sanction*, which would override the Salic Law for Austria and German lands,— there was nothing to prevent a woman from inheriting Hungary and Bohemia,—he would surrender Naples.

The various changes in the map of Europe in alteration of the Treaty of Utrecht, whether made in 1738 at Vienna or just before or after, were these.   Charles obtained the recognition of Maria Theresa as his heiress by the Pragmatic Sanction; but Francis gave up what remained of the Duchy of Lorraine outside the three French bishoprics, and received instead the Grand Duchy of Tuscany, which was a fief of the Empire and was vacant through the recent death of the last of the Medici. Poland being held by Augustus II of Saxony, Stanislas received Lorraine for his life, and then it was to lapse to France[1].   Don Carlos, son of Philip V and Elizabeth, was King of Naples and Sicily; Don Philip, their second son, was Duke of Parma; thus the Bourbon family gained a third throne, and was planted in Italy as well as in France and Spain.   The Duke of Savoy received Sardinia in place of Sicily, and took the title of King of Sardinia; he also gained some frontier places towards Milan.   But the Emperor retained Milan.   These arrangements last down to the wars of the French Republic.

It is by considering the Italian question and the Pragmatic Sanction that we can understand why Austria did less in the Balkans than she could have done.   During the Spanish Succession, as during the Thirty Years, the

[1] This happened in 1767.

THE BOURBON CROWNS

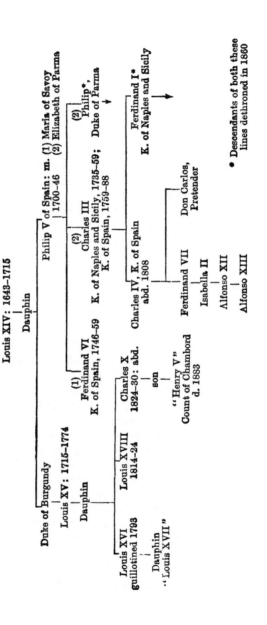

Louis XIV: 1643–1715

Dauphin

Philip V of Spain: m. (1) Maria of Savoy 1700–46 (2) Elizabeth of Parma

Duke of Burgundy

Louis XV: 1715–1774

Dauphin

Louis XVIII 1814–24

Louis XVI guillotined 1793

Dauphin "Louis XVII"

(1) Ferdinand VI K. of Spain, 1746–59

Charles X 1824–30: abd.

son

"Henry V" Count of Chambord d. 1883

(2) Charles III K. of Naples and Sicily, 1735–59; K. of Spain, 1759–88

(2) Philip*, Duke of Parma

Charles IV, K. of Spain abd. 1808

Don Carlos, Pretender

Ferdinand VII

Isabella II

Alfonso XII

Alfonso XIII

Ferdinand I* K. of Naples and Sicily

* Descendants of both these lines dethroned in 1860

Turks had missed their opportunity and done nothing to harass Austria in the rear. But no sooner was the Spanish Succession settled than they attacked the Venetians in the Morea. Venice appealed to Austria, and Prince Eugene won new laurels by beating the Turks out of south Hungary and winning a notable victory at Belgrad in 1717. It was impossible, however, to help effectively such a state as Venice in her dotage. The Turks kept their hold over Greece for another century. In truth the Austrian efforts towards the Balkans were feeble, and just when it seemed that the Turkish power would collapse and the Christian races be freed, the Emperor drew back. It was a blunder on his part. Russia was just beginning to get within striking range of the Balkans. But there was not then an Eastern Question as we know it to-day, when the Powers form and re-form in groups according as they pose as the rival champions of the Christians or bolster up the Turks. Austria alone was then in a position to be the champion, and Charles drew back because of Italy and his ambition for Maria Theresa. Of course that country is the happiest that has only one frontier, but Austria has always been distracted and unable to devote herself to one question at a time. Thus Belgrad remained in the Sultan's hands, and the *Treaty of Belgrad* in 1739 marked the cessation of the Austrian advance down the Danube.

The period both in England and France is celebrated not so much for the many political intrigues as for the strange mania for speculation which came upon the two nations. In each case there was a fear that the national debt was too great for the country to bear. In England the South Sea Company, in France the Mississippi Company under the control of a Scot, John Law, offered to take over the whole of the national debt and convert the creditors of the government into shareholders in these trading and colonial companies. The companies were genuine and their trade was genuine, but there was such a rush for the buying of shares that they ran up to abnormal values in a short space of time, the natural trade was not sufficient to give the extravagant profits that were expected, and after a period of speculation came, according to a modern phrase, a bad slump and large numbers of people lost their all. The cleverness of the Whig financier, Sir Robert Walpole, saved England from any serious trouble, but in France matters were very bad, and the affairs of Law's company had not been straightened by the time that the French Revolution broke out.

The fact that these financial schemes were based upon colonial trade is a reminder to us that we are coming now to the period when the colonial interests of England and France would clash. During the 17th century the colonial power of each country had been gradually growing, but there had been no serious collision between them so as to involve the mother countries. The English colonies in N. America, whether under the Crown, or under charters which gave them something like democratic rights, or proprietary, lived each its own life, and there was no bond of union except the mere fact that they were all English. In the extreme north of America the Hudson's Bay Company had a footing in the cold regions and dealt in furs. Along the east coast, from Nova Scotia, acquired at Utrecht from France, down to Georgia, the youngest, each colony or plantation or possession had its own system of government, and they were mostly jealous one of another. In the West Indies were Jamaica, acquired by Cromwell, and various islands of the outer ring, which had in the past been mere buccaneering stations and acknowledged, some more and some less, the authority of the Crown. The traditions of Drake and Hawkins remained amongst the buccaneers and pirates of the Caribbean Sea, but there had not yet been any serious trouble with regard to France. The French had the royal colony of Canada, which was simply the St Lawrence valley. Explorers from Canada were beckoned on by the call of the great unknown west, sailed the lakes, found the headwaters of the Ohio and Mississippi, and thus reached the mouth of the latter and founded Louisiana, where the regent's name was given to New Orleans. Law's scheme was to bring all the French colonies into one great *Compagnie des Indes Occidentales*. In spite of his failure French trade flourished in the sugar islands, Hayti, Martinique, Guadaloupe, St Lucia. Indeed the English traders had serious rivals. The keystone of English[1] commercial policy was the Navigation Act: all our trade was to be in our own ships, not colonial ships, nor French ships. It was to stop the French sugar trade with our colonies, as much as for other reasons, that the wars of the 18th century came about, and the merchants of Bristol, whose chief interests were in the West Indies, could put pressure on the home government to support their views. The Navigation Acts, rather than the Stamp Act or the Tea Duty, caused American Independence.

As regards Spain, it had been settled at Utrecht that our South Sea Company should have the sole right, enjoyed between 1701 and 1711 by the French Guinea Company, to provide negro slaves to Spanish America, also to send one ship a year of general merchandise. But this did not satisfy the English of the West Indies. Drake and Hawkins had begun the tradition of forcing our trade upon Spanish America against Spain's will. Cromwell and Charles II in turn offered alliance to Spain if she would allow free trade. Then, even when by treaty certain privileges were obtained, smuggling and

---

[1] Since the Union with Scotland in 1707, the correct word would be "British." But the Navigation Acts were English measures to protect English trade with English colonies. Scotland was no longer a foreign country under the Acts, but had not yet gained profit from them.

buccaneering continued. "Villainy is inherent in this climate," wrote our admiral from Jamaica. The Spanish coast-guards retaliated, and one Jenkins had his ear cut off. Excitement blazed up in England. Walpole was forced into war in 1739, and it was an unsatisfactory war, both from its disgraceful cause, and because the science of the time could not stay the ravages of yellow fever among our sailors. But most important is the fact that, owing to Spanish and French Bourbons drawing close together, we were sure sooner or later to be dragged into war against France also. Walpole was forced to resign.

This local and naval war coincided with a general European conflagration. Charles VI died, and he had obtained distinct recognition of the claims of Maria Theresa by the Pragmatic Sanction. At once Bavaria and Prussia took advantage of Maria's isolation. Charles Albert, "the Bold Bavarian" of Dr Johnson's satire "The Vanity of Human Wishes," laid claim to Austria on the basis of the will of the Emperor Ferdinand I of 175 years ago. Later on he was elected as Emperor. Saxony, and of course France, supported Bavaria. Frederick of Prussia, without any claim at all, played openly for his own hand; he had the army which his father had carefully nursed, and he invaded Silesia in 1741. It seemed madness for so small a country to plunge recklessly into war, but Austria was distracted by the attitude of Bavaria and France, and the loyalty of Hungary was by no means certain. But Great Britain and Hanover and Holland were true to their obligations, and, as in the "Spanish Succession," so now in *the War of the Austrian Succession* stood by Austria. It was clear that Great Britain must be the ally of Maria, not only because Hanover had to observe the balance of power and feared Prussia rather than Austria, but also because we had to be on the side opposite to France. Of the ministers who succeeded Walpole at least Lord Carteret saw that British interest

demanded that we should strongly support Hanover and
Austria, continuing the policy of William III and Marlborough to weaken France. When he was attacked as a
pro-Hanoverian who was sacrificing British interests to
a useless alliance, Pitt being one of his fiercest opponents,
even then the ministers who succeeded him were committed
to the war and could not withdraw. Almost unwillingly
our country had to continue the struggle of which the prize
was colonial expansion.

Frederick won the battle of Mollwitz in Silesia in 1741,
rather by the excellence of his disciplined Prussians than
by his skill in leadership. Then he invaded Bohemia.
But his allies did not cooperate with him. Maria, sorely
pressed and against her will, bought him off in 1742 by
the surrender of Silesia. This province is separated
from Bohemia by a range of mountains; towards Prussia
it is open and connected by the river Oder; so nature
seems to demand that it should be Prussian rather than
Austrian. Probably Maria gained far more than she
lost in this war. Previous to her reign every Austrian
sovereign had found Hungary a source of weakness rather
than of strength, and Hungarian patriots had often been
ready to receive the help of the Turk rather than remain
under the Catholic rule of Austria; but Maria in her
extremity appealed to the loyalty of her Hungarian
nobles, and they answered in the true spirit of chivalry.
Freed from the pressure of Prussia, she was able to turn
all her strength against the Bavarians and the French,
and Charles Albert was crushed. Britain helped Maria
by distracting the attention of France, and in 1743 an
army of British and allied Germans headed and drove
back the French upon the river Main at Dettingen; the
general plan of this campaign, though Dettingen was not
a great victory, is not unlike that of Blenheim, for a French
army striking at Austria through Bavaria was intercepted
and forced back. Then in 1744 Frederick declared war

again on Maria, and again had to be bought off by a confirmation of his right to Silesia.

In 1745 Austria and Great Britain and Holland remained in arms against France. The centre of the war was shifted to the Netherlands, where Marshal Saxe attacked the border fortresses. The Allies advancing on him as he besieged Tournai on the Scheldt, he beat them back at Fontenoy. Then the Jacobite rising compelled the withdrawal of the British troops. Our Sea Power was sufficient to localise the war at home, and the Highlanders of the Young Pretender were no longer to be feared when once they turned back from Derby. But things went wrong for Maria without any help from Britain. She saw her Austrian Netherlands overrun by Saxe, and it appeared as if the work of Marlborough had been undone. Yet in Italy the Austrian troops gained some successes; and British naval squadrons contributed to the weakening of France, and small yet important victories won by Hawke and Anson in the Bay of Biscay brought the ministers of Louis XV to think of peace. In India indeed the French were successful, and Labourdonnais captured Madras. But across the Atlantic an expedition from the colonies of New England captured Louisbourg, the French fortress on Cape Breton Island which stands as a sentinel at the mouth of the St Lawrence. By a general treaty of peace in 1748 at Aachen, otherwise Aix-la-Chapelle, it was agreed that there should be a mutual restoration of all conquests. The French restored to us Madras, and we restored to them Louisbourg; the French evacuated the Austrian Netherlands, but Maria had to guarantee Silesia finally to Frederick. The difficulty about the Empire was solved when, on the death of the "Bold Bavarian," the Electors chose Maria's husband, Francis of Lorraine.

Before we enter upon *the Seven Years' War*, which was the great deciding conflict of the 18th century, it would be as well to pass in review the various combatants and the resources at their disposal. Prussia, we have already seen, was a country which owed everything to its dynasty. A poor soil was worked up and transformed; manufactures on a small scale were introduced. Foreigners of all kinds, whether the Huguenots as in the days of the Great Elector, or Germans who were enticed by royal bounty from Rhineland and elsewhere, were made welcome. The Kingdom, in fact, which was a mere agglomeration of German and non-German lands round the nucleus of the old Mark of Brandenburg, was gradually receiving unity from its dynasty. But the one great institution upon which all its success was based was the army. In previous wars it had acted merely as an auxiliary or even as a mercenary force; now it became under Frederick the Great the principal military factor in Europe. It had been brought to a pitch of excellence by very severe training. About half the men were Prussians and Brandenburgers, and half foreigners, whether adventurers who served for the love of fighting, or mercenaries, or vanquished enemies forced into Frederick's ranks. For instance, the majority of the Saxons when their country was overrun in the war now to be described were converted into Prussian soldiers. But, whether natives or foreigners, the men were all drilled with the utmost rigidity. The principle was taken from Leopold of Anhalt who is always known as "the old Dessauer," who had served under Eugene at Blenheim and Malplaquet, and was connected with the family of Orange. Frederick's principle was that of good shooting, quick loading, and vigorous attack. He reduced the ranks to three and introduced iron ramrods, which enabled the men to load more quickly and more surely. It is not to be supposed that Prussians only profited by the example of the old Dessauer. For instance, Marlborough's infantry in the War of the Spanish Succession required no training beyond his, and both at Dettingen and Fontenoy, and in the war which is to come at Minden and Quebec, a very steady and well-maintained infantry fire was the mark of the British armies. But in the 18th century, after Marlborough's time, the British had no influence upon continental warfare. Our greatest victories were won, either when the native British in our armies were few in comparison with the number of subsidised allies, or when they fought in Canada and India. Stiff drill and steady fire, therefore, are characteristically Prussian. Next Frederick trained a heavy cavalry which was able to stand the shock of the keen light horsemen, better riders and more skilful swordsmen, which the Austrians were always able to put into the field from their Hungarian and Croatian provinces. As regards Frederick's tactics, he thought out what he himself called an oblique order, by which he refused one wing to the enemy and strengthened the wing which was to attack. The essence of this plan is that by very rapid marching Frederick could hurl the whole of his force upon one flank of the enemy, and so partly defeat and partly neutralise a much larger force. It was in the battle of Leuthen that he carried out this manœuvre to perfection. Lastly, we must note that Frederick's military successes would have been slight in spite of all the cleverness with which he took to himself and developed Leopold's ideas, if he had not such excellent material to work upon. The more volatile French armies would have been crushed by such discipline and unable to show their national élan. The steady and more phlegmatic peasants and serfs of northern Germany formed excellent material upon which Frederick could work.

On the other side the Austrians were much more prepared for the Seven Years' War than they had been for the first Silesian War. Maria had been looking forward to her revenge upon Frederick, and her officers had been getting ready. They were not overwhelmed at once by the Prussian charge as they had been previously, and in particular the cleverest of Maria's generals, such as Laudon, developed a power of counter-attack, upon occasions attacked on their own initiative, and were not already beaten beforehand through want of confidence. Frederick could never entirely worst the large bodies of the light Austrian horse. We also find that the Austrian generals had increased and improved their artillery to a great extent.

In the first Silesian war Frederick had had allies, and Maria was distracted by enemies in every direction. The position was now reversed. The allies were Maria's, and Frederick could only look to Britain and to Hanover. All the power of Russia was arrayed against him. Partly this was indeed in Frederick's favour, for very rarely did the Russians and Austrians combine; but when they did combine, he was almost at his last gasp, though such occasions were rare. On the other hand as fast as he made head against the Austrians in Silesia or Saxony he was recalled to face the Russians in the valley of the middle Oder, and it was impossible for him to follow up his victories over one ally in front as long as the other ally threatened his flank. That he had not more trouble and that France had not the deciding voice in the war by attacking Frederick's western flank is due to Great Britain. It was necessary for us to have the alliance of Prussia for the defence of Hanover; therefore Pitt subsidised large numbers of Germans. Frederick lent a general in the person of Ferdinand of Brunswick, and the result was that, except on one occasion, he felt safe as against France.

It was a new France where there was as much display and show as under the great Louis but very much less ability and patriotism, a France exhausted by the cruel wars in which Marlborough and Eugene played so conspicuous a part, unable to pull herself out of the slough of exhaustion because her social institutions were so bad, paralysed not only by the appalling wickedness of Louis XV, but also by the spirit of utter frivolity and lack of seriousness which seemed to find that a defeat was a joke, so that the nation could not rally. There were the elements of greatness in many a Frenchman, but the court of the fifteenth Louis was a sink of iniquity and the great men were not allowed to come to the front. Thus the national characteristics, French dash and cheerfulness and ability to face a great crisis, had no chance to display themselves, and the middle of the 18th century witnessed the triumph of German steadiness. It is not too much to say that the French, above all nations, have always required tactful leading which will enable them to make use of their natural resourcefulness. Deprived of such leading and defeated for want of it, they are too apt to shout out, *Nous sommes trahis*.

We have thus already shown that in the Seven Years' War Great Britain would be found arrayed on the side of Prussia, and France upon the side of Austria. This was brought about simply by force of circumstances. France and Britain were rivals in India and in America. In India this is the period of Dupleix and Clive, but Dupleix had already been foiled and had returned to France deserted by his countrymen and impoverished, having exhausted the whole of his own and his wife's enormous fortunes in the service of France without repayment; thus there was no *casus belli* in India, and neither the English nor the French East India Company wanted a new war. It is across the Atlantic that we find the *casus belli*, and at last the French explorers from Canada and the Virginian backwoodsmen, who were drifting to the West across the Alleghanies, collided upon the banks of the river Ohio. War blazed out fiercely, a horrible war in which the semi-civilised trappers and the wholly uncivilised redskins could not be controlled by the few regular soldiers. A reign of terror spread along the borders of our colonies, particularly Virginia, Pennsylvania, and New York. The mother country was forced to come to their aid, for the colonies—each with its different form of government and its different religious ideas, democratic Puritans in the northern, aristocratic planters in the southern, Dutch and other foreigners between—were quite unable to help each other. Therefore Britain and France were at war.

There are two theories about the relations between Great Britain and Hanover since the accession of George I. According to some writers, Hanover brought to us neither honour nor profit, and involved us in the complicated struggles of Germany from which we could otherwise have kept free. Such a theory goes on the idea that, had it not been for Hanover, Britain and France would have fought out their colonial rivalry by sea and in Canada and in India without involving the presence of great armies opposed to each other in Germany. It is thought that, our destiny being bound up with the sea, we were brought into risks by the mere fact that the King of Great Britain was also Elector of Hanover. This theory of insularity, that our statesmen should always go upon the assumption that living in an island it is wrong for us to interfere in continental politics, has a great deal to be said for it. But it disregards the palpable fact that in the days of William III and Marlborough we gained the most substantial advantages by being one of many allies in a great land war. Although anyone who reads the Treaty of Utrecht superficially does not see where our gain is apparent, except in the possession of Gibraltar and Minorca and a few minor places in America, yet it is clear that the expansion of France was diametrically opposed to the prosperity of Great Britain, which from the reign of Anne onwards had its root in the defeat of the French land forces and the consequent disorder of the French finances. Britain had taken her share in the Grand Alliance, had created a national debt that was not at all overpowering, and as the prize of Marlborough's victories had developed a national strength which made success in the Seven Years' War possible. Lord Roberts' dictum that our armies have created our Sea Power is certainly proved by the facts. Therefore the rival theory concerning Hanover is that it was to the advantage of the British to be dragged into the Seven Years' War, when, for the purpose of defending Hanover, our statesmen were forced to make alliance with Prussia by the Treaty of Westminster, January 1756, because we had no other ally to whom to look.

In the same way these two theories about British insularity or interference in foreign wars meet us in connection with Austria. The critics of the Duke of Marlborough and the promoters of the Treaty of Utrecht argued that it was not to our advantage to spend our blood and treasure in fighting the battles of an Austrian Archduke so as to make him King of Spain. Naturally our Austrian allies, left in the lurch when the Treaty of Utrecht was made, considered that we had deserted them. Again, Britain had once been the ally of Maria Theresa, but had most strongly advised her to come to terms with Frederick by the surrender of Silesia. Therefore it seemed to Maria that both her father and herself had been the allies of Britain for the advantage of Britain only, and that Austria had lost. Moreover, the possession of the Austrian Netherlands was not thought to be of much value, being so very far from Vienna. Maria and her minister, Kaunitz, would have liked to have handed over the Netherlands entirely to Bavaria and to have received compensation in South Germany. Here again it seemed to Maria that the benefit was Britain's and not Austria's, for it was Britain that was so keen that the Netherlands should not fall into the power of France. But of course the leading motive in the Empress-Queen's mind was revenge. Probably she would have sacrificed any or every ally to get back Silesia from the power of the hated Frederick. And so was brought about that most remarkable alliance, quite unique of its kind, the alliance between France and Austria, which indeed was not actually signed until May 1756, four months after Frederick had already come to terms with Britain, but which Frederick and Britain had already anticipated. The high-spirited and noble Maria actually came to be the ally of Louis XV and Madame de Pompadour. The third ally was also a woman, Elizabeth, the Tsarina of Russia. The lead given to the Russians by Peter the Great was still followed. Russia was to expand towards the sea, and wished to secure a long stretch of the Baltic coast; the power of Sweden was now trifling, and it was Prussia that stood in the light of Russian expansion. Next we take Saxony, whose Elector was likewise King of Poland, that vast and loosely knit country which could by no means cure herself of the inherent faults of her government, whose nobility quarrelled and thwarted her kings, and which had no middle class between nobles and serfs, yet was strong in numbers. Saxony herself lay straight in the path between Prussia and Austria and could not be neutral. Lastly Sweden was swept into the net of the Allies, for Sweden feared that a further development of Prussia would lead to a complete conquest of the rest of Swedish Pomerania.

Thus the Seven Years' War opened in 1756. Frederick was perfectly ready to begin, and threw his armies into Saxony before Maria's alliances had been really formed. He simply crushed Saxony, and drafted the Saxon soldiers into his own ranks. The first battle of this war, at Lobositz, was very fierce. The Austrians encountered the Prussians at their best, yet were not beaten. They

9—2

had learnt Prussian methods and were armed with iron
ramrods like the Prussians themselves. The slaughter
was great and equally divided between the combatants,
but the campaign for the occupation of Saxony was
entirely successful.

In 1757 Frederick made another step forward and
invaded Bohemia. This year he was less successful, and
at the battle of Kolin, trying to work round the Austrians
and take them in the flank, he was badly beaten and had
to evacuate Bohemia. At the same time the Swedes had
a force in Pomerania, and the Russians were threatening
East Prussia. But the enemy that was nearest to Frederick
was a mixed army of French and Germans advancing into
mid Germany. But it was a force badly led and not
united. The German element was simply an amalgama-
tion of various contingents of small German States,
summoned from the various "circles" of the Empire to
come to Maria's assistance. They were hardly trained at
all, and had no power of cohesion. Frederick lured this
army to attack him, and as they made a wide sweep
round his flank to cut him off and envelop him, he hid his
men behind a hill, suddenly dashed out upon the French,
and scattered them with hardly any loss to himself; so
was fought the battle of Rossbach, the first great engagement between France and Prussia as principals. Immediately Frederick returned eastwards, where he found
that the Allies had not gained as much ground after the
battle of Kolin as he would have expected and, coming
upon them at Leuthen in Silesia, not far from Breslau, he
carried out with conspicuous success his favourite oblique
movement by which he turned and crushed the whole
of the Austrian left wing, and then reformed his front
against their centre.

In the meanwhile his ally had so far done very little
to help him. In this same year, 1757, a Hanoverian force
had been compelled to surrender to the French on the

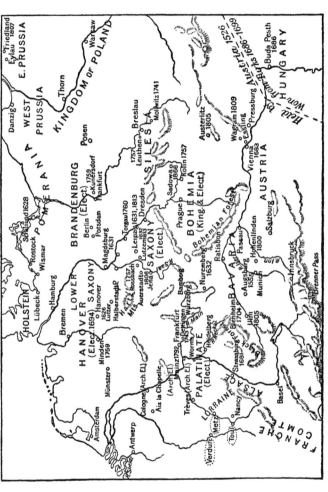

Germany

lower Elbe.   Minorca was lost, and Admiral Byng was sacrificed to satisfy the angry cries of the nation.   The American colonies were still scourged by the attacks of French and Redskins.   The ministry of George II was absolutely incompetent and had no nerve.   Yet a change was made and confidence restored to the nation almost at once.   After various squabbles amongst the various fragments of the Whig party, at last a place was found in the ministry for Mr Pitt, and Pitt could not only borrow money for war through his relations with the merchants of London, who had confidence in him, but he also had a great eye for the choice of the right men for the right positions.   When once the Newcastle-Pitt administration was formed there was no looking back, and a war policy was formulated, based upon our undoubted Sea Power. The British would keep the French fleets chained to the French coast by a series of blockades and of raids upon French ports; they would pour men into America; and in the meanwhile would contribute a small force of men and a very large amount of money to raise an army in Hanover which would secure Frederick's western flank. Thus had Pitt seen the error of his earlier days when he had attacked Carteret as a pro-Hanoverian.

Therefore Frederick in 1758 had only to face the Austrians and the Russians, but the task was one of appalling difficulty.   Every savagely fought battle cost him so many veterans and native Prussians that he could not expect the same exploits and the same devotion as a new year of the war dragged on, and as soon as he had fought the Austrians on the one side, he had to dash off to fight the Russians on the other.   Every battle fought against the Russians, who were slow and apparently lethargic but terribly obstinate, thinned his ranks cruelly. The same criticism is true of the year 1759, when the Russians at Kunersdorf, close to Frankfurt on the Oder, repulsed the Prussians after a terrible flank march of

several hours over shifting sandhills, and then an Austrian
contingent, headed by the most dashing of Frederick's
enemies, General Laudon, turned a repulse into a crushing
defeat. It seemed as if all had been lost. Had the
Russians been a little more quick and a little less fond
of booty, one hardly sees how Frederick could have survived at all. But the Russians and the Austrians simply
could not coalesce; they fought as separate armies, and
after victory they had their own interests to consult. It
is certainly true in history that rarely does an alliance
work smoothly, as when a Marlborough and a Eugene, or
a Wellington and a Blucher, are combined. Another
terrible defeat was inflicted upon the Prussians in 1759 at
Maxen near Dresden. Frederick, however, had one bright
gleam of success when the army of Ferdinand of Brunswick won a much needed victory at Minden on the Weser,
where some British and Hanoverian infantry by some
mistake charged straight against the French cavalry and
entirely broke it.

The British share in the war, of which Minden is but
one detail, is of great interest. The use of Sea Power
requires intelligent application, and therefore the study of
the war when a great statesman thoroughly understood
how to apply it interests everyone. Sea Power is the
control of the greatest highway of the world; it is of no
value unless along that highway the forces of the controlling nation are moved for a definite purpose. Pitt had
such a purpose, and to him Canada was the heart of the
war, the alliance with Frederick a means to his end.
France was distracted towards a land war by the army
of Ferdinand. The coasts of France were threatened by
various expeditions to Rochefort, Saint Malo, Cherbourg,
and Le Havre, sometimes unsuccessful, sometimes appearing to be mere raids to do wanton damage, yet always
distracting the French, who never knew where the next
blow would fall. The main fleets kept watch, the one in

the neighbourhood of Lisbon or Gibraltar, the other off
Brest, effectually prevented the French fleets from combining, and won victories in 1759 in Lagos Bay and
Quiberon Bay. Meanwhile men were poured into America;
Louisbourg fell in 1758, Quebec in 1759, two months before
the victory of Quiberon Bay, and Montreal in 1760. Pitt
was almost too successful. Frederick in later days seemed
to think that the British had only been making use of
him so as to crush French colonial enterprise; the argument is unsound, for our aid was of great benefit to him,
and he had no right to expect it to be given to him without our gaining corresponding benefit for ourselves. But
the worst result was that the younger Pitt, imitating his
father yet misunderstanding his main purpose, frittered
away the British resources in 1793 onwards. Much of the
bad feeling that has prevailed in Europe against us has
come from the idea that we enjoy our island position to
take advantage of European wars, and use our Sea
Power to advance our empire under cover of the distresses
of others; for this the second Pitt is largely responsible
when he pilfered French sugar islands, in place of concentrating all the strength of Great Britain to check the
conquering career of the French Republic.

In 1760 Frederick found the Russians less willing to
fight and the Austrians less adventuresome. At Liegnitz
in Lower Silesia, after a campaign in which his 30,000
men were manœuvred in the midst of 90,000 Austrians, he
defeated his old enemy, Laudon, who attacked uphill,
while another Austrian force under Daun, which ought
to have co-operated, had not reached the scene of action.
It was not a decisive victory like Leuthen, but it had a
great result, for Daun henceforward could not be brought
to offer open battle, and Frederick got a breathing space.
Late in the same year, in Saxony, the initiative passed
once more to Frederick. Daun was encamped at Torgau,
in a position apparently impregnable. Frederick with

the main army marched clean round the Austrians under the cover of forests and attacked from the north. The rest of the Prussians, under Ziethen, were to take the enemy in the rear from the south. The two forces were widely separated and had no means of communication, but Ziethen, though late, struck in at last just when Frederick seemed to be unable to carry the slopes upon his side and, after what is said to have been the bloodiest battle of the war, Frederick was at last able to hold up his head.

In 1760 died George II, and the advent to our throne of his young grandson George III brought about new political combinations which ended in the break up of the Newcastle-Pitt administration and brought about peace. The old arguments against Marlborough were renewed; Britain, it was said, was fighting only for the benefit of the King of Prussia and had gained all that Britain wanted to gain. So a separate treaty was made between Britain and France, and once more the disadvantage of insularity was shown, for though it is said that Frederick at the time was content that Britain and France should pair off, leaving him face to face with Austria alone, yet in after days he would have nothing to do with any British ministry, seeing that under our party system Tories suddenly made peace after a Whig war, and regarding Britain as a bruised reed on which he could not depend. The end of the war from our point of view was remarkable for the entrance of Spain upon the scene under the conditions of the Family Compact, and our fleets secured for us both Havana and Manila. By the *Treaty of Paris* in 1763 Havana and Manila were restored to Spain; Guadaloupe, Martinique, and St Lucia in the West Indies, Pondicherry and Chandernagore in India, were restored to France; but Canada remained ours, and Minorca was restored to us. Also during these years the French, and the native Rajahs who were supported by France, had been badly beaten in India. The battle of

Plassey, 1757, was followed eight years later by the virtual annexation of Bengal.

Relief at last came to Frederick. It was of little advantage to him that the British were so successful in Canada and India, and since the resignation of Pitt his money subsidies were cut off. Therefore in 1761 he seemed to be once more in a bad way. But early in 1762 died the Tsarina Elizabeth. Peter III, her nephew, succeeded and reversed her policy; he admired Frederick enormously and even offered military help. That same year Peter was deposed and murdered. The widow, a German princess from Anhalt, now began her famous reign as the Tsarina Catharine II. She gave no actual help to Frederick, but she stood neutral, and he was left alone to face Austria. In 1763 he made the *Treaty of Hubertusburg* with Maria, and Silesia became Prussian for all time. It had been an awful war for Prussia. Yet Frederick was able now to turn all his energies to the arts of peace, and Prussia recovered and was prosperous.

The European problems between the Seven Years and the French Revolution were the Polish Question and the Eastern Question, and the chief actors were Frederick, and Catharine, and Maria's son, Joseph II. Various combinations were made, and Catharine was at one time suppressing Polish rebels, at another pressing hard against the Turks. But there was only one short period of war between the Europeans.

In 1763 the throne of Poland was vacant, and Catharine asserted the claims of a Pole, Stanislas Poniatowski, to be elected. The first partition was made in 1772, and about one-third of the country was taken by the three rivals. Prussia's share was considerable, namely West or Royal Prussia, which had hitherto been like a wedge between East Prussia and Brandenburg; but the port of Dantzig and the inland fortress of Thorn were excepted.

In 1774, after a victorious campaign against the Turks

from which the Polish question distracted her, Catharine
made the momentous *Treaty of Kainardji* with the Sultan.
The Russians now definitely got Azov and the north coast
of the Black Sea, and, more important, the Christian
subjects of Turkey were declared to be free. Therefore
they had now taken the place of the Austrians as the
chief opponents of Islam.

Joseph II, Emperor after his father's death, though
hampered in his policy as long as Maria Theresa lived,
was one of the most conspicuous of the "enlightened
despots" of the century. His general idea was to give
unity to the scattered Hapsburg dominions from the
Netherlands to Hungary and Transylvania. The work
was too much for him, for the local customs and the spirit
of nationality were too strong. The Hohenzollerns, indeed,
were able to combine Prussia with Brandenburg and out-
lying lands, for there was no special Prussian national spirit
which refused to be Germanised. But the older civilisation
of the Flemish cities and the Hungarian nobles could not
be coerced to accept a centralised government at Vienna.
Joseph would have liked to have surrendered the Netherlands altogether and to compensate himself in Bavaria.
Indeed when the line of the old Electors died out in 1777
he tried to annex Bavaria, but Frederick promptly interfered as protector of the rights of the individual German
princes against a grasping Emperor—a *rôle* which his
19th century successors exactly reversed on the theory
that a grasping power promotes national German unity
and the individual princes cause disunion. Frederick
died in 1786, Joseph lived just long enough to see the
beginnings of a Belgian Revolution which occurred with
the French Revolution, and Catharine, dying in 1796,
shared in the second partition of Poland.

The War of American Independence, caused by neither
trade restrictions nor tea so much as by temper and
character, is a fine object lesson for any who believe in

a nation's gratitude. Austria and Prussia acknowledged no indebtedness to Great Britain for services in the Spanish and Austrian Succession wars or the Seven Years; had not we fought for our own hand in each case, and deserted our allies at Utrecht and Aachen and Paris? In the same spirit the colonists, to save whom we had fought the French, had no compunction in revolting and accepting the aid of the same French. Of course when once it was seen in 1777 that the colonists could hold their own, and when, with the advantage of their forests and wide territory, they surrounded and forced to surrender at Saratoga a small British and mercenary German force that had advanced from Canada too far from its base, France was only too willing to join in the war. It has been said that France is the only nation that fights for an idea,—the idea of chivalry or of help to be given to a struggling power,—but this war was entirely dictated by the idea of revenge. More than that, France secured her revenge. The Duke of Choiseul, at the end of the reign of Louis XV, took steps to improve the condition of the French navy and the French army which had been so very bad in the Seven Years' War, and the work of reorganisation was continued under Louis XVI. The French fleets that crossed the Atlantic to help the rebel Americans were well manned and well handled. The small bodies of French soldiers that were landed on the American coast were the pick of a reorganised and improved army. It is customary to look upon the British armies in America as absolutely inefficient and led by mere court favourites and incompetent officers. It is not at all difficult to refute such an idea, for the more one looks into the details of the American War of Independence, the more one acknowledges how fine a fight the British soldiers made. But unfortunately their movements were dictated from home, and when incompetent civilians at Westminster give orders to generals 3000 miles off to the west, the result is sure to be disunion and failure. France got her revenge when a French fleet on the one side and a French and American army on the other blockaded Lord Cornwallis in York Town in 1781. But France was not satisfied, and though Great Britain was ready to grant Independence to the Americans, she was forced to continue the war as against France, for abject submission would only have brought about the loss of all our West Indian islands. At no period in our history was such an effort made by sea for the very existence of our empire. Against us not only was the navy of France, but likewise that of Spain united to hers by the Family Compact; the Dutch, after having quarrelled with us on the question of the right of search for contraband of war, were now our open enemies; and the Baltic Powers formed against us an Armed Neutrality. Moreover in India Hyder Ali of Mysore threatened to destroy our settlement at Madras. But France and Spain did not work together. Spain demanded that an attack should be made upon Gibraltar, and not only the Spanish navy but a proportion of the French navy were kept distracted by this celebrated siege, and after all Gibraltar defied them for nearly four years, though Minorca was a second time lost. On one occasion plague broke out in the dirty Spanish ships, and was communicated to the French ships when they had the Channel at their mercy. The Dutch, keen only to maintain their trade with the rebels, were of little service to the French in the war. Finally, when Rodney's famous victory off Dominica in 1782 brought the French to reason, they made with us *the Treaty of Versailles*, and gained nothing more than honour and glory and the extra load of debt which made Louis summon the States General in 1789.

And finally, whereas the vile Louis XV after a reign of defeat and dishonour died in peace, Louis XVI, who was decent and honest and under whom France recovered herself, died on the guillotine.

CHAPTER VI

THE FRENCH REVOLUTION

THE Monarchy of France made the Revolution possible, perhaps inevitable. The system of royal administration was such that only a violent upheaval could alter it. There was no counter-weight, for the nobility as a political force was useless; its aims had been feudal, and the crown had broken feudalism; the castles had been dismantled and replaced by mansions, châteaux in a new sense; nobles crowded to court, lived a life of ostentation and extravagance, and had no voice in politics. There was no Whig party, as in England, composed of great lords whose opposition in Parliament against the Crown was traditional, and who could control seats in the House of Commons by their influence at elections; of country gentry of the Hampden or the Walpole type; and of the merchants and bankers and lesser townsfolk with their nonconformist conscience. The States General had not met since 1614. Therefore, the royal will had no opposition, and the royal waste of money in ambitious wars and court extravagance was unchecked in the absence of anybody able, by the powers accumulated through centuries, to pull tight the purse-strings. To this we add the degradation of the national character owing to the bad example of royal wickedness; Louis XIV indeed had vices, yet had ideas of the greatness and glory of France, but Louis XV was simply vicious and unpatriotic.

The Monarchy had done everything for France, given her unity and a national life and glory in politics and literature, and made men think of France rather than a single province. There was no chance of Normandy or Burgundy breaking off from France, though provincial customs might differ. So it came to pass that when there were grievances and acute discontent, when the commons got their chance and tasted power such as they were by inexperience unable to use profitably, they destroyed what they could destroy, but they did not split France into fragments. The Revolutionaries of 1792 and 1793 were for a united France; it was the Royalists themselves who were the provincial separatists in Brittany and La Vendée. Thus the Monarchy by making the country one made the Revolution solid.

Grievances were real enough, though it may be that excitable writers have exaggerated much. Of actual serfdom and restraint of personal liberty there was little, and not so many political prisoners were sent to the Bastille as to make the destruction of that fortress-prison a reason for revolt. The chief reason was the terrible weight of taxation, aggravated by bad trade regulations and the existence of customs-houses on the boundaries between province and province so that a cheap and quick interchange of goods was impossible. Grinding poverty in the country districts was such that there was little left when the King's taxes were paid. The *corvée*, compulsory service on the King's roads, still remained. In the manu-facturing districts a free-trade treaty with England caused men to be out of work, for English iron and cloth were better and cheaper; and it was poor consolation to the men of Normandy and French Flanders that the vine-growers of Gascony had the benefit of sending their wines to Eng-land unhampered by duty. But, these grievances apart, the one thing that immediately caused the Revolution was taxation; the unsuccessful wars of his grandfather, and the successful war that he had himself waged to help the Americans, made Louis XVI bankrupt, and he was living from hand to mouth. The one special feature of the taxation was that it fell solely on the unprivileged commons, and the nobles were privileged and did not pay. To this we add that haughtiness, frivolity, show, waste, and incompetence, among a caste of nobles who might have been leaders, aroused bitter feelings. Few were like the Duke of Rochefoucauld de la Liancourt, who alleviated distress among the out-of-work artisans of Normandy, and who received his reward when, after a short exile, he returned to France and found his estates kept intact for him.

The Monarchy was overthrown, therefore, partly because it was what Henry IV and Richelieu and Louis XIV had made it in promoting the unity of France, partly because it suffered for the ill-feeling roused by a privileged nobility. One asks why, with all its absolute power for good or ill, it did not suppress privileges and tax the nobility. To some extent the answer is that it was a hard thing to encounter the weight of a very numerous body,— very numerous because in France the sons of nobles were all nobles, whereas with us sons are commoners,—and there was no Richelieu to force taxation on them. But the main point is that that unique body, the *Parlement* of Paris, claimed the right to register the King's edicts. Often enough we find that, when a body has a right, it uses that right, simply and solely to show its own importance. The *noblesse de la robe* had no love for the real *noblesse*, but had control of the Parlement and liked to use its power. Louis XVI did issue edicts to remedy the worst abuses and tax the nobles, the Parlement refused to register, and he had not the force of character to compel them. The Monarchy in France, as in Russia and Prussia, and in Austria also at this date, was enlightened and benevolent. But the very wish to do good may be construed amiss, and people resent reform when forced on them from above; in another generation, or even in the later life of the same monarch, the benevolence may vanish and the tyranny remain all the stronger. Russia and Prussia might profit materially by paternal despotism, though class distinctions were clearly cut and serfdom remained. The Netherlanders and Hungarians under Austrian rule resented it. To Frenchmen it was not suited, for they were thinking for themselves, and knew how Louis XIV had done much for them but that the glamour of his age was disappearing, so that they were asking themselves whether any form of monarchy could be really beneficial or benevolent. Thus there was a current of public opinion in favour of the Parlement, obstinate and self-assertive, opposing reform which was attempted by the Monarchy for the real good of the nation, but the only body which could oppose.

The fact is that behind the question of grievances there was an intellectual movement, and the way was prepared for Revolution because men were thinking as well as grumbling against taxation. Frenchmen read and think, then when the time comes are whirled into action. They are fascinated by *les idées*, use phrases until they are almost slaves to the words, and put them into action without, it may be, either thought for the future or experience gained from the past. Unaccustomed to self-government they read from Rousseau and others that they had "natural rights," that they should return to the conditions of nature as their right. Thus when Louis XVI, at his wit's end to raise money, summoned at last in 1789 the States General, all the nation was ready to secure its rights without quite understanding what they were or how they could use them. The influence of England was great, for both before and during our civil war there had been much written about the origin of kingship, the soldiers of the Cromwellian army had in their debating society argued about natural rights, and, far more important, the revolted American colonists had issued their Declaration of Independence; Frenchmen had returned from America where they had fought for liberty, and had found in France that they themselves had no liberty though it was their natural right.

As we look back at a France grumbling and talking we wonder whether a different King could have saved her from the horrors that came, whether a second manly Henry could have done what dull Louis XVI wanted to do but had not the grit to carry through. Of course a man's character is created by the circumstances of his upbringing and subsequent life, and it is hardly conceivable that another King of the type of the Béarnais, joyous son of the south and nursling of the religious war, could be born and reared in selfish artificial Versailles. The speculation is unprofitable, yet forces itself on us, for over and over again we ask ourselves what might have happened if at this or that stage Louis had put his foot down. Well-meaning but dull he never put his foot down at the right time, and he always fell between two stools. He hated to use military force, yet threatened it just at the wrong moments; caused worse feeling against him on the part of the mob, yet did not satisfy the nobles. His brother, Charles of Artois, "jockey-breeched" Artois with the dress and the manners of a groom, had a bad influence. His queen, Marie Antoinette, the hated Autrichienne, daughter of Maria Theresa, married to him when a child as a result of the unnatural alliance between France and Austria, she whose nobly endured sufferings and death have made many forget her earlier influence for harm, could never understand the aspirations of Frenchmen. Yet, in any case, had Louis been a born leader of men and received sympathetic support in his own family, the wave of feeling would probably have been too strong for him.

France had helped the Americans to be free and had won revenge in seeing Britain humbled, yet had piled up in a successful war the extra load of debt which meant bankruptcy. The Swiss banker, Necker, could only point out how bad was the financial condition and how extravagant the court. Reform was thwarted by the obstinacy of the Parlement. At last the *States General* were summoned for the first time since 1614. There were three Orders, and each had its own Chamber or House; the *Nobles* were 270 in number, being elected by some 5000; the *Clergy* 291, whether rich and high-placed dignitaries, the relations and allies of the nobles, or humble parish priests; and the *Tiers État* or *Commons* 578, composed largely of lawyers who had influence in their country districts, with a few liberal nobles who had failed to be elected to their own chamber. They assembled on May 5, 1789, bringing *cahiers* or note-books in which grievances were set forth, and even some nobles were or pretended to be in favour of redress and abolition of privileges. The place was Versailles, the Windsor of France.

The first burning question was whether the three Chambers should sit separately or be merged into one. Louis wanted to propound his own scheme of reform, and ordered them to sit separately. The Tiers Etat, on June 20, excluded from the palace, met on the spur of the moment in the tennis-court and took an oath to uphold their policy of combining the three Chambers in one. Two days later they were summoned to hear the King's scheme and were again bidden to disperse, and then Mirabeau cried out that they would not yield except to bayonets. It was theatrical. But the Tiers Etat won, for they were joined by the poorer Clergy and by a few Liberals among the Nobles. Then Louis, too late, gave way, and bade the rest of the Clergy and Nobles unite with them. So was formed a single house, the *National Assembly*. This meant

10—2

that France would make her reforms for herself, not accept them from a benevolent despot.

Paris began to make its voice heard and the spirit of riot was abroad. Philip, Duke of Orleans, descended from a younger brother of Louis XIV, whose name has always been hated by French royalists and who was known as Philippe Egalité, was the centre of Parisian disaffection. The King, coming under the influence of Artois and the extremists, who were angry that he had given way on the question of the Chambers, began to draw troops round Paris. But the men were not to be trusted, in fact often sided with the mob, while the *Gardes Françaises*, a sort of military police of Paris, were openly revolutionary. On July 14 the rioters demanded arms, seized the Invalides, and proceeded against the *Bastille*; the garrison forced the governor to surrender, and the fall of the fortress, in which only seven prisoners were found, and they were not brutally immured in horrible dungeons, has been always marked as a symbol of the fall of the monarchy. Artois and many nobles fled to invoke the aid of foreign princes.

In Paris there were now signs of fear, for the respectable classes did not want mob-rule. Louis sent the troops away, and seemed to accept the situation. Two appointments were made; Bailly, first President of the National Assembly, became Mayor of Paris; Lafayette, who as a young and ardent noble had been in America where Washington made much of him, became chief of the *National Guard*, a new citizen police force to which the Gardes Françaises were joined as a paid battalion. Such men were not revolutionaries, and their position seemed to promise a middle-class rule and a limited monarchy. Lafayette had better have retired on his laurels as the hero of America; he had no force of character, and chiefly was fond of appearing in public in a fine uniform and on a fine horse as if he was also the hero of France. But if

Paris was quiet for a time, the provinces were in an uproar. Following on the capture of the Bastille came a series of attacks upon the country châteaux, and if in some places not much harm was done, in others there were burnings and murders in plenty. On August 4 the National Assembly was sitting to discuss the "Rights of Man," and at a moment's notice, receiving a report on the *guerre aux châteaux*, plunged into an orgy of destruction which has been called "the Bartholomew of property." Everything was abolished, feudal privileges and rights, Church and Church endowments, *corvée*, labour of any kind that resembled serfdom, purchase of offices and places in the Parlements. Once more we consider the scene theatrical; an Assembly solemnly debating on the interesting academic question of natural rights was converted into an agent of destructive revolution.

In October a new regiment was brought to Versailles, and its officers were feted by the officers of the royal guards. Excitement blazed up again in Paris, for the mob feared there was a new scheme to use military force. A crowd of women and rioters on October 5 marched on Versailles, and Lafayette was too late in coming upon the scene with his paid battalion; when he appeared, he controlled the mob for a time, but left it encamped in the open space outside the palace while he went to bed. Early in the morning of October 6 some of the mob burst into the palace, killed some guards, and nearly seized Marie Antoinette herself; Lafayette woke up and appeared at last on the scene, too late for the second time. Finally Louis, having refused throughout to use force, surrendered, and with his family was brought in triumph into Paris. Soon the National Assembly went to Paris.

After what may be called these preliminary scenes of violence,—the general impression was that the rioting was engineered by Orleans and his party,—the bourgeoisie regained power, and Lafayette kept order. The National

Assembly set to work to produce a *Constitution*, from which it has been called the Constituent Assembly, and took the whole of 1790 and most of 1791 in producing it. One cannot avoid Burke's conclusion that these men, many of them lawyers used to subtleties, hardly one of them experienced to lead, and none used to self-government, were foredoomed to failure. They decided that France was to be mapped out into new areas, *departments* in place of the old provinces, and these again sub-divided, for local government and for elections. There was to be an Assembly, *one Chamber* only. The King was to remain, but was only to have a *temporary veto* on any measure passed by the Assembly. The King's *Ministers* were not to have seats in the Assembly. The *Church* being disestablished, henceforward clergy were to be considered as civil servants paid by the state; glaring inequalities as between highly paid pluralist bishops and poor parish priests were swept away; Church lands were to be sold for the benefit of the state, and a large number of paper notes, called *assignats*, were issued, which were to be redeemed as the sale of these lands was effected. Now on almost every point English ideas were diametrically opposed, and in our own history we have acknowledged —till quite recently—the advantage of two Houses, a King's veto limited only by Public Opinion, and the responsibility of Ministers to a Parliament in which they sit. But the National Assembly deliberately rejected English ideas, even though Mirabeau debated strongly on each point. This great man had been a popular leader at the time of the tennis-court crisis, but now he lost his influence. The King and the Court party considered him a dangerous revolutionary, the majority of the Assembly thought him a turncoat because he refused to follow them. His advice to Louis was to escape from Paris to some provincial centre such as Rouen, rally to him the sound part of the nation even at the risk of civil war, swear never to restore the old privileges and inequalities, and so defy both the mob and the fanciful theorists who were creating an unworkable constitution.   But Mirabeau died in 1791.   Meanwhile the exiled nobles, Artois and Condé at their head, were trying to stir Joseph II, and after him his brother Leopold II, to save their sister Marie Antoinette, and, more important than that, to restore them to their privileges.   Meanwhile also English opinion, at first generally in favour of a France striving to be free, was turning against her, largely because of Burke's influence.

In June 1791 Louis escaped from Paris, but in defiance of the advice of his late well-wisher Mirabeau, fled, not to some French town, but towards the frontier to throw himself upon foreign aid.   At Varennes he was stopped and forced to return.   As a result the chance of success that a limited monarchy might have had was lost.   The Assembly voted itself to be supreme over ministers and officers, and the monarchy was virtually suspended.   The more rabid revolutionaries outside were strengthened. Then, the Assembly drawing near to its end, the Constitution at last framed, and the King a prisoner, a queer self-denying ordinance was passed ; no member of the *Constituent Assembly* might be a member of the new *Legislative Assembly.*

The *Legislative Assembly* met October 1, 1791.   Over two years had been spent in debates on its constitution. It was the outcome of the combined efforts of those who hoped to secure for France an ideal and permanent form of government.   And it lasted for less than a year.   The members were less experienced than even those of the defunct Constituent.   There were in it many middle-class respectable men, supported out of doors by Bailly and Lafayette, by the National Guard and all who feared mob rule.   But they were overshadowed by the *Girondists*, a party whose leaders came from Bordeaux, clever and

LATER HAPSBURGS

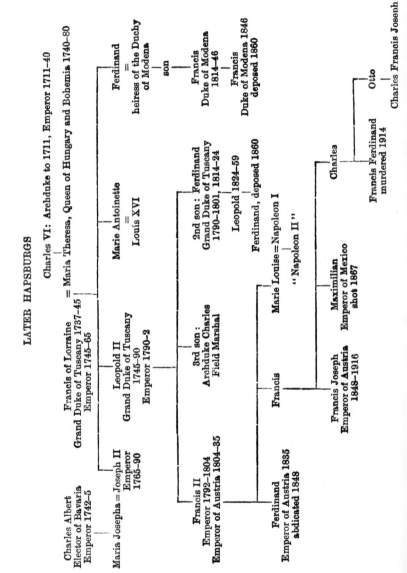

eloquent theorists with a love of words and no practical
common sense, capable of talking big and forcing France
into war, and then unable to control the war. Besides
them was the party of the *Jacobins,* whose influence was
important because they belonged to the Jacobin club,
with headquarters at Paris in the disused convent of
Saint Jacques, and with branches in all the towns and
many villages of France. Organisation and influence at
elections made the Jacobins very strong, and their representatives in the chamber were both fierce and earnest.
But at first the Girondists took the lead. The question of
foreign policy was most important. The *émigrés,* the
exiled nobles, had long been trying to force Austria into
war to restore them. The Emperor now was Francis II,
nephew of Marie Antoinette, and was young and likely
to yield to pressure. Early in 1792 the Girondists were
formed into a ministry, with Dumouriez as foreign
secretary. His language was so provocative that the
Emperor replied by calling upon the Assembly to restore
law and order in France, to re-establish the Church, and
respect the rights of certain German princes in Alsace.
The Girondists forced Louis to declare war in April,
carried away by their excitement and wish to parade *les
idées révolutionnaires.*

War once declared, the power of the extremists in
Paris grew. The Jacobins had not wanted it, indeed had
bitterly opposed the idea of defying Austria in the name
of Liberty, Fraternity, Equality. But they got the upper
hand during the excitement. First the control of the
Commune or municipality of Paris was wrested from the
middle-class respectables, then the command of the
National Guard, and these two bodies became the agents
of excesses. The Prussians made alliance with Austria,
and the Duke of Brunswick who commanded them issued
a proclamation threatening vengeance if harm were done
to Louis and Marie. On August 10 the mob burst into

the palace and murdered the Swiss guards; on August 29 the Commune ordered a house-to-house visitation to search for arms and arrest all suspected of welcoming the Prussians; from September 2 onwards the suspects were murdered in their prisons by a paid band of ruffians. Meanwhile the old royalist army, fatally weakened by indiscipline, was falling back from the frontier. Rochambeau and Lafayette, both of them heroes of the War of American Independence, were in command, but the one resigned in disgust, and the other fled over the border and was kept under arrest by the enemy. Dumouriez went to the army, and was in position at Valmy in the midst of rolling and wooded country half-way between Paris and the frontier. It is one of the mysteries of military history why the Prussians did not sweep him aside and march straight on Paris. They were jealous of the Austrians, their transport was bad, disease was rampant, the weather was bad and the ground wet. Whatever the reason was, the Prussians advanced on September 20 across a valley to attack the French position on the height; the French, mostly old royalist soldiers, but smitten with the new republican enthusiasm, stood firm and cannonaded them at long range; the Prussians retired. Such was the historic "battle" of Valmy; a very few hundreds died, yet it was far more important than any great engagement with its thousands of dead and prisoners. On September 21 met a new assembly at Paris, the *National Convention*. The Republic, One and Indivisible, was proclaimed.

Now the French retaliated. One force occupied Savoy, which was quite ready for revolution and annexation to France. Another under Custine, an old royalist soldier and noble, pressed to the middle Rhine and actually occupied Mainz. Dumouriez entered the Netherlands and won a pitched battle against the Austrians at Jemmappes near Mons, where the men charged singing a

new song that had been introduced by some volunteers
from Marseilles. The Prussians, their army spoilt by
disease, let the weight of war fall upon the Austrians and
were moreover far more anxious to prevent Russia from
annexing Poland. Thus a war, provoked carelessly by
the Girondists in their love of talk about Liberty, was so
far successful under the control of their Jacobin rivals,
bloodthirsty terrorists, but far more capable.

The National Convention was now securely seated and
dominated by the Jacobins. The *Revolutionary Tribunal*
was at work sending to the newly invented guillotine all
who sympathised with the monarchy and nobility. Louis
was executed January 21, 1793, though his death was only
voted by the Convention by a majority of one, and the
Girondist members were openly overawed by the rabble
that swarmed into the Chamber. As a result of Valmy
and Mainz and Jemmappes the war took a new character.
"Country in danger" was no longer the cry, but "Natural
frontiers." It was an obvious step, and in the language
of the time a "natural" development. No longer banded,
back to the wall, to defend France against monarchs who
were in arms to save Louis and restore the *émigrés*, the
Republic One and Indivisible would now spread republicanism abroad, assist all peoples who wanted to
shake off their kings and exchange social inequalities for
liberty, and even assist them if they had no such want.
From this to war for war's sake, to extend the boundaries
of France, to benefit themselves by invasion rather than
to confer blessings on the invaded, was but a short step
for the Revolutionaries; one more step remained to be
taken, and then would come the purely military aggression
of Bonaparte. In particular France, as ever, coveted the
Austrian Netherlands and the harvests there, for the bad
seasons and the excitement at home made famine come
very close. What touched Britain was that the navigation
of the Scheldt was declared to be open, and, if British

and Dutch statesmen objected that by old treaty the river
should be closed, the plausible retort would be that no
nations had a natural right to fetter trade, and Antwerp
must not be stifled in order that commerce from overseas
might be diverted, as in the last two centuries, to London
and Amsterdam. A military republic planted in the
Netherlands opposite to our vulnerable coast was
dangerous, and war would come in time even if the
British felt no sympathy with the royal family or *émigrés*
or ruined Church. The Convention, however, moved first
and declared war on Britain and Holland, before Pitt
could declare war on the Republic.

The war of 1793 was not so happy for the Republic as
was expected after the collapse of the Allies at and after
Valmy. Republican enthusiasm could not take the place
of skill and discipline. The Austrians defeated Dumouriez
at Neerwinden in the Netherlands, and soon he fled to them.
Mainz was recaptured by the Prussians. The peasants of
La Vendée rose and destroyed in their woods and sandy
wastes the first forces sent against them. Lyons raised
herself against Paris;—it is noteworthy that in the west the
peasants were royalist and the towns republican, while in
the south-east the great cities were anti-republican and
the peasants fierce revolutionaries; this hatred between
town and country is characteristically French, though it
seems to us the merest accident that it took one form in
La Vendée and another at Lyons. Lastly Toulon called
for aid to Lord Hood and the British fleet. But the Allies
were fatally disunited and had no common plan. Prussia
thought only of her share of Poland; the Austrians would
not march straight on Paris, but wasted time over the
border fortresses, that triple line on which Vauban had
expended all his art; the defenders of Mainz, released on
parole, were available against La Vendée, and the Breton
royalists did not move until the Vendeans were beaten;
the British army had sunk to such small numbers in

peace that it did little, while Pitt wasted what forces he had by not concentrating them at one place, let us say Toulon. But more important than the feebleness of the Allies was the astounding energy shown in Paris. The Jacobins formed a new body, the *Committee of Public Safety*, and a few resolute men able to lead worked wonders. Carnot organised camps where the men raised by a *levée en masse* could be trained, and by one means or another supplies and equipment were forthcoming. Generals might be incompetent, but could be removed or, if need be, guillotined. Aristocrats who had served the republic well, Custine for instance, were executed, for, though he had cleared Alsace and taken Mainz in 1792, he might desert to the Allies like Dumouriez or Lafayette. New men were found in time, most of them having had their training under the old monarchy. Moreau is a conspicuous instance of a civilian of no experience, like Cromwell, called by the crisis to be a great soldier. But Hoche, Pichegru, Jourdan, and above all Bonaparte, were soldiers already, though it must be added that they were of too low a rank or too young to become generals except in such a time of excitement. Another institution was the appointment of *députés en mission*, who were sent to the army to watch the generals, to see that they did their duty and did not desert, also to force both towns and country to provide supplies; they often hampered the generals, but stirred them to great energy. The chief reform in the ranks was the creation of half-brigades, one battalion of regulars linked to two battalions of volunteers. The chief reform in the field was independent fighting; swarms of skirmishers were let loose at the enemy, who took cover and shot as they could, and who thus made individual keenness take the place of discipline, so that the stiff and serried ranks of the drilled Prussians and Austrians were taken by surprise; meanwhile behind the smoke and hidden by the skirmishers a dense column could be formed, and launched at the right moment at the enemy's weak point. In general it may be said that on the one hand the ex-royalists taught the art of war to the ardent unskilled republican levies; and though there might be, owing to want of discipline, more than a little skulking and disobedience, there was on the other hand republican enthusiasm and resourcefulness. Also the armies were not encumbered with much baggage, but they made war support war, *i.e.* helped themselves. The guiding power was in the hands of the Committee whose success foretold a military despotism in the future, even as the loud cry that France was fighting to give liberty to other countries would become a cry for war for the military glory of France. In the Committee the chief figure was Carnot, "the organiser of victory."

The Republic, however, could not restore the old royal navy. The old officers were all royalists, and the old sailors had been drawn mostly from royalist districts such as Brittany. Naval discipline, once ruined, could not be restored in a day, whatever deputies on mission might try to do, and British naval victories from June 1, 1794, down to the day of Trafalgar prevented France from ever having a breathing-space in which to create a real fleet. Also the Revolution was fatal to the colonies of France. The spirit of Liberty, Fraternity, Equality, bade the freeing of slaves in French islands, and it is the boast of France that she abolished slavery at a date when Britain was only just beginning to listen to Wilberforce and his story of the iniquities of the slave-trade. But black rose against white, and premature abolition led to many horrors. Also British attacks from the sea, useless as they were for the main purpose of the war and contributing little towards suppression of the Terror at Paris, ruined the trade of the French West Indies.

During the crisis the great man in Paris was Danton, burly and strong, practical in character. To him, as a resolute leader who could voice what so many thought, and could do what many wanted to see done, while the Girondists only talked, it was due that the country did not flinch before Valmy and again after Neerwinden. He came from Champagne and was of bourgeois blood, and had purchased under the monarchy a lawyer's post. In the early days of the Revolution he was attached to the party of Orleans[1], as was Camille Desmoulins, a journalist, who became his devoted friend, and the two had very great influence in the political clubs, first the Cordeliers, then the Jacobins. The greatness of Danton is seen in August and September 1792, when in the Convention he cried, "De l'audace, de l'audace, toujours de l'audace" in face of the German invasion. He did not originate the September massacres, nor approve, nor condone; but equally true is it that he did nothing to stop them, though he later set himself against the spirit of revenge so that his party got the name of the "indulgents." In April 1793 he was one of the nine original members of the Committee of Public Safety, but he lost his seat in July and was not responsible for the fierce decrees of extermination against La Vendée and Lyons. One always admires a strong man who loves his country and liberty, who knows that great results cannot be attained unless some suffer; and let traitors suffer, he would say, if they rejoice in the advance of the Prussians who would bring us back to slavery. But the memory of his services is dimmed, when it is seen that the stone that he set rolling ground beneath it those who did not deserve to suffer. Evil passions were unchained. Marat, once a fashionable ladies' doctor, now ready for any excess, was murdered by Charlotte Corday, but the professional atheists and scoffers in November 1793 celebrated their disgusting "feast of reason" in Notre Dame. Robespierre

[1] Philip of Orleans was himself executed during the Terror, though he had been the chief agent of revolution and riot in 1789.

hated such buffoonery, and with the aid of the Dantonists sent these men to the guillotine in March 1794.

The character of Maximilien Robespierre is hard to analyse. He saw the horrors of anarchy and civil war, and therefore approved of massacre in Paris and fiendish cruelty in La Vendée if only as means to secure absolute power to the Committee. On Danton's retirement he was almost dictator in the Committee, and he wanted to promote the ideas of Rousseau, a life of nature, a reign of virtue, a worship of a Supreme Being. There was something cold and mean in him which revolts us. He attacked Danton, if motives can ever be really understood, in a spirit of paltry jealousy, and by a charge of treason in connection with Orleans and Dumouriez he brought Danton to the guillotine in March 1794. Finally he was himself guillotined in July. The party who overthrew him and stopped the worst excesses of the Terror are known as the Thermidoriens, the men of the month Thermidor.

This word reminds us what the Republic did to mark the beginning of a new age. The Christian era was given up, and a revolutionary era was substituted from the establishment of the Republic. Men spoke of the year 1 of liberty. The Roman months were abolished, and new months were named after the seasons, Thermidor being the "hot" month. Weeks were replaced by decades. Napoleon allowed this "revolutionary calendar" to disappear quietly. Of other things which were brought in at this period of change, the metre and the metric system based on it have lasted, also the division of France by departments.

We return to the military operations. In 1793 the Allies, as we saw, were slow in following up their successes at Neerwinden and Mainz, divided in their aims, and bent on obtaining each some particular advantage in place of marching on Paris. The tide turned when the British and Germans in British pay were forced to give up the siege of Dunkirk. Jourdan drove the Austrians out of north France and beyond the Sambre in the Netherlands, Hoche and Pichegru drove them out of Alsace and beyond the Rhine. Lyons was recovered and suffered terribly under a decree passed by the Convention; the same savagery was shown in the suppression of La Vendée, where Carrier earned special notoriety by the noyades when he drowned the royalists in batches. Bonaparte, only a lieutenant of artillery, breathed his spirit into the besiegers of Toulon and forced Lord Hood to evacuate it. In 1794 there were further victories; Belgium was entirely won, then Holland, and after an awful retreat in severe weather the Germans and British were driven to the Ems and Weser early in 1795. Belgium was annexed to France. Holland was transformed into the Batavian Republic. Then in 1795 Prussia made peace by the *Treaty of Basle*, acknowledging the Rhine as the boundary of France.

Here we must look to the East to understand why the Allies were disunited and therefore unsuccessful. Details of the Polish and Turkish questions are not needed here, but it is clear that these were connected, and as often as Austria and Russia turned their attention to Turkey they were distracted by some move of Prussia towards Poland. In January 1792 the Tsarina Catharine II brought a Turkish war to an end by the *Treaty of Jassy*, by which the Russian frontier was advanced to the river Dniester. Then she turned on Poland. There was a Polish crisis, an attempt to make a serious reform in the direction of a limited monarchy in imitation of the limited monarchy of France of 1790—91, the crown to be hereditary and not elective, ministers to be responsible to a diet, and the excessive powers of the nobles to be cut down. This did not suit Catharine, for anarchy in Poland was her excuse for interference. The King of Prussia offered to help Poland if Dantzig and Thorn were unconditionally surrendered;

the unlucky country was too spirited to accept; consequently he seized Dantzig and Thorn and the district
of Posen, and Catharine a large district from the river
Dnieper westwards. The years of this piece of spoliation
were the years of Valmy and Neerwinden. Austria, on
whom fell the chief burden of the French war, felt a
natural soreness when it was found out that Russia and
Prussia had thus come to an agreement. Overawed by
superior force the Poles were, however, goaded into rising
in 1794 under the patriot Kosciusko. They were no
match for the Russians, and the final partition was made
in 1795. This time Austria received a share, owing to
Russian jealousy of Prussia. It is difficult to write with
moderation on the spoliation; the Power that did nothing
in the Revolutionary war obtained most of Poland, the
Power that did little and deserted the Allies by the treaty
of Basle obtained a good deal, and the Power that suffered
most at the hands of France obtained a little on
sufferance[1].

In 1795 the Convention was threatened by a royalist
reaction. Like the Rump Parliament in our civil war it
wished to prolong its life, claiming that the majority of a
new assembly must be its members. Paris rose, and
Bonaparte, called upon to clear the streets, did so
effectually with "a whiff of grapeshot." A new constitution was framed, a Chamber of 500, a Council of
Ancients of 250, and an executive *Directory* of five. The
Chamber and Council were of no importance, and the
strong rule of a few, especially after the use of cannon in
Paris, brought France the last step nearer to military
despotism. Carnot was one of the Directors.

The year 1796 saw further victories. The Dutch fleet
was at the service of France; Spain, ever hating the
presence of the British in the Mediterranean, was openly

[1] Poland as rearranged after Napoleon's downfall was different. In
1795 Warsaw became Prussian, in 1814 Russian.

the ally of France, her Bourbon king supporting the very Republic that had done to death his French cousin. For a time, in consequence, the Sea Power of the British fleet was challenged, especially as Ireland was in a ferment and expecting French aid, and our sailors were on the eve of mutiny. Had a Nelson held full power in the Mediterranean, the coming campaign which showed the genius of Bonaparte would have been impossible. The new theatre of the war was North Italy. The mountain passes over the Alps were held by the King of Sardinia (Duke of Savoy), who was the ally of Austria. The alternative route along the Riviera was difficult in the extreme; spurs of the mountains jut out into the sea, with deltas between where the valleys open into wide mouths, and all coast traffic had to be by water. Thus a well-handled squadron would paralyse an army moving along the coast, and starve it out by intercepting the boats bringing its supplies. Bonaparte, chosen for the command by Carnot, required the coast route for a short time till he could break through the mountains into the Po valley, and at this very moment the British naval force in the Mediterranean was impotent.

Time was everything. Bonaparte had carefully studied the geography of the ground; in April, feinting towards Genoa so as to keep the Austrians to the east, he struck rapidly upwards and northwards from Savona, drove a wedge between the Austrians and the Sardinians, won the watershed, and descended the northern slopes to the Po[1]. He overpowered the Sardinians and forced a treaty on the King; and this meant that he could now communicate with France by the Mont Cenis route, and had no need to use the dangerous Riviera, so that if the British regained their Sea Power in the Mediterranean they could not cut him off from France. Once safely on the Po he could make war support war, levy forced supplies, and satisfy

[1] See map on p. 165.

11—2

his men with loot. The enthusiasm of this army, which had hitherto enjoyed none of the glory such as had fallen to the armies of the Netherlands and the Rhine, was un-bounded; it was never much more than 30,000 strong even when reinforced by drafts.

In May he found the Austrians posted behind the Po and its northern tributary the Ticino. He outflanked them by moving quickly downstream, crossed the Po, got in the rear of Milan, and carried by a sudden charge the bridge of Lodi over the Adda. Milan surrendered and the whole of Lombardy was secured.

Between Lombardy and Venetia is a narrow neck of land where the Mincio runs out of Lake Garda to the Po; next to the east the Adige descending from the Tyrol swerves aside and runs parallel to the Po. On the Mincio are the strong fortresses of Peschiera and Mantua, on the Adige and in Venetian territory are Legnago and Verona, and these make the famous Quadrilateral. Bonaparte blockaded Mantua, and disregarded Venetian neutrality by seizing Verona. The Austrians made effort after effort to dislodge him. They altogether spoilt their chance of success on the Rhine by detaching large forces from that direction, and were vastly superior to him in numbers. But to debouch from the Alps into the plain in face of an active enemy was difficult. Either a large force descend-ing by a single road would be headed off while its rear would be miles too far away to help, or two forces descend-ing by two separate roads would find the enemy between them. Bonaparte by superior marching beat them which-ever plan they tried. When it was necessary he aban-doned the blockade of Mantua, knowing that he could resume it when the relieving armies were beaten back. Finally in January 1797 he occupied the plateau of Rivoli, which stands above the Adige, while mountains overhang it like an amphitheatre, and from this central position he hurled back all the attacks from each direction; then

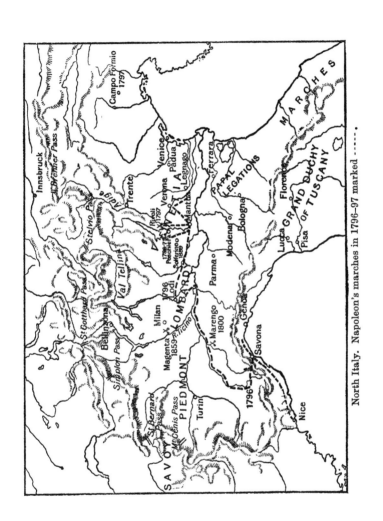

North Italy. Napoleon's marches in 1796–97 marked ······.

dashed off to intercept another army; and at last reduced Mantua[1]. Almost at once he ascended into the Tyrol and fought his way to within reach of Vienna.

Both the French and the Austrians had massed their main armies in 1796 on the Rhine. Here the French suffered from a divided command, for Jourdan on the middle Rhine was to cross and come down southwards to the Main, and Moreau was to cross from Alsace and strike towards Bavaria. The Austrians were under their best leader, the Archduke Charles, and he placed himself well between Jourdan and Moreau; he detached a smaller force to watch Moreau's left or northern flank, threw his main army on Jourdan and drove him back over the Main and over the Rhine, then returning upstream threatened to cut Moreau off from France. Only a most skilful retreat and fast marching saved Moreau. The Archduke in fact did almost exactly the same as Bonaparte. But his campaign was not so decisive, chiefly because he had to send away men to fight Bonaparte in Italy. In 1797, when Bonaparte was pushing up towards Vienna, the Archduke was called upon to oppose him and was beaten. In April a truce was made at Leoben. Hoche, replacing Jourdan, and Moreau were again over the Rhine, when the news of Leoben stopped them from advancing, as certainly they could have advanced, down the Danube. Thus it seemed that Bonaparte was aiming at more than winning victories for France; he was winning all the glory for himself, and preventing Hoche and Moreau from winning any. Hoche died this year, and a serious republican rival was thus removed from Bonaparte's path. Moreau lived to do more service for France in 1800, and to help the Allies in 1813.

In the meanwhile 1797 had been a critical year for Great Britain, the Spanish and Dutch fleets at the service

---

[1] Masséna was general of the division which did most of the marching and fighting, and later under the Empire was created Duke of Rivoli.

of France, Ireland in a ferment, and her own fleets mutinous. But Jervis in February beat the Spaniards at Cape St Vincent, and renewed our ascendancy in the Mediterranean, at the same time preventing mutiny by his iron discipline. The Dutch and French fleets did not meet for a combined descent on Ireland, the mutinies at Spithead and the Nore were suppressed, and the Dutch were finally beaten off Camperdown in October.

The five Directors could not fail to be frightened by Bonaparte's successes. Carnot fled from France, and another who was a royalist was arrested. The Councils by new elections, one-third of the members retiring every year, were becoming royalist, and Bonaparte promptly overawed them by military force. In the south-east there was a strong royalist reaction known as the " White Terror." But for the time being the main question was the nature of the definite *treaty with Austria*. This was arranged at *Campo Formio*, in north-east Italy, by Bonaparte himself, who, having now overawed the royalists, was determined to show that he, the victorious general, was master of the Directory. Austria ceded the Netherlands and acknowledged French rule up to the left bank of the Rhine; Lombardy, a part of Venetia, the papal legations of Ferrara and Bologna, and the duchy of Modena, were formed into the Cispadane Republic; in compensation, so as to keep her quiet and leave Britain the sole enemy, he allowed Austria to annex Venetia. The Batavian Republic, formerly Holland, was now virtually part of France; Savoy and Nice were already actually French; Genoa was under French control; a Roman Republic was soon erected in place of the Pope's temporal dominions; and finally the Helvetian Republic, Switzerland under a new name, was the servant of France. The *natural frontiers* had been won, and the *idées révolutionnaires* had been in theory extended to the countries whether conquered by their will or against their will. But just as Bonaparte maintained the Directory against the royalist reaction till it suited his purpose to overthrow it in turn, so it became clear that he was making a pretence of creating democracies. Money contributions, loot, confiscated works of art, poured into France. Meanwhile there was confusion and bankruptcy at home, for France was living on paper money.

Great Britain was now the only enemy of France. The Egyptian expedition followed, 1798—99. The seizure of Malta, the battle of the Pyramids, the battle of the Nile, the siege of Acre and Bonaparte's final failure, are a familiar story; so too is the capture of Seringapatam in Mysore, for our government in India was determined to crush Tippoo Sultan before French aid could reach him from Egypt. But what the Directory, or Bonaparte himself, or the British, expected to result from the expedition is not clear. Had his fleet not been destroyed by Nelson, he was not an inch nearer to India until it had sailed round the whole of Africa and taken him on board, and time was too valuable for him to wait. Probably the glamour of conquest in the East was too strong for him, and he never seemed to realise the meaning of Sea Power. At any rate Nelson locked him up in Egypt, and Sydney Smith and the Turks turned him back from Acre[1].

Naturally, Bonaparte absent, *the Second Coalition* was formed in Europe. Russia for the first time took up arms with Austria, financed by Pitt. From Holland, where a mixed force of British and Russians expected fruitlessly the aid of Dutch sympathisers, to Italy, where the genius of the savage Russian Suvaroff at first carried everything before him, there was much fighting. On the whole the Allies, in spite of failure in Holland, gained ground. In North Italy, while Suvaroff had a free hand, almost all the ground won by Bonaparte in 1796—97 was lost in 1799, and Moreau was decisively beaten. Then the inevitable

[1] The engineer officer at Acre was a French royalist exile.

happened, as in most alliances. The Russians and
Austrians were at cross purposes, and Suvaroff withdrew
from Italy. Masséna, Bonaparte's most trusted and ablest
lieutenant in 1796—97, won a victory at Zurich in Switzerland and may be almost said to have saved France. Then
Bonaparte escaped from Egypt, for a few men could slip
through the blockading squadron where it was impossible
for a whole army to escape on many transports. He came
with the glory of victory in the East, the land of romance,
and men forgot that he had completely failed there and
had had to leave behind his whole army. Posing as the
deliverer of France, as if Masséna's victory counted for
nothing, he overthrew the Directory by a *coup d'état*.
What constitutional forms he set up it is profitless to
discuss. He was the sole ruler in France with the title of
First Consul, the second and third consuls being ciphers
whose very names no one cares to remember.

In 1800 the new First Consul moved on Italy, while
Moreau crossed the Rhine. The state of affairs in Italy
was that the Austrians held all the valley of the Po, and
were with British naval aid besieging Masséna in Genoa.
A British force had occupied Minorca, the King of Naples
was our ally, and Malta was on the point of surrendering,
so that it seems to us to be a gross blunder on the part of
Pitt not to have sent a large British army to the Mediterranean to support the Austrians, for Bonaparte might
have been expected to make an effort to regain the
country where his earliest triumphs had been won. He
chose the Great St Bernard route, and in May appeared
on the Po, thus cutting off the Austrians besieging Genoa.
Masséna indeed surrendered Genoa, but he had held out
just long enough. Then Bonaparte gave battle at Marengo,
near the fortress of Alessandria, on the plain between the
Po and the Apennines. He was outnumbered and was in
full retreat, when a welcome reinforcement arrived under
Desaix, who checked the Austrians, somewhat disordered

by their pursuit, and enabled a decisive victory to be won: June 14. Meanwhile Moreau was manœuvring on the upper Danube in Bavaria over ground which Bonaparte was destined to tread five years later, and finally in December won his great victory near Hohenlinden; four bodies of Austrians advancing independently through forests were held up by Moreau's main army in front, while the French right wing worked round their flank and came in on their rear to ensure their defeat. The *Treaty of Lunéville* followed, which was more or less on the same lines as that of Campo Formio.

Once more the British alone were at war. Malta fell, and Abercrombie's expedition to Egypt was entirely successful. A naval coalition, known as the Armed Neutrality, arrayed the Baltic powers against us in protest against our claim to search neutral ships for contraband of war, and Nelson's victory at Copenhagen was the result. At last the *Treaty of Amiens* in 1802 gave a short breathing space, and by it Great Britain agreed to restore all conquered places.

The good done by Bonaparte's despotic rule to France is almost incalculable. He gave a settled government to a country sick of civil strife and changes. He restored the Church by means of the *Concordat*, or bargain, with the Pope; he recognised Catholicism, took on himself the right to appoint Bishops, and reconciled the clergy who had acknowledged the Republic with those who had been non-jurors, but he refused to restore the confiscated Church lands. The *émigrés* were allowed to return. The tangled finances were straightened out, and roads and canals were designed in a manner worthy of Colbert, for instance the upper *cornice* or coast-road from Nice along the Riviera. A system of public education, designed originally by the Convention, was elaborated. The great code of law, called afterwards the *Code Napoléon*, was drawn up by a committee of lawyers, which simplified and unified all the old

laws and customs. France was conscious that she had
order and security together with individual liberty and
equality as between man and man, and therefore probably
cared little that self-government was not general. The
critic of Bonaparte must lament that he spoilt his work
by his continued interference in European matters, his
military ambition, and his Corsican love of the vendetta,
as shown by his spite against the country which had
foiled him in Egypt, and which his lack of Sea Power
prevented him from touching.

His longing to satisfy this spite hurried him into war
against Great Britain little more than a year after the
treaty. Ordinary prudence dictated that some five years
at least were needed if he was to create a new fleet fit
to face ours. But he interfered in Holland and Switzerland and Italy, refused to make a commercial treaty and
kept British goods out of France, sent an officer to report
on the prospect of a French occupation of the Ionian
Islands and Egypt, and generally by numerous pin-pricks,
as we say now, and by abusive language in the *Moniteur*,
which was his official newspaper, drove our prime minister
into war. Addington, who had succeeded Pitt, refused
to give up Malta, though the British troops had been
loyally withdrawn from Egypt, Minorca, and all colonial
conquests such as West Indian islands and the Cape[1].
"Perfide Albion" was the phrase invented to insinuate
that the retention of Malta as security against French
aggression was wrong, and the First Consul has seemed
to some historians, even British, to have been in the right
simply because he could use words recklessly. The
Whig party believed that Great Britain and not Bonaparte was the aggressor, in fact that we should keep the
Treaty of Amiens to the letter, and leave him free to
violate treaties and again secure Egypt. The renewal of
war came in May 1803.

[1] By the Treaty of Amiens we kept the Spanish island Trinidad and
the Dutch island Ceylon.

The story of the assembling of the *grande armée* on
the coast, the great works undertaken at Antwerp, the
camp at Boulogne and neighbouring ports, the collection
of boats and war-material, the blockade of the main fleets
in the ports of Toulon by Nelson and Brest by Cornwallis,
and the impossibility of an invasion until those fleets could
break out and secure the Channel, need not be repeated
here in detail. In the years 1803—05 Sea Power saved us
from invasion, but not till 1808 was it seen how powerful
a weapon of offence it might be made; before 1808 blows
were struck across the sea spasmodically, often not at the
right place, and hardly ever with enough force, and
therefore the full effect of our naval superiority, though
based on the triumphs of 1803—05, was not felt until the
commercial blockade and the Peninsular war together
began to drain Napoleon's strength.

In 1804 there was a royalist plot against the life of the
First Consul, and as a result Pichegru, once republican
and now royalist, was found dead in prison, and Moreau
was exiled. To strike terror into plotters Bonaparte had
the Duke d'Enghien, who was a Condé and therefore a
Bourbon, seized on German soil and then shot without
trial. In May he made the senate create him *Emperor of
the French*, and December 2, though he had summoned
the Pope to Paris for the ceremony, he crowned himself
in Notre Dame. Titles and dignities were created for
his supporters, and eighteen generals were raised to be
marshals. In consequence of Napoleon's new title the
Emperor Francis styled himself Hereditary Emperor of
Austria. The Holy Roman Empire was already disappearing in the midst of the great commotions before the
campaign of Ulm and Austerlitz.

CHAPTER VII

AGAINST the new Emperor was formed the *Third Coalition* by Austria, Russia, Great Britain and Sweden, created and financed by Pitt, who returned to power in 1804. What mostly interests us is to determine when Napoleon gave up his project of invading England so as to pounce on Austria instead. Clearly it would have been madness to cross the Channel, even if he could, and so cut himself off from France and leave her open to a Russian and Austrian invasion. It was probably in the spring of 1805 that he thought that Germany would be the better battle-ground, and was planning to make the pounce before Villeneuve broke out from Toulon and was pursued by Nelson to the West Indies. Or, ever having two strings to his bow, he was ready according to circumstances to invade England or Austria. In the summer, as Villeneuve tarried and the preparations of the Allies were going forward, he made his final plan.

His campaign depended on the attitude of Prussia. At all costs Prussia must be prevented from joining the Allies. But there was no difficulty. The partition of Poland had proved the selfishness of Prussia in 1792 and 1795, and Napoleon cleverly found another bait in 1805. He had already occupied Hanover. So he threw out the hint that he would allow the King to annex Hanover as the price of Prussian neutrality, while he turned his Boulogne army against Austria. The special advantage

of the plan was that no British force could be brought to
co-operate in Germany as long as Prussian ambition coveted
Hanover; otherwise Pitt, slow as he was to risk a counter-
stroke by land, had plenty of men ready at Hythe, who
could easily be shipped across as soon as the Boulogne
camp was broken up.

Not only were the Prussians neutral and the British
thereby unable to help, but the Austrians and Russians
were far separated. There were two Austrian armies, the
one being organised by the Archduke Charles in Venetia,
the other under Mack in Bavaria, out of touch with each
other, and far away from the Russians, who were slowly
coming from the east. In August Napoleon put in motion
his various army corps from Boulogne and Antwerp and
other places from which they threatened England, and
each under its marshal they poured out towards the Rhine,
thence through the Black Forest, each by its own line
and ready to concentrate at a given point. The corps
in Hanover joined in the movement, violating en route
Prussian neutral territory. They burst into north Bavaria
and cut Mack off from Vienna; then, sweeping round him
and advancing westwards up each bank of the Danube,
they cornered him at Ulm. The Austrian army was
annihilated, and finally at Ulm some 23,000 men, the
remnants left after a fortnight's fighting, surrendered on
October 20. Next day Trafalgar was fought.

Pitt thought that, when the King of Prussia was angry
at the neutrality of his land being violated, it was a good
opportunity to send over a British force. But the usual
troubles occurred. The Swedes and Russians did not
co-operate as he hoped, Prussia was again deluded and
remained neutral, and the army of 14,500 British and
12,000 Hanoverians was finally brought home in the
February of 1806, after Pitt's death. Long before that
month Napoleon had entered Vienna and pushed on to
Moravia. The Archduke Charles left Italy and was

rallying the Austrian forces in Hungary. But the Tsar, Alexander I, was keen to strike a blow without waiting for him. Napoleon feigned to be retreating and drew back his right wing under Davout; Alexander fell into the trap and threw forward his left to encircle the French; promptly Soult dashed against the Russian centre and broke it, and thus cut off the strung-out left; Davout faced round again. This was at Austerlitz on December 2, 1805, the first anniversary of Napoleon's coronation.

The Austrians at Ulm and the Russians at Austerlitz having been routed separately[1], Napoleon had no more need for Prussian neutrality. He had let the King of Prussia think that Hanover would be given to him, and thus kept out the British troops. Now there was no need to prolong the deception, and neither the British nor the Russians could help. The mask was thrown off, and the King was goaded into war. The Prussian army under the Duke of Brunswick advanced through central Germany to cut Napoleon off from the Rhine; Napoleon out-manoeuvred them and threatened to cut them off from Prussia. They were encumbered by heavy transport and dared not let him get in their rear, while he was so used to make his men live on the country invaded that he had no fear. So they retreated and were falling back down the Saale to reach the Elbe. He swept eastwards, then northwards round their flank, and sent Davout ahead to cut across their path. On October 14, 1806, Davout, far ahead of the main army, held back and finally routed at Auerstadt 60,000 Prussians with his one corps of 27,000 French; he was energetic and put in his last reserves, while the aged generals opposed to him were slow and did not use all their resources, especially their great superiority in cavalry and guns. The same day Napoleon swerved to the west, crossed the Saale at Jena, and pene-trated through a forest; his leading corps under Ney was

[1] There were comparatively few Austrians at Austerlitz.

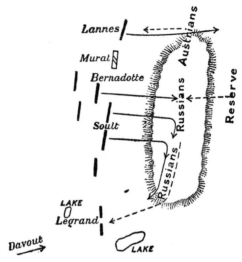

Battle of Austerlitz, December 2, 1805

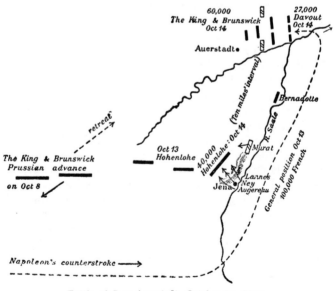

Battle of Jena-Auerstadt, October 14, 1806

at first in great danger until he himself brought up some 80,000 men to overwhelm 40,000. The two sets of fugitives met and the rout was complete. Murat was then let loose with the cavalry, fortresses and towns surrendered, and Prussia was crushed at once. Thus the old army, formed on the ideas of Frederick the Great, drilled and fashioned into obedience by severity, but rusty for want of use, fell at one blow before the quickness of the French who had been learning new ideas and practising them for fourteen years. The horrors of conquest fell on Prussia, and Napoleon trod her under an iron heel, treating her indeed much worse than he treated any other conquered country. His motive was probably jealousy of the memory of Frederick. Whatever the motive, Prussia suffered, and the bitter thoroughness of the war of 1870 was the result of the rout of Jena-Auerstadt.

Too far away to help the Austrians at Ulm, too impetuous to wait for the Archduke Charles at Austerlitz, again too far off and not ready to help the Prussians at Jena-Auerstadt, Tsar Alexander was still in arms, and a certain number of Prussians rallied to him in East Prussia and Poland. In February 1807 the French attacked him at Eylau and were victorious, but at an enormous cost in valuable lives. Napoleon, exhausted by continuous fighting in winter, fell back to recover. Dantzig was besieged and fell in May. In June the Russians, badly posted at Friedland, with a river in their rear and a gorge dividing their left from their centre, were thoroughly beaten. Alexander expected British aid, and our Sea Power was such that it could easily have been given; an army could have been landed which would have had no long and dangerous land march by which to reach the Allies, and there was no acute Hanoverian problem as in 1805. Such a force, if not in time to turn the scale at Eylau, had plenty of time to save Dantzig or reach Friedland. Disappointed and

sore Alexander had an interview with Napoleon, and his
first words were "I hate the English." The *Treaty of
Tilsit* was the result, and Russia was for some years the
ally of France.   Meanwhile the British strength was
wasted by Pitt's successors, as in previous years by Pitt,
in many little expeditions; to Italy, where an army too
small to save Naples from the French won a victory in
July 1806 at Maida, proving that it could fight well, but
reaping no benefit; to Egypt and to the Dardanelles,
where disaster ensued; to the Cape, which was won for the
second time and permanently; to South America, where
the army was entangled in the streets of Buenos Aires
and forced to surrender.   The ministry seemed unable to
understand that there was no need to hurry to conquer
places overseas, for our navy was able to take a land
force anywhere and at any time, but there was an urgent
need to concentrate all our strength at that one time and
place to help the Russians.

Napoleon by the Berlin Decree in 1806 set up the
Continental System by which he meant to ruin our country
by shutting out our commerce.   No British goods were to
enter the ports of France, of the allies of France, or of the
conquered nations.   At Tilsit not only the Tsar agreed to
bar out our trade from Russia, but also to make Sweden,
Denmark, and Portugal, the three remaining free countries,
do the same.   Canning at once replied by an expedition
against Copenhagen, where the Danish navy was seized
and carried off, and fortifications and stores destroyed,
lest they should fall into French hands.   In consequence
the name of England was hated, for we had used promptly
all our force against a little state, whereas a few months
earlier the same promptness and show of force might have
saved the Russians from collapse.

With Napoleon at the height of his power, yet beginning already to show signs of the weakness that would
cause his ruin, it is a good opportunity to discuss his

means. He had inherited the republican enthusiasm for France rather than for liberty, for military glory and ascendancy; the republican institution of the conscription, military service for the nation's good; the republican idea of *la carrière ouverte aux talents*, all men able to rise if they were capable, witness Ney and Soult, the one a private and the other a corporal of the old royalist army. He had by acknowledging the Church and recalling the *émigrés*, if they chose to return, mitigated the wrongs done by republicanism, yet without restoring confiscated lands. He made his allies to be devoted to his cause, particularly the second-rate German powers, Bavaria, Saxony, Wurtemberg, whom he favoured at the expense of Austria and Prussia. He aroused devotion in Poland, though without restoring the monarchy. He could command the services of these Germans and Poles in war, and they were especially valuable because of their excellent cavalry, the arm in which France was weak.

To get an idea of his methods we must go back to the Republic's war. When once the bad effects of indiscipline wore off, or partially wore off, this remained to the good that republican soldiers fought in loose order with individual initiative, acting like a mass of skirmishers rather than as a formed army, every man taking cover for himself, whilst behind them a main attacking column could be formed. Republican generals with the fear of the guillotine before them always took the offensive, as suits the French character and a loose formation. To this we add the great mobility of their armies, forced as they were to march without large baggage trains and for the most part living on the produce of the countries invaded. Frenchmen, by nature active and difficult to repress, might under these conditions give trouble to their officers, and even under the Empire their discipline was not perfect, but their *élan* had free play. General Bonaparte won his first victories in Italy by using this material, studying the

12—2

nature of the ground so as to drive a wedge between his
enemies, marching his divisions separately, but concentrating them for battle at the right moment on the right
point. The Emperor Napoleon, disposing of larger forces,
created *corps d'armée*, each of some 30,000 men under
a marshal, and each fully composed of foot and horse and
guns, to do the same thing on a wider scale. But this
involved great trust in his marshals. When things went
well men such as Davout and Lannes could be trusted,
Ney marched to the sound of the guns at Eylau and came
in on the Russian rear as they were in the act of envelop-
ing Napoleon's wing, Davout won at Auerstadt by putting
in his last available reserves. But in general he preferred
to keep everything under his own eye, and often he even
interfered with the marshals; towards the end of his reign
he distrusted most of them. Consequently he drew closer
his line of battle, whereas the republican armies covered
a wide front. This means a greater depth in proportion
to breadth, and French armies began to fight in column
rather than in line[1]. At Marengo, for instance, two
battalions were deployed for attack with one in column
in reserve; at Austerlitz Soult advanced in columns with
a covering screen, then threw the whole into line as the
attack developed; but at Eylau an entire corps was
launched straight at the Russians in close column and
lost 5000 out of 12,000 men. Thus the principle of the
tactics was changing. The new idea led to victory of
a decisive nature if a charge was successful, but an enemy
who was well posted and could fire coolly would be able
to overpower the column before it deployed. At Wagram
in 1809 we shall find part of the army in line and part
in column; in the Peninsula and again at Waterloo
Wellington delivered his counter-attacks just as the

[1] In the little fight at Maida in South Italy, June 1806, the French
were in line three deep, apparently the normal formation and naturally
adopted where Napoleon was not present.

French were in the act of deploying heavy columns or just before they deployed.

Ulm, Austerlitz, Jena-Auerstadt, Friedland, are great names in French history. Yet one must repeat that the Allies altogether failed to co-operate in these two years, and the story of Leipzig will be different. Moreover Napoleon bought his victories at a great price. He was using up his best men, the very thing that happened to the Swedes after the death of Gustavus, and to Frederick after his first few campaigns. French conscripts and allied Germans, Italians, Poles, Danes, were not equal to the veterans who fell at Eylau, and in all his subsequent battles he had too many young French and too many non-French; this criticism should not be taken as referring to German cavalry who were most helpful to him. Another innovation may or may not have been really useful. He detached the grenadier companies of his infantry[1] to form a choice body, then organised it as his guard, and constantly raised it till the Old and Middle and Young Guard amounted to a large army corps consisting of cavalry and artillery as well as infantry. It is possible that the creation of a *corps d'élite* did harm by weakening the other corps in proportion and causing jealousy.

We may here also discuss the new map of Europe. The Holy Roman Empire had already disappeared, there were no Electors, no Diet, no Archbishops or other clerics as sovereign princes with temporal power. France had already the left bank of the Rhine since 1795, and Hanover had been conquered in 1803; to these lands were added in 1810 the north coast and the great free cities, Bremen, Hamburg, and Lubeck. The Emperor of Austria was

[1] The hand-grenade that gave them their name had long ago disappeared, but the right-hand company of each battalion was still composed of the best and biggest men called grenadiers. Our " First Guards " have been styled " Grenadiers " since Waterloo.

still hereditary ruler of Hungary and Bohemia and
Croatia, but lost the Tyrol. Prussia was reduced to East
and West Prussia, Brandenburg, and Silesia; her King
might not maintain an army of more than 40,000, who
were at the service of Napoleon, and was burdened by an
impossible fine so that, owing to his inability to pay, the
French troops remained permanently in garrison. Saxony
was made a Kingdom, and the King was also Grand Duke
of Warsaw. Bavaria was made a Kingdom, and increased
by the annexation of the Tyrol at the expense of Austria;
but the Tyrolese[1] revolted in 1809, and fought so bitterly
for the cause of Austria that they only collapsed when
the patriot, Hofer, was betrayed and shot. Wurtemberg
became a Kingdom, and Baden a Grand Duchy. In all
these the rulers were Germans, though Napoleon's allies.
But in central Germany he carved out a new Kingdom of
Westphalia from Magdeburg and Halberstadt, taken from
Prussia, together with Brunswick and Hesse Cassel, and
his brother Jerome was King. Between the Rhine and
Westphalia was the Grand Duchy of Berg, conferred on
his brother-in-law Murat, his great cavalry leader. The
four new kingdoms, five grand duchies, and several smaller
states, were formed into the *Confederation of the Rhine*,
and had to supply soldiers at Napoleon's call.

In place of the Batavian Republic we now find the
Kingdom of Holland under his brother Louis; but the
Dutch merchants hated the Berlin Decree and wanted
commerce with England; Louis supported them and resigned when unable to influence the Emperor, and then
Holland was annexed to France. Denmark was the
devoted adherent of France because of the British attack
on Copenhagen. Sweden refused at first to obey the

[1] In the war of the Spanish Succession the Tyrolese were devoted to
Austria, and again in 1848, a curious refutation of the idea that
mountaineers always love liberty or that Austrian rule was always
tyrannical.

Berlin Decree, but was overawed by the Tsar Alexander; British help, sent under John Moore, was of no avail as the King was insane; in 1810 Napoleon consented to Marshal Bernadotte, a Béarnais of humble birth, accepting the title of Prince Royal[1] of Sweden. In the South, Savoy and Nice were already in France, and Napoleon added Piedmont, Genoa, Parma, Tuscany, and Rome; thus the farce of a Cispadane Republic disappeared. He formed Lombardy, Venetia, and the Papal Legations, into the Kingdom of Italy, and he himself was King of Italy, with his stepson Eugène Beauharnais as viceroy. The Kingdom of Naples he gave to his elder brother Joseph. Across the Adriatic the Illyrian coast and the Ionian islands were administered as provinces of France. Only Sardinia remained to the House of Savoy, and Sicily to the House of Bourbon.

From 1807 onwards the question was, how long can this state of things last? That France did an immense amount of good in breaking down old feudal ideas, out-of-date survivals, and inequalities and injustices of all kinds, is beyond doubt. But Frenchmen were much in evidence, and probably showed a great deal of contempt as haughty conquerors, besides living on the country when there was actual war. How far this feeling was general no one can decide, for French geniality and *camaraderie* might in time have won affection in Germany and Italy, even as in Belgium and Alsace. The answer to the question is that time was needed if France was to be popular and abate her military arrogance, but meanwhile two things made her unpopular, the call on her allies for troops to serve in Napoleon's wars of ambition, and the loss of English trade. Not only by his decree no cheap English cloth and cutlery could enter Europe unless smuggled, but also English ships could retaliate effectually

---

[1] He became king in 1818, and the present royal family is descended from him. He came from Pau, and in 1789 was a sergeant-major.

by preventing all neutral and colonial commerce in tobacco, coffee, sugar[1], and the like. Here again we see the importance of time. Could Napoleon remain quiet long enough to ruin British manufacturers by keeping their goods out of Europe, and to create new European manufactures? England had the start in being the first to open her coalfields and manufacture goods by steam machinery; could she stave off bankruptcy, which overproduction of vast quantities of cloth and other articles must cause in the absence of markets in Europe, by mere smuggling and by the discovery of new markets in the revolted colonies of Spain? Napoleon gave the answer. He invaded Spain and offended the Tsar, and the Peninsular War and the catastrophe of Moscow ruined him. Meanwhile by his rearrangements in the map of Europe he was creating everywhere a new national feeling. The United Italy and the German Empire of the 19th century were by him first made possible. If it is a doubtful point whether the French were really popular in Bavaria or Italy, there is no doubt at all that they were loathed in Prussia.

When Napoleon sent Junot to invade Portugal in 1807, he was merely carrying out his commercial policy by conquering our last ally and market. But when he dethroned Charles of Spain and his son Ferdinand, so as to give the crown to Joseph[2], he was at least not wise. So many nations had given way to him that he expected no resistance, and for a long time Spanish soldiers had been considered worthless. The uprising of Spain was a surprise, and was due to wounded national pride and

---

[1] The discovery that sugar could be made from beetroot dates from about 1760, but of course the culture of beet received a great impetus in Napoleon's time. Only in our own days, however, has it been found possible to make sugar from beet almost as well as from cane.

[2] When Joseph moved from Naples to Spain, Murat was made King of Naples.

resentment against French military contempt and love of
plunder, and against the military government which
Napoleon never allowed Joseph to alter. Moreover the
Spaniards, devoted to the Catholic Church and regarding
all Frenchmen as atheists, were on fire with religious
enthusiasm. They cared little enough for the Bourbons.
"They fight for freedom who were never free, A kingless
people for a nerveless state." But "Pride points the
path that leads to liberty." Suddenly in July 1808 the
French in Andalusia were beaten at Baylen by the
old royal troops of Spain, a disaster due to carelessness
indeed, yet reflecting great credit on the Spaniards, and
then were forced to capitulate. The British government,
already beginning to send help, saw their chance to strike
a serious blow at Napoleon, for this was the first nation
that had risen against him as a nation and it had risen to
some purpose.

The great hopes conceived were soon dashed. Portugal
indeed was freed from the French when Junot, beaten at
Vimiero by Wellesley and his newly landed army, signed
the Convention of Cintra. But Napoleon appeared in
person with some 250,000 men, whether of the army of
invasion or in the rear in France, burst into Spain,
shattered the regular armies who had hoped to win a
second Baylen in the north, and drove a wedge through
to Madrid. Soult turned westwards against Burgos, and
Lannes eastwards to besiege Saragossa. The details of
this siege are wonderful; when the outworks of the town
were won, soldiers and citizens and peasants defended the
streets with barricades, and the French had to fight every
inch of their way till there was nothing to capture but
a mass of ruins and putrefaction; of more than 30,000
regulars in garrison only 8000 able-bodied men finally
surrendered, and enormous numbers of irregulars and
civilians had perished, and the French lost about 10,000.
Meanwhile, the Emperor himself pushing on to Madrid,

Sir John Moore advanced from Portugal towards Burgos. Too late to help the already scattered Spaniards he drew upon him Soult's corps, then turned and retreated on Corunna, fought and lost his life January 1809; but he had disorganised Napoleon's plan by dragging Soult into the bleak corner of Spain which it was profitless to the French to occupy. Behind him Napoleon had marched some distance, but had handed over the command to Ney and returned to France.

We know that the Peninsular War, now begun, was the Spanish ulcer that sapped Napoleon's strength. But Canning and most people at home looked on Moore's expedition as another failure. Luckily Lord Castlereagh had the wit to trust Wellesley, and grit enough both to defend Moore's reputation, which even some modern historians are too ready to slight, and to see that success in the war was not hopeless. Moore had said that the open frontier of Portugal could not be defended, and by this expression of opinion the government was seriously influenced. Wellesley so far agreed with Moore, but thought that something could be done at least to save Lisbon if the Portuguese army were reorganised with British help. Castlereagh prevailed, and sent out Wellesley, with the result that we know; he was a thorn in the side of the French who were conquering and holding Spain, for he defended Portugal till he could take the offensive against them.

Soult had fought Moore in January 1809, and in March he occupied Oporto, but was quite out of touch with the French armies in central Spain. In March Wellesley had his instructions, in April he reached Lisbon, in May he drove Soult in headlong flight from Oporto. Then he pushed up the Tagus to support the Spaniards, and repulsed Victor at Talavera in July. But Soult made a fine rally and came in on his rear. So he was forced to fall back to Portugal. He saw that this would always happen,

that an advance into Spain with his small numbers would
bring a superior force of French concentrated upon him,
and that it would be better to defend Portugal alone at
present. Without him the Spaniards raised army after
army and were always beaten. Yet the French gained
ground very slowly, for it was difficult for them to live on
the country, and in parts of Spain an army might appear
and win a battle, then have to march elsewhere, and at
once the Spaniards would regain what they had lost.
Bands of irregulars carried on a guerilla warfare, cutting
off stragglers and intercepting supplies, so that more
French soldiers were needed to hold the lines of communication than to fight battles. Still the work of
conquest went on gradually. Large towns and the chief
valleys were occupied. The French held the country
between Bayonne and San Sebastian and Burgos in force
so as to keep open their connection with France. From
Burgos to Madrid, from Madrid down the Tagus valley
to the Portuguese frontier, from Burgos by a line through
Valladolid and Salamanca across several tributaries of
the Douro, from Madrid by roads over the mountains
to Seville and Andalusia generally, we find them in
possession 1809—12. But the mountains of the north they
occupied only partially. The eastern parts were very
slowly conquered. Cadiz, supported by the British and
connected to the mainland by a narrow isthmus, never
fell. The whole war took up the energies of 300,000 men
on an average year by year.

Napoleon had quitted Spain in 1809; it may be that
he had no taste for a midwinter pursuit after Moore, but
he had a genuine reason in that trouble was brewing in
Austria. The Spanish war was due to national feeling,
and it seemed as if a national rising might occur in
Germany. However, the King of Prussia was timid and
was persuaded by the Tsar to remain quiet, and only
the Austrians armed. For the fourth time, therefore,

Napoleon took the field against them. The Archduke
Charles invaded Bavaria, where at first only the two corps
of Davout and Masséna were at hand. But Napoleon
came up quickly, soon followed by Lannes from Spain,
and he concentrated rapidly. In April three corps of
French, the Guard, and three corps of South Germans,
drove the Archduke back with great loss[1]. Napoleon
entered Vienna, while the Archduke stood at bay to
dispute his passage of the river a few miles downstream
at the island at Lobau. Masséna, followed by Lannes,
reached the far bank in May, and fought desperately
with 50,000 French against the Archduke's 80,000 at the
villages of Aspern and Essling; but his pontoon bridge
was broken by fire-ships and flood, and 15,000 valuable
French lives were lost while Masséna lost or regained
Essling[2] a dozen times, and Lannes was killed. Napoleon
then withdrew from the north bank, and, having fortified
the island of Lobau, held on for six weeks while reinforcements were arriving. It was a great triumph for
the Archduke, and it was seen that Napoleon's power,
with so many men absent in Spain, was on the decline;
there were too many allied Germans in his army, too few
good French to stand the brunt of such fighting. But
the Archduke did nothing more than hold his ground for
those six weeks. Then Eugène arrived from Italy, and
Marmont from the Adriatic. In July Napoleon had
three solid bridges between Lobau and the south bank.
Suddenly he threw four bridges to the north bank, and
passed 180,000 men across. The battle then raged over
a front of eight miles between Essling and Wagram, the
French in a great convex curve, the Austrians in a con-
cave. On the right Davout pushed ahead, on the left

[1] Davout was created Prince of Eckmühl for a victory at a village of
that name near Ratisbon : he was already Duke of Auerstadt.
[2] Masséna was created Prince of Essling: he was already Duke of
Rivoli.

Masséna once more held Essling with desperation to prevent the enemy from breaking between the army and the river; then Napoleon launched a mighty column of French and Italians and Bavarians, supported by the Guard, on the Austrian centre, and though it suffered severely it won the day, and both Davout and Masséna struck in from the wings. The Austrians were not even now entirely overwhelmed, but made peace. The Emperor once more seemed to be invincible.

This year the British government made a serious attempt to help the Austrians by a descent on the island of Walcheren, on the Dutch coast. It was a costly failure. Antwerp, the objective, was never in danger. The men fell fast by marsh fever, and our military strength was for a time crippled, for the Walcheren men when afterwards sent to Portugal were still liable to fever. But Castlereagh, who was responsible for the expedition, was quite right to do something to help our allies, however badly the plans were laid. It was Castlereagh also who pinned his faith to Wellington, seeing that the policy best suited to the war was one of serious undertakings on a considerable scale. But he fought a duel with Canning over the Walcheren question, and both ministers resigned.

In 1810 everything depended on Wellington, on whom the home authorities threw the responsibility of the decision to defend Portugal. Masséna, fresh from winning honours at Essling, was sent to finish the war, and we know how he failed before the lines of Torres Vedras. Not only had Masséna trouble with Ney and the generals in his immediate command, but there was no union between the many armies in Spain. Soult, in command in Andalusia, thought only of that country and the siege of Cadiz, so that his attempt to help Masséna came too late and was fruitless. In fact the master mind was required there. Even Napoleon could not direct the war from Paris, and in his absence the rival marshals could not see what should be given up for the greater ultimate good. We can see that the conquest of Andalusia might have been postponed and Soult's forces joined to Masséna's to effect the more important conquest of Portugal. But there was also the serious difficulty ever present that too large an army in one district would starve.

In 1811, having followed Masséna out of Portugal, Wellington was, however, unable to retaliate successfully in Spain. But his great year was 1812. He based his plans on the fact just mentioned, the necessity imposed on Soult and Marmont, who had succeeded Masséna, to scatter their forces, partly to hold down the country, partly to feed the men. Having his own men well in hand, his Portuguese brigades under British training quite efficient, and his rear and lines of supply safe, with his northern force he dashed at Ciudad Rodrigo and took it by assault; then he crossed the mountains, joined Hill, who commanded the southern army, and took Badajoz by assault; each fortress falling before Marmont on the one side, or Soult on the other, could concentrate an army to save it. Leaving Hill again to face Soult, he moved into Spain from Rodrigo, and overwhelmed Marmont at Salamanca, his first decisive and offensive battle. He advanced and entered Madrid. That Wellington saved Spain in a large measure, and that the Spaniards did not solely save themselves from the French by their incessant efforts and devotion and the ubiquity of their guerilla bands, is proved by what now happened; King Joseph abandoned Madrid and retired eastwards, and Soult entirely evacuated Andalusia to join him. Hill came up the Tagus to Madrid. Wellington pushed northwards to try to occupy Burgos. But the further the British advanced the smaller was their striking force, especially as the French rallied and concentrated. Hill fell back from Madrid before Soult, Wellington from Burgos, and both retired to Ciudad Rodrigo, the retreat, as has often happened with British

armies and as happened with Moore in his march on
Corunna, being quite disorderly. It seemed as if Wellington had after all failed. But he had won the two great
border fortresses, he had destroyed great magazines in
many towns, the loss of which crippled the French, and he
had cleared Andalusia. Yet while pointing out what he
did for Spain in a few months,—more than the native
forces could have done in years, for Soult could have held
Andalusia indefinitely if it had not been for Wellington,
—we have to acknowledge that the scattering of the
French armies owing to Spanish patriotism and energy
enabled him to do so much. It also has to be remembered that two entire army corps, one under Suchet, the
other in turn under Augereau and Macdonald, were
occupied with the conquest of eastern Spain, and the
Spaniards continued their defence, though town after
town was taken, throughout the years 1809—13. British
aid on this side was very slight and intermittent.

Meanwhile 1812 is the year of the Russian war. The
rupture between Napoleon and Alexander dates from
1810, when, after the divorce of Josephine owing to her
being childless and the Empire needing an heir, Napoleon
made overtures to marry Alexander's sister, and then in
fear of a refusal almost at once asked for the hand of
Marie Louise of Austria. It was Marie Louise that he
finally married, and she, the great-niece of Marie Antoinette, bore him a son, the ill-fated " Aiglon." The Tsar
would not have liked his sister to be empress, but was
angry at the way he was treated. The serious reason of
the war was Russia's need of British trade. The Continental System was simply fatal to Napoleon, for Holland
and Germany were demanding cheap British manufactures and colonial produce, and he could only stop
smuggling by stringent regulations and by the burning
of the goods when discovered. He made his brother
Louis resign the throne of Holland because he was not

keen enough to suppress smuggling, and he annexed all
the North Sea coast of Germany. The same irritation
was felt in Italy. It existed also in France, where was
an equally strong hatred of the Conscription and of the
Spanish war. But national risings against Napoleon for
the sake of commerce were not yet possible. Russia was
the only country that could defy him, and on Dec. 31, 1810,
Alexander declared his ports free to British goods, a date
when Masséna's army lay impotent in Portugal, and over
300,000 men were locked up in the Peninsula. Bernadotte,
Prince Royal of Sweden, later threw in his lot with
Russia. Prussia was not in a position to fight, and the
Emperor of Austria was at present bound owing to his
daughter's marriage.

The grand army of 325,000 men crossed the Niemen in
June and July 1812. " Other forces, following as rearguard and reserves, raised the total numbers to more than
600,000 men. About 250,000 were French, 147,000 were
Germans from the Confederation of the Rhine, 80,000
Italians led by Eugène and Murat, 60,000 Poles, besides
Illyrians, Swiss, Dutch, and even a few Spaniards and
Portuguese, while Prussians on its left and Austrians on
its right were to guard its flanks[1]." The transport service
broke down at once, horses died, and the army could
hardly be fed. But, luckily, for all his haste Napoleon
could not catch the Russian armies. He was lured ever
forwards by their retreat, past Wilna, Witebsk, Smolensk,
until at last in answer to the Russian outcry that the
country should be defended the Tsar replaced his retreating general, Barclay de Tolly, by a fire-eater, Kutusoff.
Then a battle was at last fought at the village of Borodino,
on the river Moskva, 530 miles from the Niemen, 80
miles west of Moscow, on September 7, that is 75 days
from the commencement of the passage of the Niemen.
The Russians, 140,000 strong with 640 guns, held a

[1] Rose, *The Revolutionary and Napoleonic Era*, p. 248.

semicircle of heights strengthened by several redoubts. A murderous attack, a counter-attack which was all but successful, and a second attack led to their withdrawal after nine hours. But Napoleon had lost 30,000 out of about 130,000, and he had refused to allow his Guard to charge to complete his victory. He entered Moscow on September 14, with about 100,000 effectives and many sick.

The celebrated fire broke out that same night and raged for five days. More important than the fire was the systematic devastation of the country in direct imitation of Wellington's devastation of Portugal up to the lines of Torres Vedras. Possibly had there been no fire the retreat might have begun somewhat later, that is when the cold weather was nearer, and then the whole army and not merely almost the whole of it would have perished. Napoleon marched out on October 19, hoping to take the southern route to Smolensk. Kutusoff occupied so strong a position across this line that he had to take the route by which he had come, completely stripped already and bare. By November 6 the army was reduced to 55,000 men, and then and not till then the frost set in. November 27 and 28 the river Beresina was bridged and crossed by some 28,000 in an heroic struggle against 70,000 Russians; then one bridge broke and the other was burnt, and crowds of stragglers were sacrificed. Figures are now of very little use to us. The remnant of the grand army, also the various bodies left en route as rearguards and now falling in with the fugitives, were driven along and got across the Niemen on December 14, and the first rally was made at the Elbe. Napoleon hastened to Paris. Of all who went through the awful scenes Ney, created Prince of the Moskowa after the battle of September 7, gained the greatest reputation as a rearguard fighter. The causes of the unparalleled disaster were not only fire and snow, but also inability to "live

on the country" as the French had always done in
Germany, because Napoleon had not prepared for a
retreat nor created sufficient magazines at frequent
intervals, and this simply means want of forethought.
He had pushed on and on as the Russians fell back on
Moscow, hoping to catch their main army and making
them, not Moscow, the object of his advance. Thus he
had not laid his plans for an autumn retreat over wasted
country.

The Russians had also had heavy losses, and were in
no position to pursue through Germany at once. It was
some little time before the Tsar and the King of Prussia
came to agreement. Meanwhile on December 30 the
Prussian General Yorck made himself a national hero
by bargaining privately with the Russians; the Prussian
army corps, raised as Napoleon's flank support on the
Baltic, deserted the French marshal, Macdonald. A
similar Austrian corps had been covering the southern
flank of the retreat, but it was more difficult to induce
the Emperor of Austria to take part against Napoleon, now
his son-in-law. Moreover Dantzig and other fortresses
were still held by the French, and some 40,000 were rallied
behind the Elbe at Magdeburg. But popular enthusiasm
was great. At last, late in February 1813, the King of
Prussia came to terms with the Tsar. In the days of
Prussia's humiliation Scharnhorst had organised a short-
service system by which 150,000 regular conscripts had
been trained, and he now provided for a second reserve
or Landwehr, and a third reserve or Landsturm. Volunteers took up the cause eagerly. As for money, few
Prussian families can be found who have not the tradition
of grandparents or great-grandparents bringing jewels
and ornaments to help the "fatherland." Moreover the
reformer Stein had brought in a scheme of self-government in towns which freed citizens and fostered civic
patriotism, a step towards the abolition of rigid class

distinctions, but a step only. The spirit of liberty was roused, and nowhere was so keen as among the students of the universities. It remained to be seen whether military skill would be found equal to the enthusiasm. The new Prussian army was led by Blucher, an impetuous cavalry officer and a bitter anti-French patriot, who had done his utmost at Jena and lived for revenge. The strategist and serious student of war who directed Blucher, but who erred rather on the side of over-caution, was Gneisenau.

Napoleon was back again from Paris with men drawn from Spain, including Soult who had quarrelled with Joseph, and the last available conscripts and confederate Germans. In May he actually won two victories, though he was too weak to pursue, and held a position in Silesia. His campaign was dictated by his anxiety to save the French garrisons blockaded in Dantzig and Stettin and elsewhere, while Davout reoccupied Hamburg and was expected to force his way through to the main army. The usual mistrust prevailed among the Allies, Prussians accusing Russians of backwardness. But Napoleon made a mistake in agreeing to a truce in June and July. In August the Emperor of Austria, influenced by his minister Metternich, and partly also by the news of Wellington's victory at Vittoria, declared for the Allies. With the Prussians and Russians in front, the Austrians in the right rear, the Swedes and some Germans under Berna-dotte[1] covering Berlin, while Davout was quite unable to break through from Hamburg, Napoleon fell back to Dresden. There he beat the Austrians at the end of August. But now the Allies refused battle where he was in person[2], while they fought and beat his marshals,

[1] Ex-marshal of France and Crown Prince of Sweden, slow in the campaign, intriguing to be King of France on Napoleon's ultimate defeat.
[2] The old republican Moreau gave this advice. He was working with the Allies and was killed at Dresden.

Bernadotte for instance driving in Ney. Next, both the Saxons and the Bavarians deserted him. Blucher planned a great turning movement by the northern flank, and Napoleon fell back again, this time to Leipzig. Again the Allies did not act well together. But numbers favoured them. After two days of fighting, October 16 and 18, Napoleon crossed the Elster by a single bridge, and when it was blown up prematurely all the corps in rear were sacrificed. "The Battle of the Nations" at Leipzig was decisive; 190,000 French had held off 300,000 Allies, but after the collapse only 60,000 recrossed the Rhine. The fortresses fell one by one, though Davout held out at Hamburg till the autumn of 1814.

Meanwhile Wellington made his great advance from Portugal. Last year he had done a great deal but had finally retreated. In May 1813 he struck from Ciudad Rodrigo, on a broad front and in a north-easterly direction, so as to get between Joseph and France. Joseph left Madrid and fell back to Burgos, thence outmanœuvred to the plain of Vittoria; again outmanœuvred and cut off from the direct road to France, he was beaten and lost practically all his army and baggage. Six weeks brought Wellington from Portugal to Vittoria, but six months were needed before he could force his way into France, for Soult, sent back to the post of danger, defended stubbornly the narrow ground between the Pyrenees and the sea.

The Allies advanced to the Rhine, and in November 1813 the monarchs and ministers met at Frankfort. The Austrian minister, Metternich, particularly wished not to humble France, for he feared Russia and had a lively sense of the grasping tendency of Prussia. The Tsar and the King were for a march on Paris and vengeance. Metternich prevailed, and terms were offered; Napoleon might retain the Rhine as a natural frontier. But he wanted more. So the war went on. Now Castlereagh

went over to Europe with full powers to act at the
allied headquarters, and he was entirely against a Rhine
frontier which would leave Belgium, especially Antwerp,
in French hands. The campaign of 1814 is one of the
most wonderful of the whole of Napoleon's career. With
his last remaining troops, a remnant of his Guard, conscripts and national guards, he dashed from side to side
at the Allies as they were strung out over a wide front,
and won such victories that a retreat on their part seemed
possible[1]. But the Tsar was firm and Castlereagh supported him. Holland rose against the French and
received help from England; Murat turned traitor in
Italy and checked the loyal Eugène; Wellington, blockading Bayonne, pushed into south France, everywhere
greeted as a saviour. Thus in spite of his victories
Napoleon was at the end of his resources, and when
Blucher was strongly reinforced Paris surrendered on
March 31. Then Napoleon gave way. But Wellington
fought Soult for the last time at Toulouse after the actual
abdication.

The exile to Elba, the weary inaction there, the sudden
landing on the south coast of France on March 1, 1815,
the welcome accorded by Ney and the soldiers, the surprise of the Allied Sovereigns and the ministers who
were sitting in congress at Vienna rearranging the map
of Europe, lead us up to the Hundred Days. Napoleon
had now some 200,000 men, many quite young conscripts,
but also many good soldiers restored by the peace from
their prisons in England and Germany, including the late
garrisons of Hamburg, Dantzig, Magdeburg, and Stettin.
His army was all French, a great advantage to him. But

[1] Prince Schwarzenburg, the Austrian general, was commander-in-
chief of all the Allies, and his was a most difficult task with three
sovereigns present and the aspirations of three nations to satisfy. He
was also a humane man and hated bloodshed, and therefore was out of
place.

it was ill assorted, and had to be organised so quickly that the marshals and officers and men did not know each other well. The Allies also had not sufficient time to get together their best men. The British were near at hand, and Wellington went straight to the Netherlands from Vienna; but most of his old Peninsular veterans were in America[1], and his troops were, if the phrase be allowed, a "scratch" lot, many regiments quite raw, many officers and especially the staff unknown to him. The Prussians were occupying Rhineland and were therefore ready for action. The Netherlands being obviously the best meeting place for Blucher and Wellington, Blucher occupied Liége and Wellington Brussels, and their armies were spread over many miles till they should be ready to concentrate and cross the frontier into France. Blucher had with him some Saxons who were half-hearted and might desert; Wellington had the Dutch and Belgians, a good number of Hanoverians, and other Germans who were not fond of Prussia, and the first brigade of veterans from America actually marched on to the field of Waterloo a few hours before the great battle began[2].

Time was of the utmost value to Napoleon while the Austrian and Russian forces were still far away. He concentrated 125,000 men on the Belgian frontier, and on Thursday, June 15, he crossed the Sambre at Charleroi so as to strike his favourite wedge between Blucher and Wellington, before they could concentrate and invade France. Grouchy's two army corps, supported by the reserve and Guard under Napoleon's own eye, were on the Friday launched against Blucher at Ligny on the road to Namur, and were victorious late in the day; Ney attacked with one army corps a weak force of

---

[1] A war against the United States was caused in 1812 by the commercial blockade which the British kept over European ports, cotton and sugar and tobacco being excluded to the anger of Americans.

[2] Several thousands arrived after Waterloo and marched to Paris.

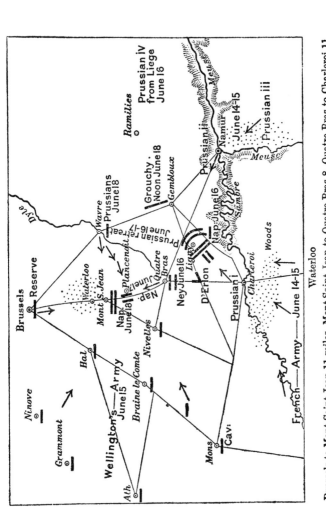

Waterloo

Brussels to Mont Saint Jean 11 miles, Mont Saint Jean to Quatre Bras 8, Quatre Bras to Charleroi 11
Wavre to Plancenoit 8 miles; Grouchy to Plancenoit (across country) 12

Wellington's command at Quatre Bras, but D'Erlon's corps wandering between Ney and Napoleon took part in neither battle, and as the British came up during the afternoon Wellington held his own. A controversy of some importance requires notice here, for German critics accuse Wellington of having deceived Blucher and induced him to make a stand at Ligny by promises of help from Quatre Bras. It is true that he reported to Blucher that his various brigades were nearer to Quatre Bras than they really were; but he was himself deceived by the incompetence of his own staff-officers, he had not been at once informed by the Prussians that they had sighted the French on Thursday, he had considered Blucher's position at Ligny ill chosen and likely to cause defeat, and had promised to help him only if not attacked himself. When two generals combine against a common foe it is but natural that one should have the harder task for a time, but if good combination is successful in the end it is no dishonour that he was beaten at first. There is plenty of glory for both Germans and British in the Hundred Days, and co-operation was so rare in the wars against Napoleon that it seems petty to us now to attribute wanton deceit to Wellington whose whole career is above suspicion. Gneisenau[1], chief of the Prussian staff, wished to retreat from Ligny eastwards towards the base and reserve corps at Liége; Blucher, wounded and in pain, overruled him and retreated northwards on Wavre so as to keep in touch with Wellington, calling up his reserve from Liege.

On the Saturday Wellington fell back on Mont Saint Jean three miles south of the village of Waterloo, followed by Ney's two corps and Napoleon's reserve and Guard; Blucher reached Wavre, followed by Grouchy's two corps,

[1] One cannot avoid the conclusion that Gneisenau's mistrust was due to Wellington's prophecy that the Prussians in a badly chosen position at Ligny would be beaten, and modern historians repeat the insinuations to take attention away from the defeat.

but at a very long interval as Grouchy was slow in dis-
covering the line of retreat. Wavre is eight miles from
the extreme left of Wellington's position, but the ground
between was soaked with the rain that fell in torrents on
the afternoon and all night, and there were no good paved
cross-roads.

On Sunday June 18 Napoleon delayed his attack on
Wellington till midday when the ground was a little less
sodden. Blucher, marching across, was on the French
flank after 4 p.m., had a second corps up after 6 p.m., and
was in such overwhelming force by 8 p.m. that the French
were driven in headlong rout. The critical moment for
Wellington was about 6 p.m. when Ney, by the capture
of the farm La Haie Sainte, seemed likely to pierce his
centre, but Napoleon was then using up his reserve
against Blucher; yet it has also to be remembered that
Wellington still had in hand his strong and unbeaten
right wing which so decisively crushed Napoleon's Guard.
Perhaps after the battle Englishmen boasted as if they
alone won at Waterloo, disregarding the many Hanoverians and Brunswickers and Nassauers who fought well
alongside them, and also making light of the help given
by the Prussians. To-day German critics speak of the
Prussians saving the British from destruction. Of course
in either case the value of loyal co-operation in war is
forgotten. As regards Grouchy and whether he ought
to have marched to the sound of the guns, common sense
tells us to reflect that an army with artillery and waggons
cannot move across soft ground at a great pace, and he
could hardly have reached Napoleon before sunset; that,
if critics now cannot decide on the exact meaning of
Napoleon's orders to him, he must then have been in a
cruel state of uncertainty; that, if he had marched
across and found Napoleon victorious, as naturally every
Frenchman expected, he would have been blamed for not
advancing straight on Wavre; and finally that the fault

was Napoleon's for not covering the country with cavalry
to find where the Prussians really were, for certainly on
Sunday morning he thought he had Wellington at his
mercy and did not expect either Blucher or Grouchy to
come.   There remains the argument that Grouchy in
trying to come across might have helped Napoleon by
drawing on to himself the main body of the Prussians;
but then Blucher, unless seriously thwarted by Gneisenau's
remissness, could still have had in position plenty of men
both to drive in Napoleon's flank and to fend off Grouchy.

What Great Britain in general and Wellington in
particular did for Europe in those days was acknowledged
then, for the custody of the Emperor was entrusted to the
British, and Wellington was made commander-in-chief of
the allied army of occupation in France.   Systematic
belittling of the nation and the man had not yet begun.

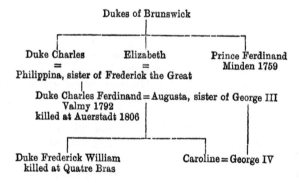

CHAPTER VIII

WHEN Napoleon fell in 1814 the Allies drew up with
Louis XVIII the Treaty of Paris. Their war had been
against the Empire, not against France; therefore no
territory was taken away, no war indemnity was imposed,
Great Britain restored most of the colonies; indeed France
was a little larger than in 1789, for Avignon remained
hers and did not go back to the Pope. After Waterloo
there was a period of military occupation, also a large
fine was inflicted, and works of art stolen by the Republic
or the Emperor were sent back to the places to which
they belonged. Yet even then the boundary of France
was not altered. Lorraine and Alsace were still French.

The Allied Powers in 1814 sent representatives to a
Congress at Vienna, Castlereagh and Wellington being
ours, to rearrange the map of Europe. Partly they had
to see that France could not again start a war of aggression, partly they wanted to secure, each power for
itself, such new territory as would reward it for its
exertions in war. Now both Republic and Emperor had
aroused the feeling of nationality. Whether released by
revolutionary armies from their monarchs, or conquered
and treated as subjects by imperial armies, Poles and
Spaniards, Germans and Italians of all kinds, were all
conscious of their nationality and aspiring towards freedom. But the Great Powers at Vienna treated the smaller

states as if they had no right to aspire, and a determined move was made to check democracy and freedom.

The House of Orange was restored to Holland, but the Stadtholder disappeared in the King of the Netherlands. Belgium was incorporated with Holland; the Emperor of Austria did not want a country so distant from him, it was out of the question to restore it to Spain, and Great Britain was determined that France should not hold Antwerp. Thus for a short time the Catholic Belgians, whether Flemings or French-speaking Walloons or formerly bishop-governed Liégeois, were put with the Calvinistic Dutch. In the same way Norway was added to Sweden.

In Italy the House of Savoy regained both Savoy and Piedmont, thus controlling the western Alps; Genoa and the Riviera were added, giving access to the sea; and Sardinia had never been lost. Thus the Kingdom of Sardinia was compact, and by its geographical features strong, and the arbitrary inclusion of Genoa not only gave a most valuable port but also was a promise of future expansion. The Emperor of Austria regained Lombardy and secured Venetia, so that with the Dalmatian coast he controlled the upper Adriatic. Southwards the Bourbon Duke of Parma and the Hapsburg Duke of Modena and Grand Duke of Tuscany were restored to their respective hereditary possessions; the Pope once more ruled from Rome to the middle Adriatic and up to the lower course of the Po; Naples and Sicily were once more joined under the House of Bourbon in the person of Ferdinand I; all these were practically under the protection, or rather supervision, of Austria. The Tyrol also, her link with Italy, was recovered by Austria.

In Germany it was clear that the electors and prince-bishops could not be restored. The King of Saxony, the King of Bavaria, the King of Wurtemberg, though old allies of Napoleon, retained each his title. George III was restored, not as elector, but as King of Hanover. The King of Prussia wanted to secure Saxony for himself, but other powers opposed him even to the point of being ready to fight. The Kingdom of Saxony that we know was settled. Prussia however received a large part of Saxon territory, recovered Magdeburg and much of central Germany, and, most important of all, got West-phalia on the right bank of the middle Rhine and the old electorates on the left bank. Being the most powerful military German state Prussia was thus definitely made the champion of Germany as against France, taking over Rhineland as a bulwark of German independence against any future Napoleon and thus being responsible for the safety of such fortresses as Coblenz and Mainz. More-over Prussia was thus marked as the destined head of a United Germany, especially as these Rhinelanders were Roman Catholics; in the Empire of 1871 Lutherans and Catholics came together without trouble.

German Unity was now an idea as strong as any idea that had driven revolutionary France to war in 1792 and 1793. But ideas usually lead to practical success only if they work slowly. In 1814 Germans were conscious of their common nationality, as most of them had risen against their French despoilers; yet some had been the allies of France, and had received benefits from France who had upset old out-of-date tyrannies. Moreover there were jealousies, especially between Austria and Prussia; Austria had her gain in Italy, Prussia in Rhineland, and thus it seemed to be the destiny of the one to look to the south and access to the Mediterranean, of the other to be the champion of Germany at home. But fifty years were yet to pass before Prussia could make a United Germany. Meanwhile there was no longer a nominal "empire" as in 1792, a mere assortment of 200 or 300 fragments great and small. A Federation or Bund was created by the Congress of Vienna, with a Diet as governing body, and

composed of 38 members; Austria, though her Emperor
ruled over many non-German countries; five kingdoms,
Prussia, Saxony, Bavaria, Wurtemberg, Hanover; several
grand-duchies, such as Baden, Hesse Darmstadt, Hesse
Cassel, and the two Mecklenbergs; duchies, such as Saxe-
Coburg-Gotha; four Free Cities, solitary representatives
of the self-governing commercial centres of old Germany,
viz. Frankfort, Bremen, Hamburg, Lubeck; while the
King of Denmark was a member by holding Holstein,
and the King of Holland by holding Luxemburg. The
very existence of a Federation, though a mere name,
disappointing patriots like Stein, ignored by the King of
Prussia and the Emperor of Austria who certainly would
not submit to orders from the Diet, at least accustomed
men's minds to the idea of national unity.

Poland was divided. Prussia finally gained Dantzig
and a part of the Vistula, Austria kept Galicia though
Cracow was for the time a republic, but Russia had the
Grand Duchy of Warsaw.

Perhaps, however, the map of Europe as rearranged
in 1814—15 is not so important—for the whole course of
19th century history shows us nations bent on rearranging
it further—as the conflict between the ideas of constitutional liberty[1] and repression. Memories of the Terror
were such that democracy to many minds seemed to be
equivalent to revolutionary violence, and it was a sort of
article of faith that mobs should be at once suppressed by
the military. Yet prospects were fairly bright in France
herself, for Louis XVIII granted a Charter; there was
to be a Chamber in control of taxation and legislation,

[1] The word "liberal" came to be definitely applied to the nationalists
in European countries who aspired to be free and self-governed. In
English it was first used as a translation of *libertados* or *liberales*, usually
by monarchical writers as a term of reproach. Lastly it was applied to
the political party of reform, as "Whig" was out-of-date and meaningless
in the 19th century.

religious equality, and absence of class distinctions; lands
sold since 1789 could not be violently resumed by the
returned exiles. It was for the time a minor point that
no man had a vote for election to the Chamber unless he
paid £13 a year in direct taxes, which meant that about
a quarter of a million of Frenchmen voted. There was
naturally a royalist reaction, and many suffered, for
instance Ney who was shot as a scape-goat for the nation.
But "France has seldom had a better government than
it possessed between 1816 and 1820[1]." The Tsar, im-
pulsive as ever, swayed by the influence of the moment
as at the time of Tilsit, gave a Constitution to Poland.
The King of Prussia promised a Constitution. But hopes
were soon dashed.

In 1815 Tsar Alexander drew up a *Treaty of Holy
Alliance* which he presented to the Emperor of Austria
and the King of Prussia. It was an expression of religious devotion in condemnation of the irreligion of the
Republic and Napoleon. Metternich styled it "verbiage,"
mere words. But gradually this clever politician, whose
influence over the Emperor was already great, cast his
spell over the King and the Tsar. Young German
students were noisy and riotous in celebration of liberty;
an anti-national newspaper writer was suddenly murdered
by a keen young nationalist. So the three Sovereigns,
led by Metternich, feared riot and murder as signs of
revolution, forgot the devotion of their peoples in the
national rising against Napoleon in 1813, and became
despots. Constitutions were either revoked or never
granted. More than that, the Sovereigns bound themselves to suppress popular risings in other countries. The
Austrians crushed movements in Piedmont and Naples,
and the French royal troops were commissioned to restore
Ferdinand of Spain. This union of crowns to overawe
nations has been popularly but wrongly known as the

[1] Fyffe, *Modern Europe*, chap. XIII.

Holy Alliance. Meanwhile several countries were well governed on the whole, and in an age of peace material prosperity was undoubted. Yet free speech, free press, right to vote under a popular government, would satisfy humanity more than commercial gain, especially the educated and the student classes. In England when reform is in the air we think of the middle classes or the working classes as demanding votes, that is a voice in elections to a 600-years-old House of Commons; in the Germany and the Italy of Metternich's period of power there was a yearning after an ideal that had never yet existed, freedom to speak and write in demand of some national Parliamentary scheme, and the would-be revolutionists were strongest in the Universities.

The first blow to Metternich's policy came from the revolted colonies of Spain, and here we have to discuss the policy of British statesmen. Castlereagh and Wellington were firm to suppress riots at home, and thus gained a reputation for needless severity; abroad they were credited with subservience to the will of Metternich and the three Sovereigns. Yet they only joined with the three so far as to be ready to crush any new revolution in France, and they did not slavishly follow Metternich either in the suppression of Naples or in that of Spain. Between 1816 and 1820 Canning was in the ministry and equally responsible with them. Then he resigned, but after Castlereagh committed suicide he returned to office and took a strong line; he recognised in 1823 Argentina and Mexico and other revolted colonies of Spain as independent states, and thus confined the action of the Allied Sovereigns to Europe. Then President Monroe of the United States issued the celebrated declaration, known by his name as the Monroe Doctrine, that his country would prevent any European power from founding a new colony, or from interfering with the politics of the Latin American states. Brazil also broke away from

Portugal, John being King of Portugal, and his son Peter
Emperor of Brazil. We are accustomed to sneer at Latin,
i.e. Spanish and Portuguese, America as a land of many
pretentious states continually engaged in civil war and
corrupt in tone. Yet even unstable states have the right
to work out their own redemption according to their own
ideas. Later, in 1826, Canning sent British troops to
Portugal to help the young Queen Maria, Peter's daughter,
against her uncle Miguel.

More important were the affairs of Greece. The
problem of the subjection of Christians to the rule of
the Sultan has always been thorny. The very idea is
hateful, and in addition there is the memory of the days
when the Turks were conquerors continually menacing
Europe and the Mediterranean trade. Mohammedan rule
was not in general very grievous; but the Turks have
always been fatalists, it is the will of Allah, no reform
can or need be made, though much may be promised
when the indignation of Europe is aroused; worse than
fatalism is the periodical outbreak of fanaticism when, in
obedience to the original idea of their faith, they wave
the Koran and the sword as alternatives to the "Giaour"
or infidel. The Christian races of the Balkans have been
various; Greeks, with traditions going back to the days
of the old glories of Athens in art and war, and of the
Eastern or Byzantine half of the old Roman Empire
which for 1000 years survived the barbarian conquest of
Rome herself, a race still Hellenic at heart though much
mixed by intermarriage with non-Hellenic peoples from
the North, conscious of unity in that they are members
of the Eastern or Greek Church with their Patriarch in-
stalled at Constantinople, prosperous enough in their way
since the collapse of Venice gave to them the coasting-
trade of the Levant—the Greeks of purest blood and
readiest spirit of adventure are the sea-loving islanders—
but with a reputation for being frivolous, fond of the

pleasure of the moment, untrustworthy, and ready to cheat, which indeed they have only lived down in our own days; Serbians, belonging to the great group of Slavonic nations, akin to the Croats of the southern districts of the Austrian Empire, conscious that they had once formed an empire before they were overwhelmed by the Turks in the 15th century, hating the Turk, and hating also the German and the Hungarian in turn, according as they fear the interference of either; Rumans, whose name tells us that they once were subjects of the Romans and whose language is partly derived from Latin, a mixed race of partly Roman and partly barbarian Dacian blood, with many of their kin in eastern Hungary, sometimes afraid of and sometimes ready to make use of Russian interference; Bulgarians, a peasant race descended from barbarian hordes who had burst into the Roman Empire, held down by the Turks more severely than their neighbours. For us it is difficult to think of the year 1820 without reference to 1876—78 and 1912. Yet one fact stands out; the Christians of Europe have always been so jealous of each other that, just as in the days of Charles V or Louis XIV the Turks conquered, so in the 19th century they remained in power though they have been conquered. Up to the middle of the 18th century Austria was the champion against Islam, after that date Russia came on the scene, and each has wanted and still wants to reach to the sea. France has a traditional interest in the Eastern Mediterranean, which dates from the Crusades. Britain has always thought of India, and three great men in turn, Wellington, Palmerston, and Disraeli, have looked to an intact Turkish Empire as the best barrier against Russian expansion. It follows that, whatever benefits Austria and Russia may have conferred on the Christian races in the past, Serbia ever feared the neighbouring Austrians and looked to the Russians, Rumania feared the Russians and looked to the Austrians.

We, after a century's experience, have at last made up our minds as a nation, being forced by recent events to acknowledge the inherent rottenness of the Turkish Empire. But we are now concerned with the fortunes of Serbia and Rumania and Bulgaria, whereas in 1820 only the Greeks were moving.

A consciousness of their nationality in spite of their mixed blood, a revival of interest in the old Greek language and literature, a belief that the power of the Orthodox Greek Church justified their ambition to raise a Greek Empire on the ruins of the Turkish, led to revolt. Secret societies were at work and the Greek mind was stirred. The rebellion of Ali Pasha in Albania—the wild mountain land opposite to Italy, "rugged nurse of savage men" like their ancestors of the time of Alexander of Macedon and Pyrrhus, Mohammedans by conversion and enemies alike of Christians and of Turks—showed that the Turks were not invincible. At first the Greeks failed, for Tsar Alexander was under the spell of Metternich and believed that rebels against the Sultan were as bad as rebels against the Kings of Spain and Naples. But in 1821 so fierce and widespread was the rising in the Morea that the Turks were driven to their fortresses, and Tripolitza, a central inland stronghold, was captured. North of the Gulf of Patras the headquarters of revolt was at Missolonghi, known to all because Byron came there to die. Cruelty and massacre stained the Greek name. The Turks in retaliation massacred at Constantinople and elsewhere, especially in such islands as they controlled. But the best Greeks were the islanders who gained several successes with devoted courage and great skill. In 1822, Ali Pasha being crushed, two regular Turkish armies advanced against Tripolitza and Missolonghi, but were beaten back. Then came a period when the victorious Greeks quarrelled amongst themselves. The Sultan applied for help to Mohammed Ali of Egypt, his

14—2

nominal vassal, really an independent prince who had both fleet and army. Mohammed sent his adopted son, Ibrahim Pasha, to conquer Crete, and the disciplined but savage Egyptians overran the island with frightful cruelty in 1824; next year the Morea was invaded; from 1825 to 1826 the Turks besieged Missolonghi in vain, but then Ibrahim came across and destroyed the inhabitants when they made a desperate sortie; in 1827 Athens fell to the Turks.

At last Europe was aroused, and Metternich's theory that all rebellions were wicked could not be maintained in face of the monstrous atrocities committed. Tsar Alexander I, champion of the rights of sovereigns, died in 1825; Nicholas I, his brother, succeeded. Russia and Great Britain drew together to mediate on behalf of Greece, and Charles X, the new King of France, joined them to draw up a treaty in London. This was the work partly of Wellington, but chiefly of Canning; Wellington did not incline to strong measures beyond offers of mediation, lest Russia should profit; Canning died before the policy of force was successful. Too late to save Missolonghi or the Morea from Ibrahim's first savageries, the united fleets of Britain, France, and Russia, at last arrived in the autumn of 1827 and entered Navarino Bay. The army of Ibrahim still held the land, but the Turco-Egyptian fleet was annihilated. What happened next is galling to our national pride; Canning being dead, the British ministers withdrew from the war, and left Russia to continue it alone. In 1828 the Turks held their own in Bulgaria; in 1829 the Russians beat them badly, crossed the main line of the Balkans, took Adrianople, and pushed a vanguard towards Constantinople. But it is notorious that this is a difficult country, and the approaches to the capital are nearly impossible to carry. The victors, far from their base, and not in strong numbers, were in some danger. The Sultan, however, was not prepared to fight to the last. The Tsar made a show of generosity in offering terms. The result was the *Treaty of Adrianople.*

By the treaty the Turks definitely gave up Rumania. Free trade and free navigation were granted to ships of commerce of all powers in the Dardanelles, Bosporus, and Black Sea. Above all, the Independence of Greece was assured. It was difficult to decide what next should be done. The crown was offered to Leopold of Saxe-Coburg, finally to Otho of Bavaria; in 1863 George, son of Christian IX of Denmark and therefore brother of our Queen Alexandra, became King.

In France Louis XVIII died in 1824. The last brother, the "jockey-breeched" Artois, who had been the most rabid of the anti-revolutionists and *émigrés* of 1789, succeeded as Charles X. France had been fairly quiet after 1815, with a Parliamentary government but high franchise. Now under Charles X the royalist reaction was more pronounced, and he tried to weaken and even destroy the Constitution. In 1830 there was a day of riots and barricades, the troops were badly handled and even deserted to the popular side, and the Louvre and Tuileries were seized. Charles resigned in favour of his grandson, the Count of Chambord, known to all French royalists as Henry V. But finally Louis Philippe, Duke of Orleans, son of "Egalité" who played so mean a part in 1789, was accepted as King "of the French," not "of France." In the eyes of true legitimists he and his line have always been renegades unworthy of respect. He was accused of having promised to support Henry V and then betrayed him. But he was certainly honest, though dull and unable to inspire enthusiasm. Accepted as King he waved the tricolor from the balcony of the Hotel de Ville, and was publicly embraced by the aged Lafayette. Charles X fled to England, and later died in Austria. Henry V, sole hope of the white flag and golden lilies of the senior line of Bourbon, died childless in 1883.

In 1830 also the Belgians rose to throw off their connection with Holland. A strongly Catholic people they had been in 1814 put under the House of Orange, though their ancestors had preferred the rule of Spain and their fathers had been content to be incorporated with France. Their grievance was that the Dutch language was used officially and Dutchmen were put into all high offices. Britain and France interfered to help them, and the Dutch garrison of Antwerp had to be besieged and forced to surrender. Louis Philippe wished to make one of his sons king, but the Powers were hostile though the Belgians themselves would have accepted him. Finally Leopold of Saxe-Coburg[1], who had refused Greece, was made King of the Belgians. Under their German kings the Belgians have prospered exceedingly; they have made the most of their coal and iron, and after the lapse of some centuries have proved that they possess

[1]

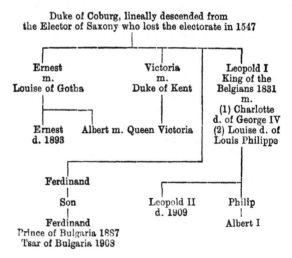

Duke of Coburg, lineally descended from
the Elector of Saxony who lost the electorate in 1547

Ernest
m.
Louise of Gotha

Victoria
m.
Duke of Kent

Leopold I
King of the
Belgians 1831
m.
(1) Charlotte
d. of George IV
(2) Louise d. of
Louis Philippe

Ernest
d. 1893

Albert m. Queen Victoria

Ferdinand

Son

Leopold II
d. 1909

Philip

Ferdinand
Prince of Bulgaria 1887
Tsar of Bulgaria 1908

Albert I

by heredity the manufacturing skill which made medieval Flanders famous. This did not indeed result at once, for the Dutch, being enemies and commercial rivals and holding the mouth of the Scheldt, prevented Antwerp at first from having a free commerce. But in 1863 by treaty tolls on the river navigation were removed, and since then the trade of Antwerp has advanced enormously, so that she has been a serious rival to London. But it has always been to our interest to protect Belgium, and up to 1914 no armed power had violated the neutrality of her soil, not even in 1870.

A third event occurred in 1830, a revolt in Poland; of course the revolution in Paris which turned out Charles X precipitated both the Belgian and the Polish movements, but this one came two years too late, for in 1828 the Russian forces were locked up in Turkey but in 1830—31 were free to act. Alexander I had allowed a Diet to sit, and he had ruled as King of Poland, not as Tsar; but Nicholas I governed more directly by Russians. The Poles fought well but were beaten. This was in general a period of unrest. Great Britain was in a turmoil over Catholic Emancipation and the Reform of Parliament, which came on top of years of discontent caused by consciousness of bad laws and customs and by the use of steam machinery. Secret societies, particularly the Carbonari, *i.e.* Charcoal-burners, were plotting in Italy; there was an insurrection at Bologna in the Papal States which was suppressed by the Austrians. Mazzini, the ardent Genoese patriot and arch-conspirator, came to the front and preached a high ideal of nationalism, but the House of Savoy did not sympathise and Mazzini was for a time imprisoned. In Germany there was much excitement and talk, and risings took place, but the Federal Diet, if useful for nothing else, was used by Metternich to empower the German sovereigns to use force each in his own state. However, one good thing was seen; under the lead of Prussia was formed the *Zollverein*, the Customs-Union, which treated Germany as a whole so that foreign goods were taxed at the common boundary only, not at the frontier between state and state. This was a great step towards a political pan-German Union. Prussia was despotic but enlightened as regards commercial progress, and doubtless increasing wealth compensated for lack of free speech and a free press. But Austria held aloof, and the time was foreshadowed when the Zollverein would become an Empire excluding Austria.

For eighteen years, 1830—48, France settled down under a constitutional and unexciting government. Louis Philippe was *le roi bourgeois*. The one really important fact of his reign is the conquest of Algeria, whose appearance to-day is a fine tribute to French energy and ability to rule, where the army has had a sphere of activity—much severity was at first shown towards the Arab tribes, but this may be forgotten in consideration of what France has done for Africa—and where engineers have had their chance to make barren places fertile. The conquest had begun under Charles X, but the real work was done under the Orleanist. In 1839—40 French attention was drawn to Egypt, as to a magnet, for Bonaparte's invasion of 1798 seemed to mark the country as France's own. Ibrahim Pasha invaded Syria, and four Great Powers combined to force him to retire. For a time it seemed as though France, as Egypt's natural protector, would defy Europe and support him. But the danger passed away, though there was talk of revenge for Waterloo and anger at having to submit to Europe's dictation. In 1846 Louis Philippe trickily brought about the marriage of one of his sons to a Spanish princess in defiance of his pledged word, and his minister Guizot[1]

---

[1] One of the greatest historians that France has produced. Thiers and Hanotaux have also shown that statesmen can be deeply learned

1848 THE YEAR OF REVOLUTIONS 217

came badly out of the business. Our foreign minister on these two occasions when British and French interests clashed was Lord Palmerston.

Since the failure of the movements for reform in 1830 there was up to 1848 a seething of discontent. Mazzini was preaching in exile his ideal of a Republican United Italy, and prisons in Rome and Naples were full of conspirators. Others looked for the deliverer to Charles Albert of Savoy and Sardinia. A new pope, Pio Nono, elected in 1846, released political prisoners and was hailed as the coming champion. "Little was done; not much was actually promised; everything was believed[1]." Kossuth was at the head of a new movement in Hungary to combine the ideas of liberalism, as in western Europe, with nationalism, that is to say to reconcile democracy with the aristocratic feelings of the Hungarian nobles, who disliked Austrian rule, yet did not wish their own peasants to be free. In France the writings of leaders of thought, some of them men of abstract theories on socialism, some practical socialists such as Louis Blanc who preached "the right to work," were as important as the writings of Rousseau in preparing the way for revolution.

The explosion suddenly occurred in Paris in February 1848. Louis Philippe promptly fled, and as he had invested much money in England during his reign he and his family were safe and well off. A provisional government sat, Lamartine the poet and Louis Blanc the socialist were members, and a Republic was certain, for no change of dynasty was possible as in 1830. But was it to be a Republic of extremists under the red flag, or of moderates under the tricolor? Lamartine spoke burning words against the red flag. But the ideal of Louis Blanc was

writers. In our own country, though many of our statesmen have been delightful men of letters, only Lord Bryce has rivalled the French as a scholar and historian.

[1] Fyffe, chap. XVIII.

put to the test, and, as has so often happened in France when a phrase runs from mouth to mouth, the putting into practice of "the right to work" led to results both ludicrous and tragic. It is very easy indeed to sneer at "national workshops," where workmen were paid but might or might not work, at commerce and industry thrown into confusion, private enterprise at a standstill, and workmen flocking from the country into Paris where the "right to work" meant pay for no work. But the scheme was not loyally carried out by the minister charged with the work, and he simply put crowds of men to clear the ground for two railway stations and, when that job was finished, to dig up earth and put it back again in a great open space. In May 117,000 men were working for eight francs a week, mechanics and artisans all put to useless unskilled labour. Failure was inevitable, but Louis Blanc had the right to complain that his idea was merely caricatured. Worse still, the men were put into the National Guard, armed but not uniformed. An Assembly met, and in the voting every Frenchman over 21 years had a vote, *i.e.* universal manhood suffrage. The middle classes were frightened, the peasants were angry because the Parisian workmen were paid for doing nothing. So the Assembly closed the national workshops. The result was inevitable as the workmen had arms; barricades appeared in the streets, and the only remedy was military force. General Cavaignac was given a free hand, and in four days after desperate fighting he stormed the barricades, June 23 to 26.

The extremists and socialists were now crushed, and thousands were deported without trial. A Constitution was drawn up, and France was to be governed by a Legislative Assembly and a President; but unluckily the relations between Assembly and President were left vague. Louis Napoleon, son of the ex-King Louis of

Holland, nephew of the great Napoleon, came to the front. At the presidential election under manhood suffrage he received 5½ millions of votes, Cavaignac 1½ millions, the Republican leaders merely a few thousands. Moderates, royalists, imperialists, had combined to vote for him for various reasons; fear of a new Terror and Jacobinism, disgust at the socialistic fiasco, the revival of the "Napoleonic legend," that is to say remembrance of the old days when France was glorious under the uncle, all helped the nephew, and in particular the peasants, devoted to peace and security and strongly anti-Parisian, were solid for him. He was only known for having twice tried to raise a military revolt against Louis Philippe and twice failed abjectly. But he believed in himself as "the man of destiny," and France seemed to see in him and his name her sole defence against a "Red" Republic.

In Italy revolution, inspired by what had happened in Paris, broke out first in Milan in March. Barricades were run up in the narrow streets[1]; the Austrian troops were powerless and evacuated the city. Venice rose under Daniel Manin and proclaimed the Republic of St Mark. In Vienna there was also revolution, and Metternich fled. Tension between Austria and Hungary was acute. Therefore when their tyrant was in difficulties—and Austria was to Italians the arch-tyrant, ever supporting the Pope and Dukes and King of Naples—it was not in human nature to be prudent. Charles Albert of Savoy, deaf hitherto to the idea of freedom, saw his chance to head United Italy, put in motion his regular army, and entered Milan. Volunteers swarmed in; all Lombardy was roused, and even the Pope—Pius IX it must be remembered was thought to be a liberal—and Ferdinand of Naples sent troops to the Po. But the ardent Republicans of Italy did not like the idea of a king leading them, and it would

---

[1] Many modern Italian towns have been entirely rebuilt with very wide streets, and in the Milan of to-day barricades would be useless.

have required great military skill to use so mixed a force. The Austrians did not evacuate Italy, but lay in strength in the fortresses of the Quadrilateral, Peschiera and Mantua on the Mincio, Verona and Legnago on the Adige, a country which had taxed all the energy of Bonaparte in 1796—97. Their veteran General Radetsky, reinforced from Austria, began to make head against the towns of Venetia, and in July beat Charles Albert at Custozza near Mantua. The great movement now collapsed. Charles Albert fled, and did not attempt to make a stand at Milan which the Austrians at once regained. If Radetsky had not had his hands full, Venice still in arms, flying bands still covering the country, the government of Lombardy to be reorganised, he could easily have invaded Piedmont and reduced Charles Albert to extremities.

Rioting and barricades were also the order of the day at Vienna and Prague, and the rioters were both students and workmen; the bitterness of the poorer educated classes against nobles and government officials and the military, against the gagging of free speech and free press, was always a factor in continental revolutions. General Windischgratz conquered Bohemia in June, but not till October did he attack Vienna where an Assembly of revolutionists was sitting. Everything depended on the Hungarians. In the first place the Hungarians had their Constitution, but the Diet was controlled by the nobles, and noble land was free from taxation; the patriot Kossuth had been working to make the Hungarian government national, to secure rights and equal laws for towns and peasants, and he was not satisfied with mere material prosperity under noble monopoly[1]. Secondly,

[1] To Széchenyi, a noble, was due the improvement of Hungary before 1848, e.g. the construction of the Buda-Pesth bridge and the blowing up of the Iron Gates in the Danube. "He was no revolutionist, nor was he an enemy to Austria." Fyffe, chap. xviii.

in Hungary itself and in the neighbouring countries,
Bohemia, Austrian Poland, Transylvania, Croatia, was
and is a large non-Hungarian population, mostly Slavonic,
which resented Magyar or native Hungarian supremacy.
The result was that while the Hungarians were excited by
these two questions they missed their chance of actually
waging war on Austria, and Prague was captured and
Charles Albert was beaten in Italy, so that the Emperor
had a breathing space. Jellacic, a native of Croatia, was
appointed to be "Ban" of Croatia, and the Hungarian
government objected; the Emperor promised to suspend
him, but later broke his word. Therefore Austria had
now a valuable ally in Jellacic as leader of the Slavs of
Croatia and elsewhere, and this implied the loyalty of the
Croatian regiments, to which we must add the constant
loyalty of the Tyrolese. When in October Windischgratz
advanced on Vienna to crush the revolution and the
Hungarian army came to help the city, Jellacic came to
take the Hungarians in the rear; they were beaten,
Vienna fell, and a reign of revenge began. In December
the Emperor was forced to abdicate, and was succeeded
by his nephew Francis Joseph aged eighteen years[1].

The year 1849 saw Austria and Hungary openly at
war. Still compelled to keep a force in Italy the Austrians
were unable to prevail unaided. Finally the Tsar interfered, and between their Austrian and Russian enemies
the resistance of the Hungarians collapsed. Tales of
heartless cruelty were spread throughout Europe, and
General Haynau gained a name for peculiar ferocity.

In 1849 a Roman Republic was set up, and Pius IX
fled; the Grand Duke fled from Tuscany; Charles Albert
took up arms again. Radetsky promptly crushed Charles
Albert at Novara, between Milan and Turin, in March,

---

[1] He died at last in 1916, and therefore his is the "record" reign of
our days, having lasted 67 years. Victoria reigned nearly 64 years,
Louis XIV 72 years.

and then proceeded to restore the Grand Duke of Tuscany. Once more Piedmont was at his mercy, and once more was spared, partly no doubt because, as in 1848, he had too much to do and the throne of Francis Joseph was by no means secure, partly because there was ever a fear that France would interfere to help the House of Savoy. Charles Albert abdicated, and left his son Victor Emanuel to be the future unifier of Italy.

But it was to Rome and her heroic Republic that all eyes were turned. The movement seemed to be mad. No outside help could be expected except possibly from France, for, though British sympathies were with Italy, the British government was under the spell of the idea of insularity or non-interference. Suddenly the new French Republic's President decided to fight in Italy, not for Italian liberty as his uncle would at least have made pretence to do, but against. Louis Napoleon was afraid of the socialists and red republicans at home, anxious to prove to the world that a Napoleon could be a good Catholic, ready to sacrifice the chance of a lifetime in order to conciliate the moderates of France. He sent an army, much too small, to take Rome. Mazzini was there, and patriot volunteers from the conquered parts of Italy who had nothing left to hope for or to fear, and above all Garibaldi, who had spent his best years in exile in South America and had returned a little earlier to raise a corps of volunteers against Radetsky. The French advanced against the higher ground of Rome on the right bank of the Tiber, where the medieval wall was strong; if once the position was carried, low-lying Rome on the left bank was doomed. But they were few, and Garibaldi's desperate men repulsed them. They fell back, and terms of peace were discussed by de Lesseps, the canal-maker of the future, while reinforcements were arriving. Then came the second attack, which lasted just a month. Heroism was unavailing, the French broke in, and Garibaldi fled to the mountains and was hunted till he managed to escape. Shortly afterwards Venice fell to the Austrians after a siege of over a year. Italy was prostrate; Pius IX, cured of all desire to be a reformer, was supreme at Rome, Ferdinand in Naples and Sicily, the Austrians in the north. But the mad resistance of a few thousands behind the old wall of Rome was no more useless than Charles Albert's campaigns had been. Italians had a brave attempt to which to look back. The ideal of devotion to a losing cause often brings about final success.

Germany had her problems in 1848—49, but no violent war resulted. The King of Prussia was forced at first to grant a Constitution, and an Assembly met at Berlin. A Federal Diet met at Frankfort. Neither body was successful. The King at the end of 1848 suppressed the Berlin Assembly by military force, and then proceeded to grant a Constitution on his own plan, thus keeping up the Prussian ideal that the monarchy should do every-thing for the people and the people nothing for themselves. The Frankfort Diet could come to no decision; it was a grand thing to have a United Germany; but firstly was Austria to be included, and secondly could the Emperor of Austria, despotic ruler as he claimed to be over his Empire, submit to be merely a member controlled by the Diet? In 1849 the sovereignty of United Germany was offered by the Diet to the King of Prussia. He refused it. As in Berlin, so in Frankfort, he would not be an elected sovereign, and if Prussia would ever attain the headship she must win it as her right by the superior might of her reigning dynasty. The Hohenzollerns have ever believed in their divine right. Thus the Frankfort movement failed, for a body of members who only talk, who are disunited in their aims, and who cannot provide the force to secure obedience to their decisions, is out of place. There is also this to be said; the reigning King

of Prussia, Frederick William IV, had not the force of
character which we usually associate with the Hohenzollerns. Under him for the next ten years Prussia was
quiet. In 1858 his brother William became Regent, in
1861 King, in 1871 German Emperor. The realisation of
German Unity had to wait for the right man, but in the
meanwhile the idea was in men's minds.

While Germany and Italy were quiet and subdued,
waiting for William and Victor Emanuel, France was the
moving force in European politics. Louis Napoleon had
appealed to the moderates in crushing the Roman Republic and restoring Pius IX. His term of office as
President would expire in 1851, and though he had sworn
to uphold the French Republic he thought that he was
justified in violating its constitution; he was the only
possible centre of law and order and a settled government;
republicanism, as the experiences of 1792—99 showed,
seemed to imply constant changes; he was the heir of
a great name, but he would base his authority ultimately
on the support of the people. How far he was self-
deceived in believing himself to be the man of destiny
whose mission was to save France no one can determine.
We know the events up to 1870 which have made his
name hated and ridiculous, and the events since 1870
which have shown that a Republic can last for over forty
years and give peace and prosperity to France; but in
1851 insecurity and republicanism seemed to be the same
thing. He ingratiated himself with the army, and planned
a *coup d'état* or military revolution. On the night of
December 1, 1851, he arrested several liberal opponents,
occupied the Parliament house, seized the printing press,
and turned out a proclamation dissolving the Assembly
and appealing to the people. Between December 2 and
4 Paris was overawed, and much innocent blood was
shed. In the course of the month he appealed to the
people, instituting what was to be his favourite device to

show that the nation approved, a *plébiscite*[1]; 7,000,000 votes were given in his support. Then on December 2, 1852, the anniversary of his uncle's coronation, a second *plébiscite* authorised him, again by 7,000,000 votes, to make himself the Emperor Napoleon III. In our eyes the title is ridiculous; Louis XVI died on the guillotine and his son in prison, so his brother in 1814 called himself Louis XVIII; it was rather a feeble imitation of what the legitimate dynasty had done when Napoleon III insinuated that the great usurper's son had a right to be Napoleon II. To combine strict heredity with military seizure of a throne is contradictory.

"The Empire is Peace" said Napoleon III, and he plunged into three great wars in Europe, and a lesser one in Mexico. But at first people believed in his star; even shortly before 1870 English public opinion, as seen in a cartoon in Punch, thought that his last successful *plébiscite* made the throne safe for Napoleon IV. He had his chance to show that the *coup d'état* was merely a cruel necessity so that France could have a strong government. But he had no directing power, no gift of organisation, nothing but a name. He could use phrases but not act up to them. Each of his successful wars he left unfinished. Designing men could easily influence him, and his Spanish wife Eugénie also had a bad influence; it is always said that the extreme Catholics dictated to him through her. Corruption was supreme in the army and the civil service. Thus he came to be regarded as an untrustworthy ally by England, Italy, Austria, and Bavaria in turn, ready to desert a cause when difficulties arose. He was an ordinary man pushed into a high position which he had not the power to fill worthily, yet not the unmanly traitor that the shrieks of 1870 proclaimed him to be.

[1] A special vote on one point alone, corresponding to the *referendum* of which much is heard now.

As if he were determined to be the worthy nephew of his uncle, he looked for a chance of distinction and seemed to waver between a wish to avenge Waterloo and a wish to avenge Moscow. With him *la revanche* took the place of *les idées révolutionnaires* under which his uncle gained his first laurels in 1796. Tsar Nicholas helped him to make his choice.

It was quite easy for any Tsar to meditate a new attack upon Turkey by straining the terms of the treaties of Kainardji and Adrianople[1]. He had only to claim a sort of general championship of all the Christian subjects of the Sultan, and thus would have an excuse to satisfy the traditional policy of Russia, to expand towards the sea. The particular occasion was a dispute as to the rights of the Greek or the Roman Catholic monks at Jerusalem to have the keys of the Holy Places; Nicholas supported the first; Napoleon, already offended because Nicholas did not acknowledge him as a "brother" sovereign, saw his chance in supporting the second. The Sultan gave way to France. Then Nicholas meditated an attack upon Turkey, "the sick man" of Europe, and suggested to Lord Aberdeen, our prime minister, that Russia and Great Britain should unite to partition the country. He liked our country and people; he remembered how his brother Alexander, our warmest ally against the great Napoleon, had been welcomed in London in 1814. So he thought it natural that he should make the other Balkan provinces as independent as Rumania was already, even occupy Constantinople for a time, and give the British a free hand as regards Egypt and Crete. What he failed to understand was that the British were no longer so well disposed towards Russia as in 1814, regarded him as a cruel despot, and remembered the Holy Alliance and the merciless suppression of the Poles and the Hungarians. Wellington's policy of keeping the

[1] See pages 139 and 213.

Russians away from the eastern Mediterranean was now supported by two energetic men, Palmerston who was most influential in Aberdeen's ministry[1], and Lord Stratford de Redcliffe[2] our ambassador to Turkey. The cry was to uphold the integrity of the Turkish Empire, and this just suited Napoleon III. Thus, in place of joining an old ally against an old enemy, the British government drifted into alliance with Napoleon, who on his side was ready to avenge Moscow rather than Waterloo. It was at least to the good that Britain and France could be allies. Otherwise our statesmen were committed to an impossible task, namely to bolster up an oriental government, which never could, and never wished to, reform itself. Of course it is difficult to criticise our statesmen of 1853—54 without thought of 1876—78 or 1912—18, and we must remember that Gladstone in 1876, even in his fiercest speech against the Turks, said definitely that he believed the Crimean War to have been really necessary, and that he accepted fully his responsibility for his share in it. Having so many Mohammedan subjects in India our statesmen could not refuse to help the Turks simply as being Mohammedans. Thus to-day it is not for their religion, but for their failure to reform after all the help given to them by the western nations, that they have lost the sympathy and support of the West. Lastly, British enthusiasm for war is curiously spasmodic. In 1853—54 public feeling seemed to be set on war as if we had had enough of peace since Waterloo, as if we were ashamed of being a nation of shop-keepers devoted only to free trade and manufacture, and required a little excitement and glory.

Thus, when in 1853 Nicholas demanded not only the Holy Places for the Greek clergy, but also his right to protect all the Christians of Turkey, the Sultan, relying

---

[1] Palmerston, who had gained a reputation for being too headstrong as Foreign Secretary, was Home Secretary in 1854.

[2] Sir Stratford Canning, cousin of the late premier George Canning.

on Lord Stratford, refused. Russian armies appeared on the Danube. British and French fleets appeared off the Dardanelles, and then passed through the straits; but they were not promptly sent forwards, and the Russians destroyed the Turkish squadron at Sinope, a port on the south shore of the Black Sea. War was inevitable, and the general impression left on our minds is that none of the powers engaged expected war, or thought that the others meant war, and so they all drifted into war. In 1854 the Russians besieged Silistria on the Bulgarian bank of the Danube, and the French and British armies arrived at Varna on the Bulgarian coast. Now the Emperor of Austria played his part; if the Tsar could have calculated on the help of any monarch at this date, surely the Emperor of Austria was that monarch, for the Russians had helped him to crush Hungary. But he demanded the evacuation of Rumania, and Nicholas had to submit. Henceforward Austria was always up to 1918 Russia's opponent in Balkan problems.

The Allied armies still lay at Varna, and what more could they do? To call them home, now that the Russians had left Rumania, seemed to be a feeble ending after much excitement, and Nicholas might begin the war again at any moment. So the demand was made that he should give up his right to protect the Christians. He refused. Thereupon both armies were ordered to the Crimea to destroy Sebastopol, the one great arsenal and place-of-arms on the Black Sea. It was now late in the year, cholera was raging at Varna and would accompany the troops, the climate of the Crimea was unknown, stores for a long siege were not ready. Thus it is difficult to acquit the governments of a blind eagerness to prolong the war to satisfy the excitement at home, France being critical about the new Napoleon, who had yet to prove himself a great ruler, Britain bent on proving herself not wholly given to trade and manufacture. The armies

landed to face the unknown, each about 30,000 strong.
Marshal St Arnaud commanded the French, but he was
at death's door; Lord Raglan, aged 66, who had seen no
service since Waterloo, commanded the British; our allies
had mostly had much experience in Algeria, but only
a few of our officers and men had been in India and all
our traditions were of the Peninsular War forty years ago.
One has to emphasise this point, for the military administration was rusty, and the economy of a nation devoted
to trade as a sacred duty until the blaze of excitement
came had prevented efficiency. It must be noticed here
that this is the first war when all the infantry had muzzle-
loading rifles; in our ranks it was quite a new weapon,
except for a few special regiments, for Wellington had
resolutely refused to discard the old musket, and he had
only recently died.

Advancing southwards along the coast the Allies found
the Russians drawn up on the far bank above the river
Alma. The British, September 20, made a straight frontal
attack on the left; the French on the right by the sea had
a steeper bank to climb, and were just threatening to
outflank the Russians when they retreated. But the
beaten enemy refused to let themselves be locked up in
Sebastopol and retired inland, leaving in the place, under
the command of Todleben, a garrison and the sailors of
the fleet and a small army of trained workmen. Ships
were sunk to block the mouth of the harbour, and
Todleben worked hard to throw up fortifications. He
said himself that the Allies could have rushed the
northern defences at once. But they swept round, and
occupied an upland in front of the south side of the
harbour, the British on the right with their base at
Balaclava, a small and distant harbour, the French on
the left resting on Kamiesch Bay close to them. While
they waited for their siege guns, Todleben dug and built.
Meanwhile St Arnaud died, and Canrobert took his place.

Siege in the ordinary sense of the term there was none. The Russians always held the north side of the harbour, and there was free access across by a bridge; reinforcements and supplies could enter Sebastopol during all the eleven months. The Allies, having received their guns, simply bombarded and prepared to assault. As fast as they destroyed the works by day Todleben rebuilt by night, and the wooden warships, trying to force the harbour mouth, were powerless against the land forts above it. Then on October 25 the outside Russian army crossed the river Tchernaya and tried to capture Balaclava, that is to say tried to cut off the British from their base; they were repulsed, but held a strong position on our rear. On November 5 an attack from Sebastopol and the outside army fell on the British extreme right on the upland at Inkerman, and was repulsed with greater difficulty. Before the bombardment could be renewed came a storm of rain, which converted the upland into a sea of mud. Siege works were out of the question when stores and food could hardly be moved. The horrors of the winter, semi-starvation, disease, lack of clothing and drugs, loss of stores in bad weather at sea, frost and snow in the trenches varied by mud after a thaw, utter inability to help the sick and wounded, congestion at Balaclava when the stores did arrive but could not be distributed, the awful story is only too well known. Miss Nightingale arrived in November at the hospital at Scutari, on the Asiatic shore opposite to Constantinople, but it was some time before her influence was felt. In January 1855, Lord Aberdeen resigned, and Palmerston formed a new and more energetic ministry. In March died Tsar Nicholas I, and Alexander II succeeded.

Things were very much better for the Allies in the spring. The French, who had suffered less, were strongly reinforced till they had in May about 100,000 effectives; the British after all their losses, having sunk as low as

12,000, numbered 30,000; about 40,000 Turks arrived whose services were considered to be worthless, and 15,000 "Sardinians," for Victor Emanuel, who had no quarrel with Russia, wanted to put both France and England under an obligation to the House of Savoy. Consequently there were enough French and Italians to occupy the ground between Balaclava and the Tchernaya, and the Russians retired beyond the river. On the upland the British were too few to carry on the whole of the right attack, where Todleben had erected several new forts, notably the Malakoff; so the French took over the extreme right as well as the left, while our men had only the right centre. Now Napoleon interfered much with the generals, this being the first war when field armies were tied to headquarters at home by the telegraph, and his idea was to give up the siege and attack the Russian outside army. Lord Raglan was clearly right in insisting that the Allies were committed to the siege, and that the Malakoff was the key of the defence. Canrobert, distracted between them, asked to be superseded, and General Pélissier came to take command, a man of energy and fire, able to carry out his own ideas in spite of Napoleon. So the siege was pressed, but expeditions were also sent to the isthmus to cut off the ever inflowing stream of Russian reinforcements and supplies. The bombardment was far more severe than before and the siege guns heavier. Some of Todleben's forts were carried by the French. But a great combined attack on Waterloo day failed, and then Raglan died worn out[1]. In August the Russian army crossed the Tchernaya to relieve the tension of the siege, but the French and Italians easily repulsed them with great loss. After a fiercer bombardment, Todleben being wounded, the

[1] He had shown little skill or alertness in battle, but much quiet persistence in the winter months of the siege, and much tact towards the French.

final assault was made on September 8. The mighty Malakoff, occupying entirely an isolated hill, seemed to be impregnable, but the French had sapped to within a dozen yards, and its weakness was that it was enclosed all round, so that, when they rushed it under General MacMahon, they were covered against fire from the rear. The British carried the central fort, the Redan, but it was open to the rear and the Russian fire drove them out again. General Simpson, Raglan's successor, has always been unfavourably criticised, and the honour of the day belonged to Pélissier. On the other hand the very powerful British artillery had greatly contributed by its cross fire to the fall of the Malakoff.

Next day it was found that Sebastopol had been deserted in the night. The Allies spent another winter in the Crimea and there was no repetition of horrors. The British were over 50,000 strong and in good condition, and a German legion of 10,000 was in our pay, the last of those mercenary corps so common in the 18th century. But Napoleon had the deciding word, as he had constantly kept up his army to some 120,000 men and they had won Sebastopol. He seemed to think that enough had been done for glory. The Russian army still held the Crimea and was not attacked, though Russia was for the time exhausted and nearly bankrupt. Peace was made with Alexander II by the *Treaty of Paris* in March 1856; the navigation of the Black Sea and the Danube was to be free, and no Russian warships might be kept and no arsenals rebuilt on the coast.

Sea Power, and Sea Power only, had brought about this result. The Allies had had free approach to the Crimea, and, except during the first winter, had not suffered more severely than any nation in war must suffer. But the Russians had not only lost thousands of men under the terrific bombardment and in battle where they had fought in dense unwieldy masses, but also had

strained every nerve to bring up reserves from the in-
terior, all on foot, and vast numbers died on the march.
Russia lost more than Sebastopol and all these lives; she
was thrown back and did not recover from exhaustion
for many years. Yet whether the Allies gained much
thereby may be reasonably doubted.

The fact that Victor Emanuel sent troops to the
Crimea was very significant. A remarkable man had
come to the front in Piedmont, namely Count Cavour,
and he had a definite plan before him. The Kingdom of
Sardinia alone of the Italian states was free, and alone
gave promise for the future; it had done something in
1848 and 1849, and since then was being nursed to prosperity, enjoying a Parliament at Turin and a free press,
laying down railways, welcoming Italian exiles from
Austrian and Papal territory, diminishing the excessive
power of the Church within its own borders. Cavour's
idea was that an enlightened Sardinia would force Europe
to recognise that hers was the only power fit to make
Italian Unity a reality; it was only possible under a
monarchy which had won its spurs and had a past history
of freedom; Mazzini's ideal of republicanism was out of
place. But Sardinia unaided could not lead a national war
against Austria. With the wisdom bought by experience
Cavour would have no share in an heroic uprising which
could not but be crushed. An organised power must be
brought against the organised armies of Austria, and, if
need were, must be bought by some sacrifice. Napoleon III
was approached, and took the bait. In 1858 at Plombières
an arrangement was made for a Franco-Italian alliance.
The Emperor was dazzled by the chance of winning a
name in a campaign on the Po in imitation of his uncle,
yet he was not quite so soft as to do it for nothing.
Cavour and Victor Emanuel wanted him, and made the
sacrifice, namely the cession to France of Savoy and
Nice. England could give nothing but sympathy and

moral support; it is easy to sneer, for moral support is cheap, yet there is a real encouragement when one free nation wishes well to another. Palmerston probably in any case would not have fought for Italy, but in 1859 he could not because of the recent Indian Mutiny; also for a short time he was out of office.

In 1859 war was declared, and the Austrians missed their chance of overrunning Piedmont before the French arrived. At Magenta on the way to Milan Marshal MacMahon[1], who as general had stormed the Malakoff, drove the Austrians back, June 4. They abandoned Milan and all Lombardy, and fell back to the Mincio and the famous defences of the Quadrilateral. A second battle was fought on a very wide front at Solferino, June 24; it was not scientific fighting, but the French and Italians, under the eyes of Napoleon and Victor Emanuel, were victorious. There was then a halt. Suddenly Napoleon and Francis Joseph had an interview at Villa Franca and an armistice was made on July 11. Napoleon feared that Prussia might come to Austria's aid, the great fortresses of the Quadrilateral had always been difficult to win, the French army, from what we know of 1870, was probably not in condition for a further big effort; at any rate the nephew had not the uncle's determination. The chief clause of the treaty was that Lombardy was to be given to Victor Emanuel.

But in the meanwhile various states, freed from the Austrian troops who had marched to the war, declared for Victor Emanuel. Luckily no misplaced republicanism weakened the movement. The union of Parma, Modena, Tuscany and the northern Papal Legations, to Sardinia was not in the Villa Franca programme. But neither France nor Austria dared let the other interfere, and Austria was always weakened by the disaffection of Hungary. A *plébiscite* was taken in central Italy, Victor

[1] He was created Duke of Magenta. For map see page 165.

Emanuel accepted the verdict, and in 1860 met in Turin a Parliament representing Sardinia and Lombardy and Tuscany, and the other states. Cavour had resigned office for a time when disgust against him and his French ally had been strong after Villa Franca. But he returned to power, and he and Victor Emanuel had to pay the stipulated price. A *plébiscite* was taken in Savoy and Nice, and it was given out that a majority wished to be annexed to France. Napoleon having fought for his idea in 1859, glory and the honour of chivalrously helping Italy, had now his practical reward. The country is to-day genuinely French in sentiment. Yet the House of Savoy has lost its home, though the white cross of Savoy is still displayed in the red, white, and green national flag of Italy. Nice is to-day a big modern French town, a centre of local government and of pleasure, and little remains of the old Nice which was Garibaldi's birthplace.

Garibaldi served in 1859 on the flank of the main army in command of guerilla bands. He then wished to make a dash on Rome and was prevented. In 1860 he sailed from Genoa in two ships with his 1000 red-shirted volunteers, landed on the south coast of Sicily, marched across to Palermo and took it; then crossed to Italy and raised the Kingdom of Naples. Revolt had begun before he arrived in Sicily, but his energy made it successful. Victor Emanuel had no hesitation in making Sicily his own. He sent his regular troops against the Papal States, then against Naples; he wanted to secure Garibaldi's conquests to himself as national king, and at the same time to prevent mere revolution and possible anarchy. He had to stop Garibaldi from making a dash upon Rome, for Napoleon ever posed as the champion of the Church and garrisoned Rome. Finally Garibaldi retired into private life, the Bourbon dynasty was for ever expelled from Naples, and whereas in 1860 the Parliament of Turin represented eleven millions of Italians, in 1861

it represented twenty-three millions by the addition of
Sicily and Naples and the eastern Papal Marches. The
Patrimony of St Peter alone remained to the Pope, and
Venetia to Austria.

In 1862 Garibaldi called for volunteers against Rome,
and Victor Emanuel's troops had to fire on them and take
him prisoner; even a hero must not be allowed to be
a firebrand and provoke France. In 1864 Napoleon
agreed to withdraw his garrison from Rome if Victor
Emanuel would defend the Pope from invasion. Meanwhile the Italian Parliament met at Florence as more
central than Turin. But all Italians lived in hope of
some day making Rome the capital. Italy was yet "un-
redeemed."

Russia, meanwhile, was occupied by the agrarian problem. In 1861 Alexander II liberated the serfs by the
Edict of Emancipation. In Poland he tried to do his best
to govern by means of Polish officials, but the spirit of
national independence was strong, and outrage led to
measures of repression; then came revolt and more severity
of repression. The insurgents were the nobles, the Roman
Catholic priests, and the townsfolk. The peasants had
little sympathy with nobles, and often enough in the
wide districts of the old Poland of the 18th century
were not Poles by blood. The revolt crushed in 1863, the
Russian government supported peasant against noble by
setting the former free at the expense of the latter. But
at the same time the Polish language and national thought
were opposed to Russian ideas, and were therefore trampled
on, and the very class benefited by emancipation has
become anti-Russian as much as the nobles themselves.
Memories of Russian cruelty outweigh whatever benefits
have been conferred. Napoleon III and Palmerston could
not interfere as the friends of Poland, for France and
Britain were estranged as the result of the Crimean War;
the French loudly boasted of their superiority before the

fortifications of Sebastopol, and even war against us was for a short time in Napoleon's mind.

In this decade the fortunes of Germany began to attract the interest of all Europe : even the excitement roused by events in Italy paled in comparison. The spring of all action was Prussia. William I was King in 1861, and called upon the services of the then unknown Bismarck. The main idea of their policy was that the Crown should dominate Prussia, and Prussia dominate Germany ; the divine right of the Hohenzollerns should be supported by an efficient reorganised army ; for the sake of the greater good, German Unity under the lead of Prussia, a steady policy of " blood and iron " should be pursued, and the goal must be reached whoever might suffer. The Federal idea of 1814, and again of 1848, was out of place, and a Diet representing great and small sovereign states was a hindrance to unity. The national sentiment of Hanover or Bavaria tended to disunion. The Austrian Empire was largely non-German, and an Emperor could not be a mere second to a King. Therefore Prussia must dominate or conquer Austria and Hanover and Bavaria. Already Prussia had absorbed Pomerania and some of Poland, much of central Germany and Rhine-land ; her policy since the days of Frederick the Great had been to absorb. Therefore she had a large population. The Customs-Union, initiated by Prussia, had shown that prosperity follows on unity. The new railways had their influence. William and Bismarck had now to prove that Prussia was strong enough to beat down opposition, and direct the aspirations for unity into channels of their own choosing. The minister Von Roon and the strategist Von Moltke gave them their instrument, the Prussian army.

The question of Schleswig and Holstein had been of importance in 1848—49. Here were two provinces under the King of Denmark, Schleswig partly German, Holstein

purely German. The Frankfort Diet had tried to sever
them from Denmark, but nothing had resulted, chiefly
because the conflicting views of Prussia and Austria prevented action. Among outside powers Great Britain took
the lead in supporting Denmark, and in 1863 Christian IX
came to the throne and his daughter Alexandra married
the Prince of Wales. At this moment—for Christian
was only connected with the royal line through his
mother and grandmother, and had to go back 250 years
to establish a male connection—the Bund claimed rights
over the duchies and occupied Holstein. But Bismarck
was determined that Prussia should settle the question,
not the Bund. In a clever way he obtained the alliance
of Austria, and the joint armies invaded Schleswig beating
down the Danish defence. Active help from Great Britain
was expected. Palmerston and Lord John Russell promised
"support" for Schleswig if Christian gave up Holstein;
but Palmerston was now old, and after wars in the Crimea
and India and China was less energetic than before;
Queen Victoria was German in her sympathies; Napoleon
was not anxious for war, and in any case the Franco-
British entente of 1854 was no longer cordiale. So it was
given out in Parliament that "support" meant "moral
support," which was not of much value when Bismarck
had made up his mind to carry the matter to a finish.
Christian could not resist. By the *Treaty of Gastein*
Austria took over Holstein, and Prussia Schleswig. The
troops of the Bund had to retire, for they would have
been useless against the armies of the two great states.

We have to look across the Atlantic if we wish to
understand the attitude of Napoleon in the sixties. If
he was really ambitious to shine in war, he missed two
chances, now in the Schleswig-Holstein affair, two years
later in the Prussian-Austrian war, which his uncle would
have turned to account. There was trouble in Mexico,
for the Latin-American republics have had many civil

wars since Canning acknowledged them, and the half-Spanish races are excitable and resentful of established government. The lives and property of Europeans were not safe. Napoleon sent over a French army in 1863, and then offered to set up an Austrian, the Archduke Maximilian, as Emperor of Mexico. But this was done at the very worst time. The great Civil War in the United States was just drawing to a close, and as the North was victorious after a bitter struggle there was a huge army, well led and trained, well equipped with all the resources of a wealthy country, ready to carry out the wishes of the government. The United States put into force the "Monroe Doctrine" of 1823 by which the interference of European powers in Latin America was forbidden. Napoleon had no choice but to recall his army, a terrible humiliation for one of his name. Maximilian, deserted by him, was killed by insurgent Mexicans.

Both France and Great Britain were deeply moved by the American Civil War, but wisely did not interfere. It was caused by the question of negro slavery. The South or Confederate States, led by Virginia, were Democratic and stood up for the rights of individual states to govern themselves and to keep their slaves if they wished; the North or Federal States were Republicans and enforced by the sword the right of the United States as a whole to demand the emancipation of all negroes. At first in 1862—63 the Confederates beat back the Federals, yet never gained such a crushing victory as to compel peace. Gradually the Federals, having wealth and manufacturing power and, above all, naval power, hemmed in the South, and in the long run collapse came from sheer exhaustion in men and means. Now had France and Great Britain thrown all the might of their naval strength into the struggle—for quite a majority in each country sympathised with the South in the desire to be free, including freedom to have slaves—their interference might have been successful. They would have given to the South precisely what was lacking, supplies, manufactured goods, everything that naval power can give. But it would have been done at an awful cost, the undying enmity of the Northern States, the hatred which the mere thought of helping slavery would have caused, and possibly years of war. Palmerston's policy of non-intervention strikes us to-day as having been wise. He was old and less warlike, as we saw when we found him applying non-intervention to the Schleswig-Holstein affair; Napoleon could not be trusted, for in every war he was at first active and ended by being slack. So the United States ended their war by themselves after woe unutterable had fallen on the South, and then they ordered the French to quit Mexico.

Returning to Europe we see at once that an Austrian occupation of Holstein was impossible. It was miles from the Austrian frontier, and had no interest for the Hungarians and other non-Germans of the Empire. Bismarck had lured Austria into war with Denmark so as to checkmate the Bund. It was easy to quarrel in 1866 with Austria so as to settle which power was the stronger, to humiliate Austria, and then to destroy the Bund. The Prussian army was quite ready. The minor German states wished well to Austria, but Bavaria was not ready to fight, Saxony and Hanover armed but were not very strong. Napoleon was in trouble about his Mexican failure, and Bismarck tricked him into being neutral and thus losing his great chance; in 1805 Napoleon I had dangled Hanover as a bait before the eyes of King Frederick William III, so that no Prussians fought at Austerlitz; Bismarck now let Napoleon III think he would be allowed part of the west bank of the Rhine. Thus Austria had the active help of only Saxony and Hanover. Prussia secured Italy as an ally with the promise of the annexation of Venetia, and this meant that

THE SEVEN WEEKS' WAR

a large proportion of Austrian troops were required in the south.

The Prussians advanced in the end of June. A western force was sent against the Hanoverians. The main army under Frederick Charles, the "Red Prince," invaded Saxony and moved up the Elbe, and the Saxons fell back to join the Austrians. A third army was in Silesia and prepared to cross the mountains under the Crown Prince. The campaign is therefore famous for the daring strategy of Von Moltke; he was launching two armies from two widely separated bases in Saxony and in Silesia to combine in the enemy's country, Bohemia, a most delicate undertaking even though each was aware of the other's movements by telegraph. "March separately, concentrate on the battlefield" is a Napoleonic maxim, and a crushing victory will attend success; the risk is great but justifiable. On the other hand an active and ready enemy will get between the two and beat them separately, even as Napoleon himself did in 1796. On this occasion Benedek, who commanded the Austrians and Saxons, meant to throw his whole force on the Red Prince, but he was too slow and allowed the Prussians to advance too far. Meanwhile the Crown Prince crossed the mountains without loss, just where he should have been met and overpowered. Finally Benedek made his stand on the heights around the village of Sadowa where the high road runs to the upper Elbe, and in his rear was the river where the road crosses it at Königgratz; hence the battle is known by either name. Already he was despondent because in the minor actions of the previous week the Prussian breech-loader, the needle-gun, was clearly superior to his own muzzle-loader, the men firing six shots to the minute and being able to load and fire while lying on the ground. On July 3 the Austrians held their own well at Sadowa against Frederick Charles who attacked them in front, but by midday the Crown Prince

M. E. H.   16M. E. H.   16

made himself felt on their right flank; then, driven in on both sides and forced on to the river, they collapsed as badly as the French at Waterloo. The strategy had succeeded, and the Prussians had met on the actual field of battle.

The Hanoverians on June 27 held their own well against the western Prussian force at Langensalza, in the neighbourhood of Jena; but next day they surrendered to superior forces. The Italians fought on June 24 at Custozza, the place so fatal to them in 1848, and were again defeated. Their only gratification was that they had detained Austrians who were badly wanted to stem the tide of defeat in Bohemia. Their fleet also was beaten by the Austrians off Lissa. Bismarck, however, made good his promise, and when peace was made Venetia was ceded to Victor Emanuel.

The arrangements in Germany after this Seven Weeks' War were highly important. Prussia took and incorporated not only all Schleswig and Holstein, but also Hanover, Nassau, Hesse Cassel, and the great free city of Frankfort, thus securing a solid portion of central Germany to connect her with her older conquests in Rhineland. The Bund was finally dissolved. A new *North German Confederation* was created, Prussia at its head, Austria excluded. The kingdoms of Saxony, Bavaria, and Wurtemberg were left untouched; also the Grand Duchies of Baden and Hesse Darmstadt. Napoleon hoped that these would form a South German Confederation looking to France for protection. But Bismarck had only to make known that Napoleon desired to annex German territory up to the Rhine[1], and at once the South Germans were offended and each state made secret alliance with Prussia. The details of Napoleon's intrigues are difficult to follow, but at least it remains that he did nothing to help Denmark

[1] A part of the old lower Palatinate north of Alsace belonged to Bavaria, and this explains Bavaria's alienation from France.

in 1863—64, and nothing to help Austria and the South Germans in 1866, and had no one to help him in 1870.

The Austrian Empire also was influenced by the result of Sadowa-Königgratz. Ever since 1849 the Hungarians had objected to the single government which sat at Vienna, and in connection with the Italian troubles in 1859—60 it had been the fear of a new Hungarian rising that had tied the Emperor's hands when Victor Emanuel got more than the treaty of Villa Franca allowed him. On the eve of the Seven Weeks' War matters were being discussed by Austria and Hungary. The war hastened a decision, for defeated Austria had to buy Hungary's loyalty at almost any price. So was formed *The Dual Monarchy*: two Crowns, two Parliaments, two Ministries, two official Languages; but matters of common interest, foreign affairs, war, and finance, were to be treated in common. In 1867 Francis Joseph was crowned as King of Hungary. It is generally acknowledged that the system worked tolerably well, and anything was better than repression resulting in disloyalty. But Hungary still had her problem. The Slavonic peoples of Croatia and the Rumanians of Transylvania disliked the domination of Hungarian officials and language, and even in Hungary proper a large proportion of the inhabitants were still non-Hungarian.

Yet four more years were to pass after Sadowa before the great catastrophe. We have already seen the character of Napoleon III, well meaning but unable to organise or to control those whose selfishness thwarted him, keen to begin a war worthy of his name but ready to stop when a crisis arrived. He claimed that his was a "liberal empire" based on popular votes or *plébiscites*. But he fell between two stools; he neither allowed speech to be entirely free, nor unsparingly suppressed speech that was too free, and both in Parliament and in the Press anti-imperial feeling was kept alive by prosecutions, yet was punished by quite trivial sentences and always could express itself. Meanwhile France was growing in prosperity. Paris was largely rebuilt with broad boulevards and streets, doubtless with the hope that, as they could be easily swept by artillery, the days of barricades were over. Outside France, to balance the fatal interference in Mexico, the construction of the Suez Canal by Ferdinand de Lesseps with French capital was a splendid undertaking, and bid fair to give that ascendancy in the near East which France ever coveted; Englishmen disliked it, and preferred that the bulk of Asiatic trade should come round the Cape and by the Atlantic to London, but no statesman dared to oppose openly the scheme. Napoleon and Eugénie opened the canal with great ceremony in 1869. Nearer home he never wavered on one point, his support of the Pope; the very foundation of his policy was to conciliate the anti-revolutionary, therefore the Roman Catholic, majority of Frenchmen. Once he withdrew his garrison from Rome, trusting that Victor Emanuel would keep Garibaldi in check. But in 1867 Garibaldi, the irrepressible, made yet another effort. French troops were speedily sent over and routed him at Mentana; and then they garrisoned Rome once more.

The occasion of the Franco-German War was trivial. Spain had had much civil war during fifty years, a dreary and uninteresting period. In 1868 Queen Isabella was deposed, in 1870 the crown was offered to a Hohenzollern who was a distant cousin of King William of Prussia. Napoleon interfered, and the Hohenzollern withdrew. But that was not enough. As though he were seeking for war on any pretext to make atonement for his backwardness in 1866, Napoleon demanded that William should not support the cousin if he were put forward again. An account of the French ambassador's treatment by William was sent to the papers, and the spark was set to the gunpowder of national jealousy. Napoleon declared war, being falsely assured by his ministers that his army was ready, and Frenchmen shouted *"A Berlin!"* Bismarck, Von Moltke, and Von Roon had everything ready, and wanting war were only too glad to let France appear to be the aggressor and begin the war.

Napoleon was not only deceived as to the readiness of the French. He had no efficient reserves; favouritism had ruined the officers, and permission to pay for substitutes had lessened the numbers in the ranks; even his fortresses were but imperfectly equipped. But also he miscalculated his chances as to having allies. Austria and Italy had no reason to trust him, and in any case an alliance could not be made good in a hurry; moreover a hint from Russia kept Austria quiet. The South Germans had been estranged by his ambition to extend to the Rhine, and, even had they been willing to join with Austria as his allies to avenge 1866, they would have expected him at once to advance into South Germany, just the very thing he was not ready to do. Yet Europe was certainly surprised to see them arm and soon afterwards fight well and enthusiastically against France. The old idea of Louis XIV and Napoleon I that Germany should be kept disunited through the alliance of France with the second-class states against the stronger disappeared for ever. Bavaria in 1870 sent two army corps, Saxony one, Wurtemberg and Baden and Hesse Darmstadt nearly one, to fight side by side with the twelve corps of Prussia and the North German Confederation. France had but one advantage; the chassepôt was a better breech-loader than the needle-gun of Sadowa. On the other hand the Prussians had a much more powerful artillery; their officers had been more scientifically trained, and the doctrine of a great military writer, Clausewitz, had been taken to heart, namely that when one corps was engaged the others near to it must march to the sound of the guns and strike in at once to support it. Modern German critics point out the faults of 1870, and do not think Von Moltke's strategy perfect. They think that the great victories were bought too dearly. They acknowledge that the policy of attacking at once, general supporting general as a matter of course, made the victories really great, even if dear, but that a great Napoleon would have made them rue it. The general verdict is that the Germans won because the units were so well handled, as each regiment, brigade, division came into action under its own commander, rather than that the supervision of the whole campaign by Von Moltke was faultless.

War was declared July 17. In less than three weeks three great armies were converging on the frontier, the first under Steinmetz from the lower Rhine, the second under the Red Prince from central Germany and Saxony, the third under the Crown Prince partly South German and partly Prussian. Austria being quiet there was no need to watch her, and thus nearly 500,000 men were ready. On August 6 the French lay scattered, one army of 50,000 under MacMahon in the north of Alsace, another of 150,000 under Napoleon based on Metz, and more men were coming up; they were too far apart, and the various army corps were also out of touch. The main German plan was to drive a wedge between them. Thus the same day two battles were fought nearly fifty miles apart. The Crown Prince's leading corps fell on MacMahon at Wörth with inferior numbers[1], but up came more corps on each flank and behind, and the 50,000 French after defending some strong woods and slopes with great bravery were surrounded by some 90,000 Germans and ceased to exist as an army. Steinmetz[2] had a similar problem and won

---

[1] The Crown Prince himself meant to fight next day, but the corps commander by attacking brought on a general action.

[2] Von Alvensleben, commanding a corps of the Red Prince's army, marched to the guns and came in on the left of Steinmetz' battle.

a similar victory at Forbach-Spicheren. In neither battle
were the whole available French forces up in line, and no
supports marched to the sound of the guns. The defence
was now broken, but the Germans, as if out of breath,
were slow in pursuit. Napoleon had time to retreat, but
hesitated too long near Metz till Steinmetz was on him,
then he turned over the command to Marshal Bazaine
and escaped.

The Crown Prince detached part of his force southwards to besiege Strasburg, and himself pushed westwards
along the main railway line towards Paris. His cavalry
had lost touch and could not find MacMahon. But there
was no army to find, for marshal and fugitives had fled
with all speed to their reserves at Chalons. There was
a great camp at Chalons, half way between Paris and
Metz, and Napoleon and MacMahon were creating here
a new army of reserves and fugitives and militia; we
must leave them while the Crown Prince was groping his
way to find them.

Steinmetz approached Metz from the east just as
Bazaine was beginning to retreat. Meanwhile the Red
Prince was marching south of Metz so as to wheel round
and strike in to the west of it. As the French retreat
began on August 16 the Red Prince's nearest corps, under
Von Alvensleben, cut across them near the villages of
Mars-la-Tour and Vionville, and without any delay
went into action. Bazaine could have annihilated him,
but was painfully cautious, so that Von Alvensleben, in
spite of great loss and only reinforced by one other corps,
held his ground. The other Germans were arriving by
forced marches. Bazaine fell back on the 17th, and
chose the line of a valley west of Metz leading from
Gravelotte to the north[1]. On the 18th some 200,000
Germans of the armies of Steinmetz and the Red Prince

[1] Thus the French fought with their faces, and the Germans with
their backs, to Paris.

combined attacked across the valley on a front of seven miles, lost about 20,000 men, and might have been broken if Bazaine had but made a counter-attack; but they persisted, and at nightfall the Saxons, coming up on the extreme left or north, carried the village of Saint Privat. Bazaine withdrew into Metz, and was soon securely blockaded though he still had 180,000 men. The appalling losses of the Germans at least had produced a decisive result.

MacMahon had now an army of 120,000 troops of various kinds at Chalons. Common prudence and the rules of war dictated that he should take a defensive line. But Paris was in an uproar and crying out " Nous sommes trahis." The Empress Eugénie feared a revolution, and urged her husband to order an advance for the relief of Metz. MacMahon could but obey direct orders, however stupid. He marched from Chalons, and the Crown Prince, hardly able to believe that the news was true, swerved aside to head him off. Von Moltke and the King came across from the army besieging Metz. The French were edged northwards towards the Belgian frontier, beaten in several engagements, driven demoralised into Sedan, ringed in on all sides, and under a pitiless shell fire forced to surrender. An emperor, a wounded marshal, 80 general officers, and over 100,000 men were prisoners on September 2. The *Third Republic* was declared in Paris on the 4th.

There were now about 750,000 Germans in France, whether before Metz and Strasburg, or gathering round Paris, or on the lines of communication, and no formed French army to resist them. The Republicans did their best and held out for five months, after the regular armies of the Empire had collapsed in just one month from the first shot fired. It was heroic, but useless, except indeed that France can always think with pride of the raw recruits' devotion; and, after all, overpowering disaster is less galling than tame submission. But there was no

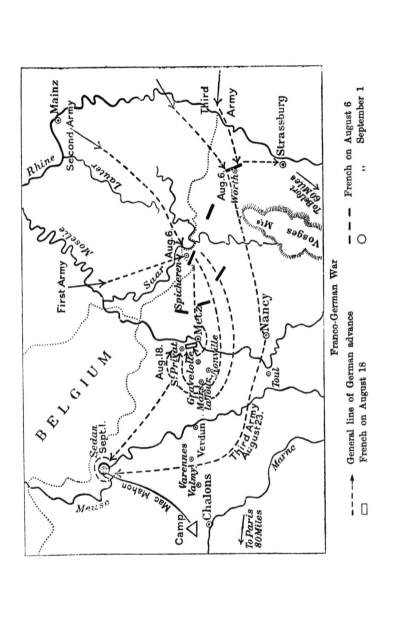

Franco-German War

- - - → General line of German advance
- - - French on August 18
☐
———— French on August 6
- - - ,,   September 1
○

Valmy and no Jemappes for the Third Republic. Indeed
the lesson of 1792 was misread. The French said that,
now that they had "it," they would drive back the
invader, and refused to give up an inch of their territory
or a stone of their fortresses. There had not been 750,000
highly disciplined Germans in France in 1792, burning to
justify themselves as a united nation, and against such the
raw recruits were powerless in spite of "it," even though
Garibaldi himself came to fight for "it." The soul of the
resistance was Léon Gambetta. A few regular soldiers
and veterans, sailors from the useless fleet, national guards,
mobile guards or militia, untried conscripts, manned the
defences of Paris or were formed into armies. General
Aurelle de Paladines actually won a battle near Orleans
on November 9, but on October 27 Metz had already been
surrendered; consequently the Red Prince was free to
bring his whole army between Orleans and Paris. Neither
Paladines, nor General Chanzy who succeeded him in
command of the army of the Loire, could break through
the Red Prince's lines so as to relieve Paris, and after
circling round from Orleans to Le Mans Chanzy lost most
of his men. His movements finally collapsed in January,
though he came out of the war with a reputation as the
ablest of the French leaders. Similarly Faidherbe raised
a northern army and tried to break through from Lille,
but was beaten in the end. The winter was appallingly
severe and all the French suffered beyond words. But
the worst horrors were in store for the last army raised
by Gambetta and put under General Bourbaki. In January
he advanced into Burgundy where Garibaldi with his
volunteers was defending Dijon, and proceeded towards
Belfort which the Germans, after the fall of Strasburg,
were besieging in the gap between the south end of the
Vosges mountains and Switzerland; it was hoped that he
would cut the lines of communication between Germany
and the besiegers of Paris, perhaps even raid in Germany.

He was beaten back after three days' assault on a position near Belfort manned by a German force barely one-third of his own army, and, as other Germans hastened up, the French reduced to 90,000, shoeless and in rags and crippled by frost-bite, straggled over into Switzerland. In these actions against Chanzy, Faidherbe, and Bourbaki the Germans had the enormous advantage of being not only well disciplined, but also well clothed and well shod, and therefore able to march quickly in the bitter weather.

Paris, from which sorties were made in vain, was surrendered at the end of January 1871. Finally, peace was made by the *Treaty of Frankfort* in May. A war indemnity of five milliards of francs, 200 millions of our money, was inflicted, and was actually paid within three years. Part of Lorraine, including Metz but not Nancy or Toul or Verdun, and the whole of Alsace, except Belfort which still held out beyond the fall of Paris, were given up to *the German Empire*. For the war was no longer against Prussia and the North German Confederation plus Bavaria and other allies. On January 18 the dream of German patriots was at last realised, when in the great hall of the palace of Versailles, the capital of Louis XIV, now the headquarters of the besieging army, King William of Prussia was proclaimed German Emperor by the King of Bavaria.

The French Assembly, which sat first at Bordeaux and returned to Versailles to ratify the Treaty of Frankfort, was mostly royalist. Europe, believing all republics to be unstable, expected that a Bourbon, whether Henry V, who was the last survivor of the direct line, or the Orleanist Count of Paris, would soon be chosen. But the immediate danger was not from monarchists, but from "reds." Early in March 30,000 Germans made a formal entry into Paris; on March 18 broke out a city revolution, and soon the forts which the Germans were not occupying and war material were in the hands of the reds, who set up the *Commune of Paris*; if we can imagine anything similar here, let us call it a violently socialistic City Council. The Communists were armed, for they were mostly the defenders of Paris against the Germans. The Assembly used against the Commune the imperial regular troops released from their confinement in Germany, and MacMahon was in command; he bombarded the western forts and wall from the Germans' old position at Versailles, broke into Paris on May 21, and stormed the barricades in the streets. The communists set fire to public buildings, such as the Tuileries, and murdered the archbishop and other priests; the troops in their turn shot men, and women too, the *pétroleuses* who poured oil to feed the fires, untried in batches. Meanwhile the Germans looked on from the positions they still held on the north and east of Paris.

Outside France the war had two chief results. The French garrison was of course withdrawn from Rome, and the troops of Victor Emanuel marched in after a slight defence by the Papalists. Since then Rome has been the capital of United Italy. Pius IX still kept the Vatican, the palace adjoining St Peter's; there he shut himself up as though he was a state prisoner, and never acknowledged the royal government. It matters little who is pope or who is king; the feeling between Church and State is still bitter. The two extremist parties, fascisti and socialisti, unfortunately damage the cause of a truly United Italy.

Secondly, the Tsar, Alexander II, now that one of the Crimean allies was humbled to the dust, thought himself strong enough to defy the other. He tore up the Treaty of Paris of 1856, and proceeded to build a new arsenal and naval base at Sebastopol, and a new fleet for the Black Sea. His instinct was quite correct, for Great Britain made no effort to stop him. We had since the Indian Mutiny clung to a policy of "insularity" or "splendid isolation," first under Palmerston, and now in 1870 under Gladstone. It seems that nobody expected that this move on the part of Russia would lead so soon to a reopening of the Eastern Question, but within six years Europe and Great Britain in particular were convulsed with new excitement.

The problem was not changed at all in its main features since 1853. The Turk still bore rule over a large Christian population, and did not on the whole rule badly, but could not reform or acknowledge the aspirations of the subject races. Rumania indeed was free, and Serbia partially free, but Bulgaria and Macedonia and other provinces were in their old state of subjection. But the position of the Tsar was not quite the same. He was, like his father, the professed champion of the Christians of the Balkans; but in the interval since 1855 he had freed the serfs of Russia. More than that, in the same interval United Germany and United Italy had become solid facts. Very naturally a similar ideal presented itself to the Slavonic nations, and there was a movement towards Pan-Slavism to match Pan-Germanism. We shall see that it has failed so far. Bismarck with his policy of "blood and iron" crushed German Austria, then created a German Empire by the exclusion of Austria and the inclusion of Bavaria and others who were excited by a crusade against France; also he was able to unite Lutheran Prussia and Saxony with Roman Catholic Bavaria. But the Austrian Empire was then a barrier against a Pan-Slavonic league under Russian leadership, for the Slavs of Croatia were Roman Catholics and devoted to Austria, whereas the Slavs of Russia were of the orthodox Greek Church, and yet the Greeks themselves are not Slavs; thus Russia failed to create a United Slavonic Empire by a crusade against Turkey.

Trouble began by the revolt of Herzegovina against the Sultan in 1875. Bulgaria rose in 1876. Then occurred the terrible Bulgarian atrocities when hordes of irregular troops, known as Bashi-Bazouks, were let loose and murdered thousands of peasants. The excitement in Great Britain was intense. Disraeli, our premier, who just at this date took the title of Earl of Beaconsfield, was thought to be very cold on the question of the massacres; it is not unkind to his memory to say that his Jewish blood made him hate Russia as the arch-enemy of the Jews, and the keynote of his policy was the integrity of the Turkish Empire as a barrier against Russia. On the Conservative side it was argued that the tale of massacre was exaggerated, that Russia was only encouraging the revolts of Christians as an excuse to fight Turkey, that our duty to the millions of Mohammedans in India forbade us to cease to support the Turks merely because they are Mohammedans. On the Liberal side Gladstone came out from his retirement, and in pamphlet and speech denounced the Turk and all his works; he should be driven out "bag and baggage"; "perish India" rather than let the needs of India, at which Russia was thought to be aiming, be an excuse for passing over Turkish cruelties. Beaconsfield retorted by calling Gladstone "a sophistical rhetorician inebriated with the exuberance of his own verbosity." Meanwhile relying on Beaconsfield's support the Turks defied Europe. The Serbians and Montenegrins armed to help Bulgaria, and were defeated, though many thousand Russians were in the Serbian ranks. In 1877 Russia declared war. Alexander II had no fear of French interference, and probably hoped that Gladstone's speeches would prevent the British from endorsing Beaconsfield's war policy.

In June 1877 the Russians reached the Danube and crossed with ease. They struck at once at the main chain of the Balkans and seized the Shipka pass, thus occupying a triangle of land, with the river as base, the pass as apex. The Turks were split apart; their main army lay

between the Russians and the sea, their reinforcements
were pushed up to the south of the Shipka, and a small
force under Osman Pasha lay at Plevna to the west.
Suddenly came news that the Russians had attacked
Plevna and been beaten back. A second attack was
made in July, and again they were beaten. In September
was a third attack, more keen and better led. But
Osman's men, shooting coolly with their breechloaders
behind the earthworks which he had thrown up, again
repulsed the assailants with enormous loss, and even
Skobeleff, the ablest Russian general, who launched forward his men in successive waves, could only effect an entry
to be driven out in turn. The position was very serious
for the invaders. The Rumanian army had to be called
in while the reinforcements were arriving. The veteran
Todleben was summoned. Two things were yet in favour
of the Russians. The reinforcements arrived by rail;
it was not necessary to tramp painfully on foot all the
way from Moscow or the north as in Crimean days.
Secondly, they were on the inner lines in their triangle,
and could still bring superior masses to defend any one
point. Thus they held the Shipka with success against
Turkish attacks as fierce as their own had been at Plevna.
The three armies of Turks were quite unable to combine
as the mountains and the Russians separated them.
Todleben arrived and undertook a regular siege of Plevna,
and at last in December after a desperate and unsuccessful sortie Osman surrendered with the remnants of his
army smitten by hunger and fever. The war showed the
exact opposite of what happened in 1870. The loss of
life was probably even greater. But the Germans always
attacked[1] and always won in spite of modern rifles; both
Russians and Turks fought best in defence.

In the winter months the Russians poured over the
Balkans, took Adrianople, and were near Constantinople.

[1] Except at Orleans, and at Belfort against Bourbaki.

Meanwhile in Asia, after defeat at first, they had routed the Turks and taken Kars. The Turks had made their great stand in each theatre of the war, had been near to winning, and had then collapsed hopelessly. Terms were offered, and at San Stefano the Sultan agreed to give independence to Serbia and Bulgaria. But the voice of Europe had yet to be heard. Beaconsfield, backed by an excited popular feeling which cried that the Russians must not take Constantinople, forgetting the Bulgarian atrocities of only eighteen months back, was even ready for war. Austria did not wish to see an independent Balkan peninsula over which she had no influence. Germany, at any rate in words, cared little for the Eastern Question, which was not worth the life of one Pomeranian grenadier, and therefore Bismarck offered Berlin as a meeting-place for a Congress. Whether Beaconsfield would have fought is doubtful, for already two members of his cabinet had resigned. But the Russians had lost very many men and were hard pressed for money, their vanguard near Constantinople was not very strong, the distance from Russia was great. Bismarck's offer was accepted, and the *Berlin Congress* met. Beaconsfield went over himself, with Lord Salisbury his Foreign Minister. The chief terms of the treaty were, that Austria should have a protectorate over Bosnia and Herzegovina; Serbia and Montenegro should be independent and have each an accession of territory; Bulgaria should still be under the Sultan nominally but have a Christian prince; but Rumelia south of the Balkans should be Turkish, a point for which Beaconsfield strongly contended, so that the passes could be held by the Turks in case of a new war; Russia should have some land at the expense of Rumania, and a large territory in Asia south of the Caucasus, including Kars and the port of Batum.

The Congress certainly was not favourable to Russia. She had spent much blood and money, yet she had only secured advantages for the Christians of the Balkans, and indirectly for her rival Austria; she gained for herself only small permanent advantage in Transcaucasia. Russian warships were, also, forbidden to sail through the Bosporus and the Dardanelles, so that she was as far off as ever from access to the Mediterranean. Perhaps in return she might expect gratitude, a notoriously brittle commodity; as a matter of fact Serbia alone has ever shown any gratitude to Russia, and Bulgaria in the Great War fought on the side of the Germans and Turks.

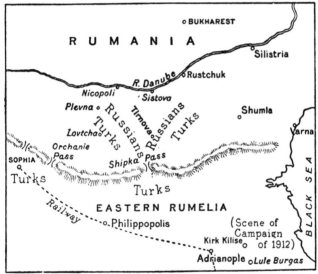

Bulgaria in the war of 1877.

CHAPTER IX

THE NEW EUROPE

THE chief thought in most minds during the "seventies" was: when will France try to take her revenge? The next thought was: how long will the Third Republic last? The five milliards were paid up in 1873, the army was reconstituted under a five-years scheme of conscription[1], and Bismarck is credited with having twice tried to provoke a new war because his enemy had recovered too quickly from her humiliation. The idea of *la revanche*, and of the recovery of Lorraine and Alsace, has always been present. But the nation showed a wonderful self-restraint, and for forty years and more there was still peace. And there is still a Republic. "Henry V" gave offence simply because his followers persisted in giving to him that name, and he died in 1883. "Napoleon IV" died in Zululand in one of our little wars in 1879. In 1882 died Gambetta, the fierce and uncompromising foe of Germany, of Monarchy, and of the Church, and not long after him General Chanzy who was marked out as the leader in any war of revenge. In 1882 was formed the *Triple Alliance*, when Germany and Austria joined together as allies, and brought in Italy so as to secure a naval ally in the Mediterranean. Also in 1882 Great Britain was forced

---

[1] Reduced gradually to two years, raised again in 1913 to three.

to take action in Egypt, thereby causing bad feeling in France.

There have been many ministries in France in the forty years, and it would be useless to name the prime ministers. At home the chief feature has been anti-clericalism, for republicans have always been indignant that clericals, while living under the republic's laws, should conspire to restore the monarchy. In foreign policy there have been periods of anti-British feeling with corresponding colonial activity, and periods of anti-German feeling. Thus the year 1882 has to be specially noticed, and later on the year 1898, because French hostility was then against us rather than against Germany. Also during the "eighties" and early "nineties" France was steadily drawing nearer to Russia, until Nicholas II finally made the *Dual Alliance* in 1895. To Russia also sometimes our own country, sometimes Germany, has seemed to be the destined enemy. But British and German interests so far clashed that at last we seemed to be committed to the support of the Dual against the Triple Alliance.

It will be found convenient to follow the course of events from the British point of view. Our policy swung from "insularity" under Gladstone to "imperialism" under Beaconsfield. He, while still Mr Disraeli, first showed his imperialistic ideas when in 1875 he bought the shares in the Suez Canal which were privately held by the Khedive Ismail; these were 176,000 out of a total 400,000 shares of the original capital, and Frenchmen hold more than 200,000, so that our government owns less than half; the price was four millions, and the interest in 1914 was one million, 25 per cent. on the outlay.

The chief result of the Russo-Turkish war was that Mohammedan feeling was strongly aroused in various countries. At the same time, the Russians, angry because of Beaconsfield's attitude to Turkey, turned their eyes to Central Asia and sought to vex our government in India.

The counterpart of "insularity" in India is "masterly inactivity[1]," and this was followed after the Mutiny. But Beaconsfield would have none of it. When the Russians intrigued in Afghanistan, he was quite ready for an Afghan war and declared that he would make a "scientific frontier." Russia was visited by the plague of Nihilism and was too hard pressed for money for the moment. Thus in 1878—80 the Afghan war was fought. Abdul Rahman was set up as amir, and, though thought to be a friend of Russia, proved for many years to be a valuable friend of British India. In fact Beaconsfield struck his blow quickly before the Russians were able to interfere, and a north-west barrier was created against them. It was not till 1881 that Skobeleff finally conquered Turkestan with merciless thoroughness, and that same year Alexander II was murdered by nihilists. Alexander III, too busy in suppressing anarchy to think of India, recalled Skobeleff. In 1885 indeed trouble occurred on the Russo-Afghan frontier, but war was avoided. The much talked-of invasion of India never got beyond words, and Russian expansion being checked in Central Asia, as it had been checked in the Balkans, tried to find its way through Siberia to the Far East; the next great war was not directed by the trans-Caspian railway towards Afghanistan and India, but by the trans-Siberian towards Manchuria and Japan.

Meanwhile the French movement of expansion by sea began when Jules Ferry, under the leave as it were of Bismarck, annexed Tunis in 1881. Gambetta opposed him fiercely as this was distracting France from her revenge. Ferry fell from power; Gambetta was premier for a time and fell in his turn, then died in 1882. Then came the outburst of Mohammedan fanaticism in Egypt,

[1] "Masterly inactivity" was the phrase used by Lord Lawrence, when Governor-General; he was the famous John Lawrence who saved the Punjab from Mutiny in 1857.

when a nationalist party arose to claim Egypt for the Egyptians as against the French and British who exploited their country for the benefit of the Canal shareholders, and Arabi Pasha controlled the native army. Gambetta would have joined with Gladstone in maintaining order and upholding the Khedive Tewfik[1]. His successor left Gladstone, a lover of peace, to suppress Arabi. Thus Egypt came under our protectorate, and the French, ashamed that they had not helped, were also sore for the next score of years because Gladstone's promise to evacuate Egypt when the Khedive was fit to govern was never redeemed. The Mohammedan rising of the Mahdi in the Soudan was due partly to the same fanaticism, partly to the wild Arab spirit which sought to enslave the negroes; after the despatch of Gordon and the failure of the relief expedition to save him the Soudan was abandoned in 1885. France, in 1883—85, under the second Ferry ministry, pushed on in Tonquin and Siam, Madagascar, and West Africa. Then came the inevitable reaction, and an outcry arose that the great loss of life from tropical disease and inexperience and savage enemies was too large a price to pay for profitless distant colonies. Ferry again fell from power and French colonial activity cooled down.

In 1885 a new Balkan problem brought the attention of Russia back to Europe. Eastern Rumelia called for incorporation with Bulgaria under Prince Alexander, and thereby the Berlin Treaty was violated. The Rumeliots are mostly Bulgarians by blood and their action was natural, but when united they controlled both the north and the south of the Balkan ridge[2]. The Tsar Alexander III was

[1] He became Khedive when Ismail, too extravagant and trying to imitate western ideas, was deposed.

[2] See page 256. One of Beaconsfield's chief aims at the Berlin Congress was to prevent the union of Bulgaria and Eastern Rumelia; Lord Salisbury, his colleague then and reputed to be his successor in imperialism, promoted the union, probably to check Russia.

angry, as though it were the duty of Prince Alexander to be the submissive vassal of Russia, and he took Rumelia without Russian leave. Serbia was tempted to attack the newly combined countries and was well beaten. Then, cowed by the Tsar's anger, the Prince resigned. Ferdinand of Saxe-Coburg[1] was chosen to take his place. This episode brought out strongly the rivalry of Austria and Russia in the Balkans. But whereas in 1870 and in 1877 Germany and Russia quietly supported each other in a time of war, in 1885 Germany by the Triple Alliance was bound to Austria. Bismarck ever wished to conciliate Russia. But another force was at work, the military jealousy between the conquerors of France and the conquerors of Turkey. It was ominous that Russian loans were now placed in France and no longer in Germany, and a Franco-Russian alliance was foreshadowed.

In 1888 died the great emperor, William I. In his old age his influence was entirely for peace, for he had won his laurels, and Bismarck's influence over him was weaker. The Crown Prince, nominal emperor for a few months, was peaceful, and also somewhat unpopular because of his fondness for England, his wife's country. With the accession of their son William II a new spirit appeared. He had been too young to serve in the army in 1870; he had not had his share of glory, and had no laurels on which to rest, therefore was less pacific. Yet up to at least 1914 he was not a fire-eater, and his chief idea had been to keep the German army ready and free from rust, not to plunge needlessly into war, but to prevent war by showing strength. Undeniably, at the same time, the German spirit was under him much more pugnacious. His first noticeable act was to get rid of Bismarck in 1890.

To think of France in the later "eighties" and the "nineties" is to remember a bare intelligible excitement, and three great scandals. Between 1886 and 1889

[1] See page 214.

General Boulanger was the central figure in France as the war minister who was the soldiers' friend, who increased the army and introduced a new rifle, who rode a fine black horse to gladden the eyes of Paris, that is to say the melodramatic figure which stood for *la revanche*. The official republicans did not want him, and therefore he was both hero and martyr, until at last ridicule ruined him and he died in exile in Belgium. But thousands of Frenchmen believed in him, especially when an unsavoury story was spread abroad that the "legion of honour," the decoration dear to every patriot, was being bought and sold. Boulanger was noble compared to the President of the Republic and his son-in-law, who dishonoured France by such traffic. Luckily steady Frenchmen kept their heads at the time of the scandal, and a new President was chosen, M. Sadi Carnot, grandson of the great Carnot of 1793, a man of the highest honour. Then came the Panama scandal; a company formed under de Lesseps to construct a Panama Canal went bankrupt, partly because of the climate of the isthmus and engineering difficulties, partly because of the terrible waste of money, fraud, and bribery of public men and newspapers; over 1250 millions of francs had been subscribed in vain. Yet we are forced to admire France. The country repudiated the fraudulent ones and justice was done. Then, perfectly solvent in spite of this loss, the French public put down their money ungrudgingly for loans to Russia. The scandals, it seems, prevented Tsar Alexander III from making a formal alliance with the Republic[1]. Only after his death was the *Dual Alliance* announced by Nicholas II.

The third scandal was the Dreyfus affair. An army captain was suspected of selling military secrets to Germany, and was convicted and sent to the horrible "Devil's Island" off French Guiana, on what has been

[1] But the French fleet visited Cronstadt in his reign, and the Russian fleet visited Toulon.

acknowledged to have been insufficient evidence. The honour of the army seemed to be at stake, and almost all French nationalists honestly believed him to be guilty; and he was a Jew whom none need pity. So men were found who went so far as to manufacture new evidence when the affair was reopened. Over all the excitement hung the fear that some carefully kept secret might be made public, and the result be a German war. The affair lasted from 1894 to 1899, the very years when the Dual Alliance was new and active. But again we see the same encouraging feature in French political life; scandals may be bad and excitement seem to be hysterical, but France rallies and regains her sense, though of course the injured are by that time beyond cure. Against the loud-voiced and insincere whose influence has passed away in time, against the supporters of Boulanger and the persecutors of Dreyfus, we put Presidents Carnot, 1887 to 1894, murdered by an anarchist at Lyons; Félix Faure, 1895 to 1899; and Loubet and Fallières and Poincaré; and the Foreign Ministers, Hanotaux and Delcassé, whose speeches at various crises in recent history have been as dignified as their conduct of affairs has been discreet. Yet the pity is that in France ministries have had but short lives, owing to the confused state of parties.

Germany in the "eighties" began to think of colonising. The reasons are not far to seek. An industrial and industrious country, with plenty of iron and other minerals and coal of her own, developing her commerce and manufactures at a great pace since her political union, she has hated the idea that, when her sons emigrated owing to pressure of population, they had only the Latin states of South America, or the United States, or British Dominions, to which to go. But entering late on the race for oversea empire she has found no land available for colonies except in the tropics. Also her methods are those of the stiff Prussian drill-sergeant, which do not encourage enterprise as we understand it. Naturally in seeking an outlet in East and West Africa, or in Samoa, German activity collided with British, and thus the two countries for the first time found their relations strained. Bismarck said that he acknowledged the good services of Britain in the past, but if Germany seriously had to defend herself against British exclusiveness in colonial matters the past services must be forgotten. It was an aggravation of the position that owing to our system of free trade German merchants could rival ours in our own lands. At the same time the national pride roused in 1870 made the Germans look down on the small British army and envious of the navy. His-torians taught systematically that those past services of Britain, which Bismarck acknowledged, were not very great, that Wellington had deliberately deceived Blucher at Ligny and was himself saved at Waterloo by Blucher, and that really Germany's services to us were the greater. We have also to mention the peaceful invasion of England by Germans, waiters, clerks, merchants, men of science and professors, and often had to feel humiliation because our own men showed incompetence or conceit and, re-fusing to learn, were ousted by them.

Before long France, recovering from her bad experi-ence of colonial expansion of the early "eighties," found that she could do well enough in Madagascar and Ton-quin. A revival of French energy was strongly marked in the middle of the "nineties." The attitude of Germany under William II was for peace. So the strange thing is that the Dual Alliance threatened at first, not Germany at all, but Great Britain; the energies of Russia were devoted to pushing on the trans-Siberian railway with the help of French gold, and to securing an outlet to the Pacific in the Far East; the energies of France were aimed at expansion from Senegal and the French Congo into the heart of Africa, with an eye to the upper Nile, and likewise at further power in Siam. It must not be supposed that, between the years of the Ferry ministry in 1883—85 and the Dual Alliance of 1895, French colonisation was at a standstill; the occupation of Dahomey, of Nigeria, of Timbuctoo, came in successive steps. But the friction between Great Britain and France was at its worst in the years 1895 onwards. Both Lord Rosebery and Lord Salisbury had to be very firm, yet careful to avoid war. Indeed it is thought that, had Russia been a little more keen to do her share in return for those French loans which created the trans-Siberian railway, war might easily have occurred. It is not out of place to notice that 1895—98 were years when the British navy became "modern." The new steel armour, steel wire-wound guns, and smokeless cordite, were in evidence in the batch of ships of the "Majestic" class, which seemed to be the last word in naval architecture at the review during Queen Victoria's Diamond Jubilee.

Acute as the tension was concerning Nigeria and Siam, the greatest danger occurred in 1898 in Egypt. Probably in any case Lord Salisbury's ministry would have pursued a forward policy. The Soudan had been abandoned in 1885, and our work had been to give good government to Egypt, to protect the fellaheen or peasants against officials, and to take in hand the work of irrigation so as to add to the country's productiveness. Yet the advance up the Nile was merely postponed. The devastating rule of the Mahdi, and of his successor the Khalifa, in the Soudan had to come to an end. The progress of the French across from Senegal was becoming serious. They were making for the upper Nile, and therefore Sir Herbert Kitchener's expedition to reach Khartum before them was necessary. Kitchener had an ordered country behind him, trained native regiments as well as British, and a railway. In 1898 he crushed the Arabs.

Proceeding up stream in a gunboat he found Major Marchand and a French force at Fashoda. War nearly resulted, yet French good sense prevailed and Marchand's men were withdrawn.

Events far more critical for the Great Powers of Europe were taking place in the Far East. The most wonderful of all modern wonders is the rise of Japan. In 1894 Japan overcame China in war, but the European Powers interfered and made her give up the fruits of victory; our prime minister, Lord Rosebery, was sympathetic but stopped short at sympathy. In 1898 there was a scramble for places, Germany secured Kiao-Chow from China, Russia got Port Arthur. Lord Salisbury, probably intent on the Egyptian question, caring little and, it is said, knowing little about the Far East, let the Russians take Port Arthur and close it against free trade; yet he was thought to be the successor to Beaconsfield's anti-Russian imperialism. In 1900, during our Boer war, the Boxers besieged the Embassies at Pekin, and a relief force was sent by all the European Powers and the United States and Japan.

Thus the harmony of the Europeans in the Far East, short-lived as it was, was in strange contrast to the sort of stale-mate at home where the Triple Alliance and the Dual Alliance faced each other. One would think that a sense of this contrast was at the heart of the Tsar when he proposed a *Peace Conference*, and the Powers sent their representatives to the Hague in 1899. Valuable as the Conference has been, and important as it is that minds should be accustomed to arbitration in place of war, there was yet no disarmament. The two Alliances lasted on. European feeling, we know well and at the time we were bitterly angry at it, was entirely unfavourable to us during the Boer war. The newspapers of France and Germany probably represented the actual state of public opinion in those countries. But our navy was undoubtedly strong. Therefore no Power could come to the point to help the Boers. And indeed one can hardly imagine a serious Franco-German combination to hurt us in a cause which concerned them so little, for the Triple and the Dual were mainly the result of Franco-German rivalry.

The outcome of the sense of isolation felt by our nation during the Boer war was a realisation that allies were definitely needed. A navy is a great thing, but in these days, when modern ships are soon out of date and it is vastly expensive to continue to build up to a standard of superiority, the nation that has no adequate citizen army must have allies. In the first place, Great Britain and the Dominions had been drawing together and discussing Imperial Defence, though a definite plan is difficult of adjustment; in the second, Great Britain and the United States were, on the whole, much more friendly than of old. But a formal alliance is binding where ties of sentiment may soon be broken, and, whether rightly or wrongly, in 1902 a formal alliance was made with Japan. Curiously enough just at that very time public opinion was changing in France, the uselessness of French and British rivalry and opposition in various parts of the world was being recognised, and the old feeling towards Germany was gaining the upper hand once more. The benefit of our rule in Egypt was acknowledged. In fact a real *Entente Cordiale* was being created.

In 1904 came the great Russo-Japanese war. Our alliance was formal and binding, but our armed intervention was only to be active if a second enemy opposed Japan. France did not throw in her lot with Russia, and therefore Great Britain had not to fight France; indeed, when Russian ships of war fired on our fishing boats in the North Sea as if they were disguised Japanese torpedo craft, the good services of France helped to settle the affair by arbitration. But if France had supported Russia and if we had not been pledged in that case to support Japan, the result of the war might have been very different. The struggle was on more than a Napoleonic scale, battles were fought on a front of fifty and even eighty miles, the Russians put into the field from first to last 1,300,000 men by means of a single line of rails. It is now generally thought that Japan could not have done much more after the great loss of life which was the result of victory, that her reserves of soldiers were used up and money hard to borrow. Therefore the intervention of France would probably have turned the scale. The British nation at first applauded our "allies." Yet second thoughts made some people hesitate; was it wise to let Russia be exhausted, and had not the anti-Russian policy of Beaconsfield gone too far? At least Russian expansion in the Far East had taken off the pressure from Afghanistan. Events have shown that Australia has disliked the Japanese alliance, has adopted a scheme of compulsory military service, and has welcomed with great cordiality United States warships. The United States, being now a Pacific power since the annexation of the Philippine Islands from Spain, and disliking very much the presence of Orientals in California, are strongly opposed to Japan. Therefore in our traditional opposition to Russia have we been hurried into an undesirable alliance displeasing alike to Australians and Americans?

It almost seems as if German influence had been deliberately used to drive Russia into this war, for William II had called upon Nicholas to maintain the cause of civilisation against the "Yellow Peril." No sooner was the force of Russia crippled for the time being than the Germans used a very dictatorial tone towards France in 1905. The immediate question was quite trivial and concerned the right of the French to interfere in Morocco. But there was more behind. The drawing together of Great Britain and France had resulted in the *Entente Cordiale*; the two countries agreed to give each other a free hand in their own spheres of influence, which meant a recognition of the British Protectorate over Egypt. The smaller countries were opposed to Germany. Even Italy was tiring of the Triple Alliance. Therefore the Kaiser felt that, strong as he was, he was being surrounded by a ring of active enemies or luke-warm allies, and must assert himself by making a counter stroke. The opportunity was too good to be lost, for Russia seemed to be prostrate at the end of a disastrous war and anarchy was rearing its head. Accordingly orders were laid on France to abandon her Moroccan policy and to dismiss M. Delcassé who was responsible for it. Finally a conference was held at Algeciras near Gibraltar. Our government stood by the French, and the German claims were abated.

The most striking development of modern Germany has been in her Navy, and the most important thing in connection with a modern navy is that it must be new and up to date. Immediately after the Japanese war we began to build vastly improved battleships of the "Dreadnought" class, and every new batch of "super-Dreadnoughts" was stronger in size and speed and gun-power, and Germany built at a corresponding rate. The very fact that only "Dreadnoughts" count told against us by making comparatively useless the older ships in which we had a great superiority. Germany had the right to create a fleet to protect her own trade. Yet it is idle to dub as alarmists those who saw in her naval preparations a menace to our trade and even to our coasts. There had been for some years a constant belittling, in German books and newspapers, of our strength and our importance in Europe, and though the more sober views of statesmen influence politics more than a wild public opinion, still there was a danger from national feeling. Denmark and Belgium, whose geographical position makes both Copenhagen and Antwerp strong for commerce and for war, feared a violation of their territory; Germans did not at all like that much of their trade passed through Antwerp, and that Copenhagen hampered their naval power in the Baltic, even though they had cut the Kiel Canal. The problem of a population of sixty millions requiring expansion was vastly serious. Already German merchants had overflowed into neighbouring countries, even into France, and in great numbers into Italy. Yet beyond national jealousy there was no excuse for war. And the strength of socialism in both France and Germany, the great expense of armaments both for land and sea—we return to our old argument that no nation yet has been able to maintain army and navy, witness the reigns of Philip II, Louis XIV and Napoleon—and the fear that a general conflict would upset international finance, all tended to peace.

Meanwhile the Balkan problem had made us forget Japan. In 1908 a revolution dethroned the Sultan, and Europe expected that the party of the Young Turks would put life into the Ottoman Empire. Austria replied by converting the protectorate over Bosnia and Herzegovina into actual sovereignty, and Germany openly stood by Austria. Prince Ferdinand of Bulgaria proclaimed himself Tsar and absolutely free of Turkey. Serbia and Montenegro were frightened of Austrian influence. Later, Italy laid hands on Tripoli. Now the hope that the Young Turks would really make proper reforms, govern properly, and sweep away corruption, was not realised; in particular the army, in spite of German advice which was given in view of a possible assistance from Turkey to Germany in case of a Russian war, was not in good condition. On the other hand the young Balkan states made decided progress. Yet when the war of 1912 broke out Europe was certainly surprised. That Serbia and Bulgaria and Greece could be allies was wonderful; that their armies would drive in

the Turks on all sides was more wonderful still. They
fought against the expressed wishes of the Concert of
Europe. How would they use their victory ? For it was
notorious that however much they hated the Turks, they
were bitterly jealous of each other, and all three desired
to secure Salonika, the only good port of the coast.

Bulgaria, it would be acknowledged, had at first the
best sympathies of Europe; on her had fallen the task of
beating the main Turkish force, her best troops suffered
terribly in action and were disorganised by the very
suddenness of her success, and the impetus of her attack
was spent before the strong lines which covered Constantinople. At last, after a pause, her army won
Adrianople. But the Greeks had won Salonika. Then,
in a fit of madness, the Bulgarians attacked the Greeks.
The Serbians supported the Greeks. The Rumanians
threatened from beyond the Danube. Their best men
already used up, the Bulgarians were beaten everywhere,
and then the Turks regained Adrianople. We have hardly
yet got the truth as to how far the various Christian nations,
learning only too well the lesson of the Turks, committed
atrocities upon the Turks when they had their chance, and
upon each other. Since Gladstone's attacks on the Turks
and their atrocities in 1876 we have been sceptical about
the word. Yet what we heard was very distressing.

The Balkan problem, otherwise the Eastern Question,
still remained. The Greeks held Salonika and the Aegean
Islands; the Serbians were not satisfied, for Austria did
not allow them access to the Adriatic; the Rumanians
wanted more land at Bulgaria's expense, although they
took no share in the original war. Meanwhile the Turks
recovered somewhat, and had a real chance to show
that they can reform as they have always promised to
do since pre-Crimean days. Amongst all the saddening
events the one ground for satisfaction was that the Great
Powers were not yet involved in war.

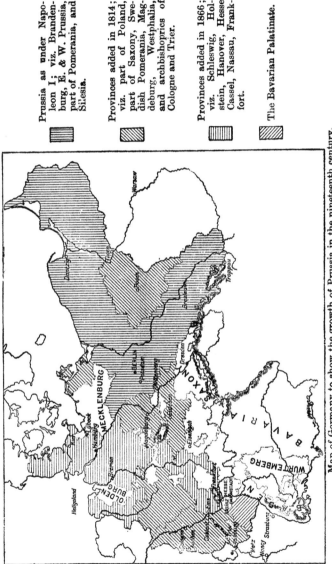

Prussia as under Napoleon I; viz. Brandenburg, E. & W. Prussia, part of Pomerania, and Silesia.

Provinces added in 1814; viz. part of Poland, part of Saxony, Swedish Pomerania, Magdeburg, Westphalia, and archbishoprics of Cologne and Trier.

Provinces added in 1866; viz. Schleswig, Holstein, Hanover, Hesse Cassel, Nassau, Frankfort.

The Bavarian Palatinate.

Map of Germany to show the growth of Prussia in the nineteenth century.

INDEX

18—3

280 INDEX

For EU product safety concerns, contact us at Calle de José Abascal, 56–1°,
28003 Madrid, Spain or eugpsr@cambridge.org.

www.ingramcontent.com/pod-product-compliance
Ingram Content Group UK Ltd.
Pitfield, Milton Keynes, MK11 3LW, UK
UKHW020320140625
459647UK00018B/1945